Respecting
The Stand

Respecting *The Stand*

A Critical Analysis of Stephen King's Apocalyptic Novel

JENIFER PAQUETTE

McFarland & Company, Inc., Publishers
Jefferson, North Carolina, and London

LIBRARY OF CONGRESS CATALOGUING-IN-PUBLICATION DATA

Paquette, Jenifer, 1978–
 Respecting The stand : a critical analysis of Stephen King's apocalyptic novel / Jenifer Paquette.
      p.   cm.
 Includes bibliographical references and index.

 ISBN 978-0-7864-7001-3
 softcover : acid free paper ∞

 1. King, Stephen, 1947– Stand. 2. Horror tales, American — History and criticism. I. Title.
 PS3561.I483S73 2012
 813'.54 — dc23   2012013247

BRITISH LIBRARY CATALOGUING DATA ARE AVAILABLE

© 2012 Jenifer Paquette. All rights reserved

No part of this book may be reproduced or transmitted in any form or by any means, electronic or mechanical, including photocopying or recording, or by any information storage and retrieval system, without permission in writing from the publisher.

Front cover image: Ruby Dee in Steven King's *The Stand*, 1994 (Photofest); cover design by David K. Landis (Shake It Loose Graphics)

Manufactured in the United States of America

McFarland & Company, Inc., Publishers
 Box 611, Jefferson, North Carolina 28640
 www.mcfarlandpub.com

To Remi,
who not only said that I could
but that I should

Table of Contents

Acknowledgments	ix
Preface	1
Introduction	5
Literature: What Is It Good For?	11
Horror: Red-Headed Stepchild of Fiction	23
King Criticism: Or Lack Thereof	30
A Defense of Escapism	37
The Stand	40
The Tolkien Connection	46
One: The Set-Up	53
Small-Town America	54
The Military	59
99.4 Percent Communicability	65
The Media	68
Two: The Players	71
Ordinary People Can Make a Difference	72
Small-Town Maine: King's Specialty	75
American Nice Guy	79
A Pawn in the Hands of Providence	86
Human Nature	90
The Sanctity of Innocence	95
Intellect Gone Awry	98
The Self-Fulfilling Prophecy	100
For Every Villain a Right-Hand Man	102
Evil Always Undoes Itself	105

Table of Contents

In the Hands of a Demanding God	107
American Evil	108

Three: The Big Picture — 112
- Good vs. Evil: Dream a Little Dream — 112
- The Problem of Choice: Predestination or Poor Judgment? — 116
- The Stand: It's the Journey That Counts — 117
- The Right to Govern — 121
- Hope vs. Despair: "Do people ever really learn anything?" — 125

Four: The Nitty Gritty — 127
- Writing Style: "The Prose Is Indistinguishable" — 127
- Genre Choice: Today Is a Good Day to End the World? — 129
- Popular Appeal: The Kiss of Death? — 130

Five: *The Dark Tower* Connections — 133
- Some New American Heroes — 134
- The Lady of Shadows — 139
- The Boy — 140
- Not in Kansas Anymore — 144

Six: All God's Chillun' Should Stand — 146
- "The Body": Ray Brower Meets a Train — 149
- *IT*: Clowns, Sewers, and Spiders — 152
- The Losers' Club — 153
- IT's Minions — 156
- "You Can't Be Careful on a Skateboard" — 157
- Grown-Ups Are the Real Monsters — 158
- American Horrors — 161
- *Dreamcatcher*: Aliens, Old Friends, and Hunting Cabins — 163
- Horror Lives Everywhere Every Day — 165
- Last Stand — 166

Final Thoughts — 168
Chapter Notes — 171
Bibliography — 177
Index — 179

Acknowledgments

I would like to thank Philip Chamberlin for the insight and encouragement, not to mention the lunches; Dr. John Hatcher, for telling me to write about something I really cared about and wouldn't get sick of; Thessaly Ann Miller and Freyja Skarsgard, for their endless unbridled enthusiasm; and Evelyn Jane Paquette, for the late night idea fests.

Preface

I have always been an avid reader — what English major isn't? — so when I received my first Stephen King novel when I was ten years old, it was the perfect Christmas present. I inhaled that story (a fabulous tale about a group of kids who defeat a scary monster as adults), and it wasn't long before I was scouring the local used book store and the library for more stories by Stephen King. As a child, I never questioned my attraction to this writer; as an adult and a scholar, I was forced to re-evaluate my opinions, to stop and ask myself if this beloved author whose works covered almost three entire shelves in my bookcase was worth my admiration.

Throughout my educational career I always tried to balance homework reading (those classics with which all English majors are familiar) with enjoyable light reading. Often, my fun book of choice would be the latest King novel. Even with my new literary perspective, I still enjoyed King's work, often applying the new techniques I learned in school to what I was reading and feeling smugly proud of myself for putting my knowledge to practical use in my real life. Unfortunately, it only took a few dismissive comments and a few more disapproving glances to ingrain the habit of reading Stephen King novels at home instead of at school. Apparently, I would have done better to bring a copy of the latest romance novel, complete with Fabio-esque cover, to read before class started than to indulge in the horror of Stephen King. Such authors were beneath the notice of proper English majors, so my professors seemed to say.

Stephen King is a touchy subject for those in academia. Some dismiss him off-hand as a genre writer, a horror hack, or an over-glorified bestseller who appeals to the lower classes (because he writes on a level that appeals to those with a liking for cheap thrills) — and those are the more positive views of America's favorite horror writer. Though there are some who will grudgingly admit that King is worth study as a cultural relic, an icon of popular culture, few are willing to address King as a serious writer, never mind a literary one. When I was finishing my classes for my doctorate and considering my dissertation, however, I never doubted that I would write about Stephen King — it was only a question of which novel I would examine. Of course, a veteran graduate student by that point, I was not entirely surprised by the reaction to my ideas.

When I first proposed Stephen King as the topic for my dissertation, there was a general miasma of groaning and uncomfortable glancing around the room, as if to make sure no one else had heard such a preposterous idea. It was only after a thoroughly exhausting research project revealing the hundreds of dissertations being written on King, along with a great deal of argument, and, to be honest, some wheedling and soapbox standing, that I was able to get this project approved at all by my committee. Even after this "probationary" approval, I had to focus on the most rigid of Formalist techniques, as if everything I used to analyze literature in my courses was too good for a study of King, and I had to restrict myself to the basic blocks of study relegated to freshman English Literature courses.

I am pleased to say that this study has grown a great deal from that initially detailed focus to include a number of other relevant issues, but the fact that there is such resistance against the serious study of King points to something more than lack of quality. Clearly, a writer who lacked quality would not have graduate students all over the country begging and arguing for the privilege of writing about him. I hope that the recent surge in dissertations that consider more than cultural studies will speak in King's defense as a writer worthy of serious literary criticism, and that someday a suggestion to study King in the classroom will not be met with raised eyebrows and exasperated sighs.

One reason (and there are many) that King finds himself in such low standings in the academic community is the genre in which he likes to write. Horror fiction written by anyone other than the Literary Greats (Poe, Stoker, etc.) is just scary stories, devoid of value by virtue of what it is. Horror fiction is escapist by nature, the flight of the reader into an imaginary world — something else that literary critics disdain. Literature should reflect the society, the real world, and to step beyond those boundaries is to go beyond where academia is willing to follow. When this study was presented at my dissertation defense, I encountered a great deal of

Preface

resistance, to say the least. One reader suggested that I was not actually talking about Stephen King at all; rather, I was defending the very notion of escapist fiction, an idea he found much more exciting than a look at *The Stand*. I argued with him then, bringing the focus back to King's epic and trying to convince professors of Austen and Yeats that King can be examined as laboriously as any author who makes the required reading list, but the idea remained with me. Perhaps this is the problem that King studies keep running into. But King doesn't need to be used as the poster child for escapist fiction; his works can stand on their own without any underlying agenda.

With these challenges in mind, I am pleased to report that the analysis that follows uses many of the tools of the literary critic, examining King's work in the same light as any English major discussing Woolf's "angel of the house" or Gilman's "madwoman in the attic." The following pages take a look at King from all perspectives, flying high above in the realm of the abstract to consider themes and symbols, hovering around the lived-in levels to examine characters and setting, and then delving into the basement to analyze sentence level details and turns of phrase. Though I would like to demand that readers take something insightful away from these discussions, I have learned to take cues from the master of this technique, and I shall let you, dear reader, take away what you choose. If anything, I hope that you enjoy the ride, and if you think more critically the next time you peer into the pages of a King novel, then my task has been doubly successful.

Introduction

Stephen King's concept of America is, many critics agree, a frightening picture. From demented madmen infiltrating small towns to rabid dogs who chew on leg bones instead of squeaky toys, Stephen King is known for his ability to make readers squirm. Not only is he an acknowledged master of horror and the gothic, King is also an unacknowledged chronicler of his nation, and an unappreciated observer of the American psyche. Though his works may follow in the footsteps of many canon-worthy greats of American and English literature, like Poe, Hawthorne, and Stoker, Stephen King seems unable to win the respect of scholars. Critics are not so eager to give King the stamp of serious literary approval, though they are willing enough to admire him for his prolific stacks of published works. Some, like Harold Bloom, argue that the popularity of Stephen King marks the downfall of the generation and the death of the Literate Reader in America, while others claim that his popularity illustrates a need within the American consciousness for gothic terror in American landscapes, thereby relegating his work to the realm of cultural studies instead of literature.

Although King has outsold most of his contemporary writers, literary critics are often displeased with his work. As Hoppenstand and Browne claim in their introduction to *The Gothic World of Stephen King*,

> Some attack his ideas, claiming that the content of his horror fiction is trite and unoriginal: *Salem's Lot* (1975) is a vampire story and vampire stories have been done to death; *The Shining* (1977) is a mere haunted house tale; or *The Stand* (1978) is simply another end-of-the-world fantasy, and who needs one of those? Other critics attack his style, claiming he has none. In a recent *Time* magazine feature article about King, several of his stylistic nuances were outlined: "The Disgusting Colloquialism," "The Brand Name Maneuver," "The Comic Strip Effect," "The Burlesque Locution," and "The Fancy Juxtaposition." Of course, if original ideas and

Introduction

writing style are valid measures of success, then William Faulkner and Henry James should be on top of the *New York Times* Bestseller list instead of King.[1]

Many American readers prefer King to the classics, with their often-hard-to-plow-through language, but some critics will admit that King does have something more to his works than the average easy-to-read bestseller, something that makes his books fly off the shelves, a quality that Hoppenstand and Browne call "the dazzle effect." King can "take the reader outside of himself with fiction" so much so that the reader becomes "oblivious to such things as style (or the written word) in a desire to be swept away by the author's vision, to be oblivious to page turning."[2] This evaluation is not so flattering as it seems at first. According to this definition, King is popular because he manages to spellbind his readers with a good story to the point that they don't care if the story is told well, as long as they get to the end. It is unclear if this view is more degrading to the American book publishing market, because readers are in such dire need of a good story that they will forego the pleasantries of good writing, or the American reader, who apparently is so deprived of quality entertainment that he is willing to accept anything that keeps the pages turning. Either scenario is not flattering and raises essential questions about the purpose of literature in the first place.

Have Americans become so accustomed to "page-turners" (entertaining though they may be) that they no longer appreciate the finer nuances of classic literature? According to a 2007 survey, three out of four Americans read books (that are not required by school or work). But when asked to specify what kind of books, two-thirds of American readers listed the Bible or a similar religious work (interpretations and evaluations of the Bible). "Popular fiction, histories, biographies, and mysteries were cited by about half, while one in five read romance novels."[3] Three-fourths is still more than the "fewer than half of American adults" who were reading in 2004; of that half, twelve percent, or twenty-five million, claimed to read poetry; while four percent, or seven million, had read a play in the last year.[4] Surveys do show that Americans are reading more now, but the quality of what they choose to read is questionable. Many works of popular fiction and mystery are not considered official "literature" according to scholars, and would be considered "page-turners" by those trained to evaluate literary matters. Just consider *Harry Potter* or the *Twilight* series. Though both series have topped the charts and prompted a new generation of school children to read a little bit more, as well as inspiring an entire host of nearly copycat storytellers, can we call these "page-turners," with their minimalist insight into the human condition, literature? Have we witnessed the death of the Literate Reader, as Bloom claims,[5] or is it simply time to reorient the definition of literature to accommodate modern expectations? This is not to advocate a complete abandonment of literary ideals, but certainly readers' expectations of "a good read" have changed over the years; and it is the responsibility of the literary critic to consider, if not condone, the needs and desires of a changing audience. If sales are any judge of popularity, which they ought to be because people *choose* to buy what they presumably *want* to read (books for school aside), and Stephen King is among the best-selling writers of his time, it makes sense that there ought to be something that so many readers find worthwhile in his work, just as J.K. Rowling and Stephenie Meyer have managed to touch a nerve in the American consciousness. In a country where most people choose television over the printed word, it is significant that King's books sell the way that they do.

As John Grisham said, it is something to be a best-selling author in a country where no one is said to read. After all, William Shakespeare, F. Scott Fitzgerald, and Ernest Hemingway were all popular writers in their time, and each is taken seriously by the literary establishment today. In September 2000, Andrew Ervin suggested that King be awarded a Noble Prize for Literature, claiming that "while popularity doesn't necessarily equal greatness ... one of the many wonders of democracy is that every once in a while, the masses get it right.... Just this once, the Academy should bestow the award upon someone people actually read."[6] Such a statement illustrates the division in American culture between that which is popular and that which is considered worthy of serious study. The "Great Divide," as Andreas Huyssen deems this schism, is clearly visible in today's universities: "Witness the almost total institutional separation of literary studies, including the new literary theory, from mass culture research, or the widespread insistence on excluding ethical or political questions from the discourse on literature and art."[7] Some of this division is a result of Modern ideals in literature — the notion that a work must have a "strong and conscious break with tradition" and must "reject traditional values and assumptions [as well as] the rhetoric by which they were sanctioned and communicated." That is, Modern works "reject not only history but also the society of whose fabrication history is a record."[8] By Modern criteria, literature ought to distinguish itself from the culture of which it is a part, focusing instead on individual concepts of reality and existence; this line of reasoning clearly leads to a rejection of anything that is obviously representative of that society—and rarely is there anything more influenced and shaped by a people than popular culture.

In addition to Modern ideals, academia has had an enormous effect on which writers and texts can make their way into a respectable anthology. Part of the reason for this is obvious—the critics who evaluate literature and publish these anthologies are academics, and academics disdain the notion of anyone common or popular being taken seriously. While this is yet another result of the Great Divide between pop culture and literature, it is also an effect of the general attitude of English graduate programs. Popular authors, such programs assume, are for cultural studies courses taught by adjuncts and graduate students; the real literature can be covered by the teacher-scholars—and inevitably presented through the narrow lenses of the faculty member's area of specialization. Such focused interpretations of the canon are worthwhile, faculty members suggest, while the interest of graduate students in popular authors was a "pastime," if they were inclined to be kind, or a waste of time, if they were not. The general attitude of faculty towards serious studies of non-canonworthy authors, or those students who dared to turn them in for credit, is to consider it the mucking about of idle children who must soon come to grips with the realities of the literary world. A sense of quiet indulgence was the most such writers could hope for, but such casual dismissal was certainly preferable to the vehement disgust shown by others in the field. Papers on popular authors have been returned with comments ranging from the blatant and powerful "F" to "This isn't literature" or "This author isn't acceptable." Despite such rigid opposition to these new studies, however, more and more students graduate each year with an interest in popular authors like King, and as they slowly replace the generation of scholars before them, there is hope that someday a paper proposal on Stephen King will not be met with such hilarity. Perhaps the Great Divide between what is seen as popular culture and what is categorized as literature will continue to shrink as studies pop up about not only the outcast Stephen King, but other newcomers to the realm of literary studies, like Isaac Asimov. Until then, readers must be satisfied with the "unauthorized exposes" that pass themselves off as literary studies and crowd the shelves at major booksellers.

Introduction

Still, these two categories seem mutually exclusive in modern times; the dominant theory today is that if a work is popular with the masses, it somehow cannot be literature. So Harold Bloom would say, but Bloom is fast becoming a voice from an older generation of literary critics. Though he decries the rise of cultural studies, blaming the realm of mass culture for the devaluation of the canon, Harold Bloom's claim for what makes literature worthwhile, a quality of arresting strangeness, "a mode of originality that either cannot be assimilated, or that so assimilates us that we cease to see it as strange" can be found in King's work.[9] It is this ability to render the ordinary extraordinary that draws readers back to King's novels again and again, where they can "feel strangely at home."[10] The question of Stephen King seems to begin with the crucial issue of where his works belong — are they merely a relic of popular culture, something to be devoured and pored over by cultural studies critics, or can they be examined through the critical eyes of literary critics and survive to actually say something about modern literature? The current criticism on King seems to suggest that the answer to this question is yes on both counts. King's massive popularity alone is worthy of study for those seeking insight into the mindset of the late-twentieth-century American. The very force of King as a phenomenon serves as fodder for those who would use King as a lens through which popular American culture can be understood and categorized.

When it comes to literary matters, however, even the pro–King critics begin to squirm. The notion of King as a serious writer is confounding not only because of reactions like Bloom's, whose standards of acceptability rule out even some authors who make the high school required reading list, but because to admit to a critical appreciation for a popular writer is only recently becoming an acceptable pastime. The climate of today's literary criticism has shifted some from the standards of Bloom's school of thought; critics are able to evaluate works considered less than canon-worthy if they so choose. With the rise of Bloom's much lamented cultural studies, there has been a sudden influx of criticism that focuses on sociological aspects of literature instead of aesthetics, and some works that would not have made the cut for their literary qualities are now being considered for their cultural qualities. Huyssen explains the reasons for a compromise in *After the Great Divide*:

> High modernist dogma has become sterile and prevents us from grasping current cultural phenomenon. The boundaries between high art and mass

culture have become increasingly blurred, and we should begin to see that process as one of opportunity rather than lamenting loss of quality and failure of nerve. There are many successful attempts by artists to incorporate mass cultural forms into their work, and certain segments of mass culture have increasingly adopted strategies from on high. If anything, that is the postmodern condition in literature and the arts. For quite some time, artists and writers have lived and worked after the Great Divide. It is time for the critics to catch on.[11]

This hope that critics would "catch on" remained only that for some time; in 1980, "even with the growing interest in popular culture, comparatively few people have chosen to study these books [best sellers] either for their own content and style or as a tool for broad analysis."[12] The explosion of study brought on by cultural studies did not arrive for another decade.

Stephen King seems lost in this shuffle. Some critics laud him as a cultural icon and examine his work in light of his success. Others focus on biographical criticism ("It's all because his father left him!") or genre studies. There is very little criticism, comparatively, on King's work as literature. This absence of serious consideration could be attributed to King's lack of literary success, a circular argument of sorts—King is not literature because literary critics have not yet examined his work seriously, and literary critics have not seriously examined his work because King just is not "literature." It is easy for literary critics to dismiss him as someone left for the popular culture specialists. This tendency to overlook King's literariness allows other critics to assume that King is not worthy of serious study and move on to other possibilities. Even so, King studies have started to gain some ground in the last twenty years, and if the rise of King-related dissertations is any indication, serious literary studies of King's work will soon outnumber cultural studies of the "Stephen King Phenomenon." This book takes the first few tentative steps into this area, showing that while Stephen King may not rank up there with William Shakespeare when it comes to literary genius, his work is certainly worth serious study as literature.

This book will show how King transcends genre, creates and maintains a viable Secondary Reality, and treats capably those literary techniques that critics expect of a serious writer. In addition, it discusses the ways in which King has secured the loyalty of his Constant Reader (the imagined reader to whom King addresses much of his introductory material—King's use of this term dates back to his earliest writings). The primary means of analysis will be through a close reading of the "expanded and uncut" version of *The Stand*, one of the classics in King's arsenal; but the discussion is broadened with a brief look at *The Stand*'s cameo in King's *Dark Tower* series, as well as the notion of "Standing" as it applies to "The Body," *IT*, and *Dreamcatcher*.

The analysis begins with an overview of the general set-up in the novel — the start in Arnette, Texas, of the super-flu, the actions of the military and media, and the 99.4 percent communicability of the flu itself. From there, it delves into detailed character analyses of the main players in the story before moving on to questions of the bigger picture — good vs. evil, the question of choice, the issue of government, and the promise of the future. The study of the text concludes with a brief look at King's style and considers the overall reasons for his popular appeal. In addition, the book considers the appearance of Randall Flagg and Captain Tripps in King's opus *The Dark Tower*, comparing these interactions to the world so capably destroyed and rebuilt in *The Stand*, and then expands on the idea of standing against evil despite the consequences as it appears in other King works.

Such a lengthy study of one of King's novels — instead of the brief chapters devoted to each of his novels in turn — as well as some of the threads that spill across the worlds of his multiverse will not only reveal the reasons why King is worthy of serious study, but will show that King's work does stand up to in-depth criticism, thereby answering one of the key questions of current King scholarship: Is there enough in King to work with? Everybody agrees that King can crank out lengthy novels without much trouble; the purpose of this study is to peek into the corners and down into the basement, if for no other reason than to find out if there really is a monster hiding in there or if it is merely an over-inflated rag doll. Either way, whether the horror be in the text or in the lack of substance in the text, it is hoped that this examination will lend new insight to the study of *The Stand* and perhaps pave the way for other in-depth studies of other King novels.

Literature: What Is It Good For?

In order to make the claim that Stephen King is literature, however, it is necessary to define the term "literature" as it is used in this argument.

Introduction

From the Greek emphasis on the aesthetic importance of *paideia*, Western civilization has the expectation that the literature of a people embodies the ideals of culture and education held by that society.[13] Writers are a product of their environment, and so the great writers are able to encapsulate the spirit of their age and culture in their works, and then share that vision with readers throughout later ages of the world. Literature, then, can be used to enhance "the process of educating man into his true form, the real and genuine human nature."[14] The Greeks believed that "the only genuine forces which could form the soul were words or sounds or both — rhythm and harmony"; hence, the position of literature was an exalted one — a form that could reach the soul more truly than any other.[15] For the Greeks, nothing exemplified this ideal of literature more so than Homer: "As Plato said, Homer was, in the full sense of the word, the educator of Greece."[16] Through his idealization of the hero, Homer taught his readers what it meant to be a man, and how to stand for the values of family and duty. And through his keen depictions of character and motivation, Homer captured the feeling of his time, allowing later readers to experience life as it was in that place and time — what Bloom would describe as making the readers feel strangely at home inside the text. Plato felt that the job of the poet, at least partly, was to educate his readers; therefore, the "aim of poetry is not essentially aesthetic, but the immortalization of the hero," and the poet must "clothe all of the great deeds accomplished by the men of old with glory, and thus educate those who come after."[17] Even though Plato decried the rise of reading and writing as the downfall of poetry, or at the very least the slow decline of memory and recitation, he was not averse to the ideas contained in stories and held the heroes of Homer as the standard to which all Greeks should aspire. By Greek standards, then, literature, whether oral or written, is a means of educating readers about life lessons and behavioral ideals.

Modernism, however, has different views of literature. In the scramble to differentiate itself from mass culture, Modernism has "constituted itself through a conscious strategy of exclusion."[18] Despite this stringent selectivity, Modern literature still aims for a broad appeal — texts that recognize the "complexity of the world."[19] The critic and poet T.S. Eliot added to this forming definition, claiming in his essay "Tradition and the Individual Talent" that new works ought to have some connection to the great works that have come before them, both so that readers can have a sense of continuity and a relationship to those great works, and to show how the great ideas of the past can indeed be reworked and re-fashioned to serve a modern world. Eliot claims that tradition depends upon an understanding of the past—that is, "This historical sense, which is a sense of the timeless as well as of the temporal and of the timeless and of the temporal together, is what makes a writer traditional."[20] For Eliot, the writer must learn to utilize the old with the new, a balance between his individuality and the inspiring forms and ideas that have come before him. This somewhat tumultuous relationship with former great writers is something that has plagued writers for ages—after all, how is a writer to balance the knowledge of old forms that have been shown to work for all time with the certainty that only a certain kind of originality will ensure access to the precious canon? Certainly a blend of some kind is required to make literature today. Harold Bloom answers this question with his theory of the "anxiety of influence," the idea that all poets (and all writers, by extension) suffer this dilemma with an anxiousness that in some ways makes their work what it is—the modern paranoia contributes to the work itself, and this quality makes the work exemplary for literature today.

Literature in a modern sense does not necessarily have to make the reader a better person, as the Greeks would have it; rather, literature is expected to have a certain aesthetic quality or stylistic strength that readers can appreciate. Typically, this "literariness is often said to lie above all in the organization of language that makes literature distinguishable from language used for other purposes."[21] According to Kant, "Aesthetic objects ... have a 'purposiveness without purpose.'" In other words, a work of literature ought to accomplish the purpose of aesthetics through the work of the parts and their contribution to the whole, not through a specific agenda (political, feminist, etc.) that takes over the text with its message.[22] Modern literature, in addition to this purposeful purposelessness, ought to prod readers towards critical thinking "by encouraging consideration of complexities without a rush to judgment, engaging the mind in ethical issues, inducing readers to examine conduct (including their own) as an outsider or reader of novels would."[23] The idea here is that literature allows readers to contemplate the world around them, to consider their own experiences through a different lens of understanding, and perhaps gain some insight into the human condition from the exposure. Perhaps the standards of an 1860 educator still stand true today:

> By converse with the thoughts and utterances of those who are intellectual leaders of the race, our heart comes to beat in accord with the feeling of

Introduction

universal humanity. We discover that no differences of class, or party, or creed can destroy the power of genius to charm and instruct, and that above the smoke and stir, the din and turmoil of man's lower life of care and business and debate, there is a serene and luminous region of truth where all may meet and expatriate in common.[24]

Such lofty notions of literature have come under fire in recent years from the same cultural studies critics that Bloom so detests. For instance, Terry Eagleton claims that this high-minded ideal for literature only serves to distract the rabble from building barricades in the streets.[25] This reaction is typical of a multicultural approach to literature — the theory is that a strong focus on classical canonized literature does not represent people beyond the traditional "dead white male," and so literary critics ought to branch out and find other works that speak more directly to readers who are not white and male, not to mention dead. Any reading list that focuses on the high-minded intellectualism of literature, according to the theory, ignores those marginalized voices who are not represented and can only be engaged in some kind of misdirection that tries to teach ideas that reinforce dominant social practices— hence the concept of literature as a distraction from the everyday. Literature can be a distraction, certainly, but to suggest that the study of literature is an exercise in denying cultural history seems farfetched; moreover, the true purpose of literature, as the 1860 speaker saw, is to lift readers out of the ordinary, show them a potential possibility, and then set them back down again armed with the memory of the experience. It is in this way that the Greeks felt that literature could truly make readers better people.

This is not to say that literature cannot be subversive or used in this way, but, overall, such agendas or conspiracies are not the purpose of literature as we understand it today — though there are certainly those authors who use this field as a convenient base for their soapbox. Even the bestselling wizard Harry Potter comments on serious topical issues, but the characters will never compare to Dickens' Pip or Faulkner's Sarty. The literature that lasts the test of time, as literature should, often distinguishes itself from these hangers-on, usually as the clingers are relocated to cultural studies (as they should be — they are reflections of the culture that happen to be in the form of literature, more so than examples of literature itself). True literature may be studied for its cultural qualities, but it will stand first and foremost as an example of the literary qualities valued for that time. Pleasing prose, well-developed characters, a sense of history

Introduction

(perhaps), and some insight into the human condition often define works as literature, whereas other popular novels (what are sometimes called page-turners) may hint at such broader issues in tiny snapshots, requiring a great deal of mining and massaging to have any kind of meaning for the readers. When readers today pick up the latest James Patterson novel, they rarely expect to learn something about what it means to be human, nor do they anticipate exposure to ideas that will make them better people. Typically, they pick up Patterson for a fast read, an entertaining, expectation-fulfilling mystery that reinforces the status quo and delivers precisely what readers want and nothing more. The best seller list is filled with such page-turners. From romance novels suggesting that passionate love can and does exist in the real world (and in fantastic worlds beyond imagination) to detective thrillers promising a written counterpoint to the ever popular initial-laden shows on television today (*CSI*, *NCIS*, etc.), today's page-turners are a reflection of the culture of which they are a product. They are literature only in the sense that they happen to be formatted as novels and have a plotline. They do not possess the qualities that make true literature stand the test of time.

Stephen King straddles this line in some ways—he is a bestselling author who writes in conventional formats and utilizes plotlines, but he also weaves tales about characters who make readers think and includes fundamental questions about human nature that allow readers to probe their own feelings about the future of humanity. In this way, he is both a popular writer and a literary writer—a sort of John Steinbeck (who was popular in his day as well) for the masses—who can keep readers turning the pages while subtly allowing them to think about bigger issues. Unlike with other, more traditional literature, King does not force readers to contemplate life's deepest mysteries, nor does he demand that readers dissect his prose to find the hidden meanings; but he does offer this option to those who choose to look deeper into his work. Most literature requires a serious consideration of what lies beneath the proverbial hood, and King does not disappoint. Even so, some critics are still skeptical. The primary purpose of this study is to point out the gears and gizmos that make up the engine of King's *The Stand*, revealing literary qualities along the way. What exactly are those literary qualities? Suffice it to say that "literature" for purposes of this argument includes works that are aesthetically pleasing, prompt intellectual curiosity, and reflect (but do not copy) a tradition of other works formerly considered great works.

Introduction

The question of Stephen King as a literary figure inevitably leads to a discussion of precisely what "literariness" entails. We can assume that the function of literature is to enlighten the reader, whether through exposure to new ideas or cultures, descriptions of events which prompt critical thinking, or references that hint at a broader world of knowledge and experience. The text need not explicitly refer to previous works of literature, but such references often reinforce the quality of the enlightenment experienced by the reader; a text with references to previous literary greats imparts a sense of history to the reader, an impression of the scope of the world of literature. However, the most important condition of "literariness" is the result of the reading — that is, the reader must gain some new insight into the human condition from the text. Ideally, a "literary" text would also be re-readable in the sense that new ideas, images, and lessons can be gleaned from each additional reading, but as long as the reader receives an impression of a wider world than he or she had previously envisioned, the work that inspired this new perspective can be considered "literary."

In opposition to Modern standards, this sense of literature does not have to separate itself from the dominant culture in order to qualify as "literary." The lens of popular culture is just as viable as any other as an appropriate means for a reader to gain greater insight into the world. The word "literature" often implies a sense of depth, an understanding that the work in question may require some intellectual effort in order to be appreciated and understood. Often, these works of "literature" require more than a dictionary to comprehend, and volumes of explicatory supplements and critical interpretations are necessary, or at least helpful, to facilitate understanding. "Literature" does not need to be dense in this sense of the word — that is, a text can be simply written and still retain "literariness" as long as the insight remains visible to the reader. Such exercises in vocabulary flexing may be "literary" in their use of language, but this style is not a requirement of "literature." In fact, it seems likely that part of the reason why Stephen King's work is dismissed as non-literary is due to his writing style, a way of telling a story that mimics the voice of the ordinary American — a tone that does not appear to be "traditionally literary" and therefore is often dismissed without further consideration.

The question of Stephen King as a literary figure, then, for this argument, rests on the result of reading his work. After finishing *The Stand*, readers have borne witness to death and destruction on a massive scale,

Introduction

and though much has been lost, they have encountered amazing characters throughout the journey. King's readers can hardly emerge from this tale unscathed, and certainly King raises enough ethical issues to promote critical thinking, not to mention the insight into human behavior his casual narrative has revealed. More importantly, though, is the manner of King's lesson — he does not overwhelm the reader with insightful observations, nor does he allow his own personality to take over the threads of the story. The reader is not forced to claw through complex phrases or convoluted theories of humanity in order to reach the meaning; in fact, King's reader rarely experiences that exasperating sense of "I get it already!" that leads many modern readers to quit in their efforts to devour the classics of literature. King never beats his reader over the head with his ideals, his personal theories, or his underlying messages. The primary focus in a King novel (and thankfully so, according to modern readers) is on the story and the characters—the basis of all fiction. The effect of the novel— what readers take away from the text — is left up to the individual. Each reader is permitted to see what he or she wants, to focus on the aspects that interest the individual instead of simply receiving the wisdom of the author in large, repetitive chunks of dogma. Such an obvious agenda is certainly a characteristic of some "literature" (take Upton Sinclair's *The Jungle*, for instance), but King's "literariness" rests on his faith in his Constant Reader to take away that which is relevant to that person's life and circumstance, gaining insight and perspective as needed by that person. This somewhat casual approach to literature is one of the reasons why Stephen King is often disdained by critics and dismissed as unworthy of study.

Today's literature is typically considered bound to the realm of the intellectual; average readers, the dominant theory suggests, do not generally reach for literature when in pursuit of their next book. If it hasn't made Oprah's Book Club, then most people assume that only academics and scholars should pay attention to it, relegating literature to the realm of learned professors and critics. This designation is problematic to America, since this country is known for a fairly strong feeling of anti-intellectualism. One of George Orwell's axioms was that "the poor, 'the ordinary people,' had a stronger sense of what he called 'common decency,' a greater attachment to simple virtues like honesty, loyalty, and truthfulness, than the highly educated."[26] A distrust of the educated elite has long been part of American history, but never more apparent than since the 1950s. The view of the lofty intellectual has certainly shifted in the last few decades: "The belief seems to be spreading that intellectuals are no wiser as mentors, or worthier as exemplars, than the witch doctors or priests of old."[27] This sentiment is certainly reflected in Stephen King's work, where he takes every opportunity to extol the virtues of the everyday American and mock the self-importance of the self-proclaimed intellectual. There is no doubt that King values Everyman far more than his educated companions. King has never hedged in his personal opinions regarding the literati, often stating his feelings with a bluntness that no doubt makes the literary critic more than a little leery of approaching his work. After all, if critics were to take their valuable time and deign to examine King's work seriously, who knows how King himself would respond to their critique? It seems a great risk to take, both in terms of respect from their fellow critics for commenting on a popular writer and from the man himself. Why take the time to evaluate a book, ostensibly helping the writer to gain a foothold in the literary world, when the writer is very likely to spit on those words with a disdain almost as great as that directed at his work by old-school critics? King's open disapproval of critics is probably a result of years of abuse at the hands of those who keep trying to pigeonhole him into the realm of cultural studies, but regardless of the cause, King's own very public views of intellectuals have certainly contributed to the spiteful reviews his work has generated. Perhaps, like the popular authors before him who attained literary status after their death, King will be easier to examine in the future when a new generation of critics can approach his work without such stigma clouding their words.

Granting King the status of serious writer may be difficult for some critics, but the time has come to consider King's literary qualities along with his popularity. Still, beyond the curious state of literary criticism and modern readers, there is no debate regarding King's success as a popular writer.

Hoppenstand and Browne posit that one of the reasons why King is so successful in a genre that is not mainstream is because he aims his stories at women and the young, and because these two groups presumably have the free time to read his works, these are the readers who make his books sell so many copies (Hoppenstand and Browne suggest that women do not work full-time as men do, a somewhat dated notion).[28] In other words, the horror aspects of the story are simply the vehicle in which King makes some kind of scathing social commentary that appeals to women readers, or has some kind of adventure that a young reader could identify with because he or she is experiencing such things every day. Apparently, both of these categories of Americans have enough spending money to purchase King's novels in huge quantities, and their devotion explains the reason for King's massive financial success.

This evaluation seems more of a justification for pigeonholing King than an honest critique, an alarming trend in King scholarship. Granted, King does appeal to women and the young, but he also finds Constant Readers among working men and retired seniors. King's audience runs far beyond the reader of horror fiction, and in the last decades, he has become an arm-chair celebrity, a writer of books to be read on airplanes, in waiting rooms, and in snatches below desks in classrooms. But he also manages to offer "more than mere escape fiction or 'adrenaline' fiction; [his work] urges readers to confront squarely and disturbingly the horror in their own lives," and "the resulting depth connects him to an audience drawn to literature more 'serious' than horror or genre fiction." In fact, King's "model has inspired enough followers to cause horror fiction to move to the front of bookstores and the top of the *New York Times* bestseller list."[29] King's audience defies description; his "dazzle effect" manages to affect almost anyone who wanders into one of his "page-turners," as his status as a best-selling author will attest.

One cannot fully address the issue of literature without at least considering the characteristics of the modern reader. Mark Edmundson has a rather depressing outlook on this figure, suggesting that today's readers, ruined by the cultural wars of their parents, do not know a good book when they read one, nor can they identify what makes a book worth reading; and though they are not to be blamed for this ignorance, Stephen King and John Grisham are the fortunate recipients of their misguided attempts at fulfillment.[30] For Edmundson, readers today "missed out" on an education that showed them what to appreciate in the classics—and also, he implies, in life. For today's reader, he says, a good read is simply something that makes the reader feel good. Quality is not of concern— only ease of enjoyment is important. In keeping with our consumer culture, he continues, publishers have continued this sham by promoting those writers who are easily digested and give readers precisely what they are seeking without asking too much of them, presumably to allow modern readers to uphold their busy schedules without the trouble of thinking too hard about something.

Introduction

This may be true to an extent. Certainly there are shelves of page-turners in the mega bookstores, novels whose sole purpose is to fulfill a basic need for a predictable story with anticipated elements, and no serious engagement with the text required. But there is a difference between a simple, cheesy page-turner and a good simple story that offers readers a choice as to whether they want to engage themselves intellectually. Not to disparage the cheesy page-turner, but there is a time and a place for everything, and when readers want to be intellectually challenged, these stories will inevitably come up short. The stories that are considered classics today—Milton, Shakespeare, Hemingway—began as all fiction does, with the intention to tell a good story, to entertain readers, and once the writer had everyone's attention, perhaps to show something fundamental about humanity or the universe. The difference is that to read any of these writers today requires effort because the world has moved on since their authors wrote them. Language has changed—not so fundamentally as it has for someone reading *Beowulf* in the original Old English—but enough to put readers on their guard. They know when they pick up a book written by a "classical" author that their brains will be required to get their money's worth out of the venture. Still, this does not mean that reading literature should require a handbook as well as a second book of explanations and footnotes (thank you for the hand-holding, Eliot).

Sometimes it is easy to forget that literature is words, and words meant to entertain us, the readers. Without that basic foundation in getting—and keeping—the listeners' attention, any tale spinner from the ancient world or the last decade would find himself without an audience. There is meaning in literature, certainly, and sometimes deep meanings that need to be unearthed, but Edmundson is right about one thing—modern readers do not always have the time nor the inclination to seek those depths. This lack of desire is not because modern readers do not know how to read critically or what terms to use to describe what is happening in the story; in fact, this type of reader is not a new creation. People have always read for pleasure, and they read what is popular and available and recommended. Today that happens to be Stephen King and John Grisham, authors who weave simple enough tales in simple enough language, but still, at least in King's case, manage to raise those same fundamental questions about what it means to be human. If readers want to pursue the depths of meaning, they are there to plumb, but if readers just want to enjoy the ride, as it were, the story is enjoyable enough on the surface.

Introduction

This cannot always be said for those works of classic literature where time makes the language difficult, or customs and context make the story seem insignificant. After all, to modern readers, why should Virginia Woolf's Angel of the House long for a Room of Her Very Own? The issues raised in the novel are somewhat dependent on the time in which it was written, and to modern readers, a main character who spends an entire novel wondering about the intricacies of domestic duties is not as engaging as a lawyer or a group of children fighting a monster (an insurance company or an actual fiend). Just as readers in Woolf's time would relate to a story that reflected their own world perceptions, today's readers are more comfortable with things familiar and known. This tendency to seek stories that reflect modern sensibilities is not a reflection of laziness in readers as much as it is a desire to use very limited free time to read a story that resounds with readers' cultural expectations and awareness.

Now, this does not mean that the story is not worth reading, or, as a product of popular culture of the time, that the story must be a "waste of time," to use Edmundson's words to denounce King's work. Shakespeare was hugely popular in his time, as was Hemingway, and to suggest that these works are a waste of time is laughable even to the most jaded reader. The attitude that today's books are easy and useless is just another way of dragging the old high art/low art argument into new rooms. The idea is always something like this: Old is good because it's old, and new is bad because it isn't old; therefore, classics must be respected by virtue of being classics, and new fiction is a waste of time and space — something for the unwashed masses to indulge in while they keep the machine of society turning (presumably society is running to support elitist intellectuals who disdain the very things that support them). The truth is that the unwashed masses read the books, and to say that popularity equals literary vacuity is to ignore the possible Shakespeares and Hemingways alive in our time. That is not to say that Stephen King will someday rival Shakespeare — he will not — but there is something to be said for the popular and literary authors in the world. To dismiss such writers because of who reads them seems another way to discredit them without a fair trial.

In addition, Edmundson decries what he considers the Narcissus obsession: "The common reader today is someone who has fallen in love, with himself."[31] Today's media, Edmundson claims, gives modern readers exactly what they want, and so everything in society is a reflection of the readers, making them feel good about feeling good. In a consumer culture like ours, this is certainly true, but the question is: When it comes to reading, why is this a bad thing? Literature is about universal values, fundamental human concerns, and good literature is always some sort of mirror reflecting society back at readers. It is not that modern readers are in love with themselves; it is that reading allows readers the perspective of the observer, giving them a chance to see the world anew by watching someone or something else follow the paths in life. Needless to say, it is a fascination with life itself, which includes readers themselves, that makes reading worthwhile.

Modern readers are not so different from their ancient counterparts, but considering how literacy rates have risen, it is curious that more people are not avid readers, especially in America. In my own experiences with college students, I have met more than one person who revealed, almost with pride, that they had never read a single book to completion. This confession always makes me a little sad inside, and when I ask why, these non-readers always say the same thing: books are boring. They have never found a story that engaged them. In most of these cases, this lack of interest is a result of high school reading lists. For most of these students, the only books they have been exposed to were the ones they had to read, and those who have slogged through those works as teenagers will not blame them too much for their disdain. To be honest, even devoted readers often have a hard time recalling a single "required" book that they actually enjoyed during their public school years. Sure, readers may appreciate Shakespeare's turns of phrase, or muddle their way through Ray Bradbury and Charles Dickens, but they generally do not really appreciate them until they are much, much older. The world experience required to really understand *Les Misérables*, for instance, does not arrive in high school, never mind the wherewithal to really grasp John Donne's musings on life and death. What teenager, rebellious by nature, can really relate to these works about life's biggest questions? Of course, there are some things that stand out, enjoyable moments within stories (the only thing remembered with any fondness from *A Tale of Two Cities* is the ending — he sacrifices himself for the woman he loves! How romantic!). Most students do not even get that far, and that was in the days before Wikipedia made every storyline available with a click (now most students do not even bother with the actual text unless their teacher gives really difficult reading quizzes with questions that are not answered online). Ultimately, this attitude, this reluctance to pick up a book and actually read it, is largely a result of our high school reading lists (combined with some laziness, of course). For someone who does not have a lot of exposure to books beyond the classroom, these samples of classics may serve to turn a potential reader away from the pastime for good. Then again, J.K. Rowling and Stephenie Meyer, whatever the inherent quality of their work, certainly inspired entire generations to read, and once they devoured those (mostly) page-turners, they may seek out other works with more depth. Popular culture has done literature a great service in this respect — readers are made every day, lured in by page-turners, yes, but some decide to stay and investigate this new world, finding enjoyment in works old and new. And whether the book is easy to read or a bit more challenging, the fact remains that while there are modern readers, literary works will be rediscovered again and again.

Horror: Red-Headed Stepchild of Fiction

King is largely credited with giving the entire genre of horror fiction a real niche in the American consciousness, or at least the inverse: "It is not so much that the reading public has developed a perverse taste for horror as it is that, emulating King, horror writers have broadened and deepened their art enough to address us all on issues of consequence."[32] As Clive Barker so aptly put it, there are typically two books in every American household — the Bible, and something by Stephen King. However, King is often dismissed from literary circles because of the very genre in which he chooses to write. Michael Collings, in *The Many Facets of Stephen King*, addresses the pink elephant in the room when it comes to King scholarship — namely, King's lack of critical success:

> The problem is that King, like his forebears in horror fiction, Edgar Allan Poe and H.P. Lovecraft, "has not been taken seriously, if at all, by the critical establishment," in King's case both because of his chosen genre and because of his enormous commercial success within it. Even when trying to separate King from the genre, Charles de Lint paradoxically emphasizes King's identification with horror by writing that ED [*Eyes of the Dragon*] proves "once and for all that while he can deliver the shocks, he doesn't need them to be one of America's premier story tellers." That is in fact the crux of the matter. King may lapse into stylistic infelicities.... He is on occasion (and by his own admission) afflicted with "literary elephantiasis." Yet, as de Lint implies and a number of other critics have admitted, ultimately those technical problems fade and the story takes over. In many

cases, the story is based on terror or horror; yet invariably, beneath the horror lies an extraordinary talent for the tale well told.[33]

The problem with King then, lies not with the quality of his storytelling, which his commercial success illustrates is spot-on with many readers, but with the literary establishment's predisposition to disregard anything that can be neatly categorized in the horror genre. It is only in the recent explosion of cultural studies that these "genre novels" have been studied as anything more than examples of their respective types; in-depth examinations of these novels as works of literature are still somewhat lacking, but with the emerging acceptance of this type of genre study, there is hope that more critical reviews are on the way.

What is it, then, that is so terrible about the horror genre that makes critics squirm? True, it is a style well known for blood, gore, and a basic plotline of "scary monster–type kills lots of characters before getting killed by hero" or the more modern "scary monster–type gets away with killing lots of characters despite the best efforts of the hero." But there has to be a reason for the longevity of the genre, a type that has been garnering fans from the 1800s. Douglas Winter, author of *Stephen King: The Art of Darkness*, a seminal work on King, addresses this issue:

> At a minimum, horror fiction is a means of escape, sublimating the very real and often overpowering horrors of everyday life in favor of surreal, exotic, and visionary realms. Escapism is not, of course, necessarily a rewarding experience; indeed, horror fiction's focus upon morbidity and mortality suggests as masochistic or exploitative experience, conjuring subjective fantasies in which our worst fears or darkest desires are brought into tangible existence.[34]

Though this is not the most flattering of explanations, Winter has hit upon the crux of the matter — horror deals with the ordinary world turned sideways, a possibility that unnerves almost as much as the saliva dripping from the monster's curved fangs. It is not the philosophical potential that critics malign, however; rather, they generally disapprove of anything that requires monsters in order to get the point across. Consider how loudly and often J. R. R. Tolkien had to praise *Beowulf*, a work organized around two monsters and a dragon, of all things, before anyone would take the work seriously as a poem (and not a great historical document depicting a defunct way of life). It was only after suggesting that the monsters were metaphors for the human experience (the dragon is Beowulf's — and therefore mankind's — struggle with mortality) that critics were able to look at the poem as literature. Literal monsters without metaphorical counterparts apparently disqualify something from being literary. To the contrary, King feels that horror reaffirms people's "self-image and [their] good feelings about [them]selves" because it allows them to peek at the monster and walk away thinking, "Hey, I'm not so bad. I'm all right. A lot better than I thought."[35] The chance to see the unspeakable allows readers to appreciate what they have, much like Aristotle's notion of catharsis; readers are exposed to a "worst case scenario," and suddenly their ordinary lives seem quite livable, even wonderful. Through the extraction of Aristotelian terror, readers realize that the real world should be appreciated if only for the sake of what could possibly happen should reality take a more sinister turn. Mapping those dark possibilities is the duty of the horror writer.

Like Tolkien before him, King works within a genre that has been traditionally ignored; even the classic Holman and Harmon *Handbook to Literature* does not have an entry for this kind of writing. Though Tolkien's genre was the much neglected fantasy, King chose to begin his career with horror, and many critics are still determined to leave him in that category. Now, as Winter claims, horror has often been associated with escape, a need for the reader to abandon the real world in favor of gore and guts. This statement is true, but only to a certain point. After all, even critics agree that there are few things more horrifying than to find elements of horror in the real world, and this integration is exactly what Stephen King does in his work. He takes ordinary American settings—small towns in Maine in particular, forgotten elbows of the landscape in general—and peoples them with recognizable American faces. The horror element arrives not in the form of a big, bad monster, though certainly those do haunt the pages of King's novels, or in supernatural events, though King has been known to toss in the odd ghost or ghoul now and then, but in the faces of one's neighbor. Sartre said that hell was other people; King has solidified this philosophy into reality. The true horror of his tales is that they begin and end with ordinary people, believable people, and readers are unable to ignore the mirror that has been brought before them. King shows the world as it is, and as it could be, and then as it just may be, if people forget what it means to stand against evil.

True, King would not be nearly as successful without his penchant for blood and gore, but it is his ability to blend such shocking scenes with the ordinary that allows him to get away with gore in front of a mainstream readership. Readers are so surprised by the emergence of the unspeakable in the midst of the regular world that they are spellbound. In King, such events are like car wrecks—readers want to look away, but they cannot, and they read onward, trapped by their need to find out what happens to everyone else. The potential for such events in the real world, however remote, manages to ensnare readers' imaginations because, after all, what if it really did happen? King's uncanny ability to blend the Primary World with his created Secondary World lets readers believe in his story enough for it to completely overwhelm them. It is this gripping madness that readers devour en masse, and the fact that the author they read so greedily is categorized in the Horror section of bookstores ceases to matter. King transcends genres just as he transcends boundaries between readers—he finds dedicated readers in housewives and businessmen, school children and retirees. Part of that appeal is due to his amazing ability to reel readers in with a good story, but there are many levels to King's allure, and the horrific elements are only the beginning.

King himself claims that his work "underlines again and again that I am not merely dealing with the surreal and the fantastic but, more importantly, using the surreal and the fantastic to examine the motivations of people and the society and institutions they create."[36] As Smith observes, this is an "artistic purpose that is a far cry from — and significantly more complicated than — churning out sensationalized gore to shock the masses."[37] Part of his appeal is his ability to create characters that readers can believe in amid the chaos of the horrific. As Gareffa put it when discussing *The Dead Zone*, "By creating a world so very close to our own existence, then disturbing it with a frightening supposition, King offers a horror no seven-foot green monster or fanged stalker ever can. After all, horror we can place in an isolation booth is one thing. Horror let loose in the real world is quite another."[38] Punter expands this to include the world of film: "There are many films of terror, Alfred Hitchcock's and Roman Polanski's among them, which ably demonstrate that fear is at its fiercest when it is seen to invade the everyday contemporary world."[39] Even King himself explains the moment he first stumbled on this idea of horror in the everyday world when he discovered Richard Matheson's *I Am Legend* and read as the narrator staked a vampire to death in the freezer of a grocery store. His young mind, he says, was intrigued and fascinated by the idea that vampires could be spending the day in such an ordinary place — a grocery store — and that such horror could fit right in to the mundane (not to mention that the staking of this customer-vampire was even more horrific because it took place amid such recognizable surroundings). Apparently, King never forgot that curious blending of horror and reality; the combination occurs often in his novels, always jarring readers into that disturbing question: what if it did really happen? It seems that King's ability to combine the ordinary world with the horrific is one of the things that makes him so successful, though his many readers could probably list numerous other appeals.

Horror fiction allows readers to face their fears in a safe environment. Unlike "ordinary" fiction, like mysteries or thrillers, where readers are shown the real world with real characters and real events, horror takes readers to the proverbial edge of the abyss and allows them to take a quick peek into what lies beyond. Popular fiction is popular fiction because it is easily recognizable. King offers readers this recognition, then teases them with a view of something beyond the ordinary. After all, "in the tale of horror, we can breach our foremost taboos, allow ourselves to lose control, experience the same emotions—terror, revulsion, helplessness—that besiege us daily."[40] King lets readers experience things they can relate to but in a context that makes it easier to digest—it is safe to watch, he assures readers, because it's only a book, after all. With any fiction, readers assume they are allowed control of the situation: they can choose to close the book if the scene gets to be too much; they can skip ahead if the description gets to be overwhelming. Such a luxury is not available in the real world. Horror fiction may appear to give readers a chance to steer the course of their experience, yet it is the virtue of the horror writer to upset that journey as much as possible. While readers may seem to be in charge of their fear intake, in truth it is the author who controls the experience; and with a storyteller as skilled as King, readers can rest easy in the knowledge that they are in good hands, aren't they? This slight uncertainty only adds to the overall experience, and this quality is another reason King can address a Constant Reader in his introductions.

Horror is often dismissed as escapist fiction. Critics say that people read horror when they need to get away from the real world. This is not exactly the case with King's work. In fact, most of his stories take place in the patently real world, and this realism is the appeal that readers respond to. Douglas Winter continues to expand on the escapist nature of horror fiction, adding:

> Despite its intrinsic unreality, the horror story remains credible—or at least sufficiently credible to exert an influence that may last long beyond

the act of reading. One does not easily forget the thing that waits inside "The Crate." ... This credibility is possible because horror's truths are judged not by the real fulfillment of its promises, but by the relevance of its fantasies to those of the reader or viewer. Although horror fiction appeals to the source of the daydreams—and of nightmares—its context is waking reality.[41]

Part of the appeal of horror, then, is not what is revealed but what the reader imagines. Unlike ordinary literature, where much value is placed on how the writer tells the story, stylistically speaking, horror fiction must be judged on what the writer chooses to omit, thereby heightening the terror and increasing the overall effect of the tale. Perhaps it is this difference that makes horror such an oddity in the world of criticism.

The horror in King's work is known for walking the thin line between fantasy and reality—monsters appear in ordinary living rooms, aliens invade recognizable back yards. Horror fiction suggests that "rationality and order are facades, mere illusions of control imposed upon a reality of chaos," and "we are clothed with the thin veneer of civilization, beneath which waits the beast, eager to emerge."[42] Winter argues that "along with its obvious cathartic value, horror fiction has a cognitive value, helping us to understand ourselves and our existential situation. Its essential element is the clash between prosaic everyday life and a mysterious, irrational, and potentially supernatural universe."[43] This glimpse of the beyond is what King reveals to readers. There are the monsters in the closet that readers expect from King, but what keeps the audience flipping from chapter to chapter is the hope that along with the horrific, King will also show them something beyond bogeymen. King delivers on this score time and again, whether it is in his vision of a world "moved on" in *The Dark Tower* series, or in the casual way the Derry residents of his many novels ignore the fact that children tend to disappear quite often in their small-town Eden. It doesn't matter if King is creating entire multiverses or describing the happenings inside one home on a quiet street; he manages to show readers another layer of reality—sometimes gruesome, sometimes shocking, but always something on the very edge of believability—and it is no wonder that King's images haunt his readers long after they have finished the book.

This glimpse into the underbelly of the American psyche is what King promises readers, and this is the quality that has earned him such a dedicated following among the masses, despite his roots in the horror genre.

For a more detailed look into the horror genre, King himself has written *Danse Macabre*, a consideration of his theory of horror — basically, he jokingly admits, horror has been here for a long time and will be here for a long time to come. According to King, part of the appeal of this genre is that "magic moment of reintegration and safety at the end, that same feeling that comes when the roller coaster stops at the end of its run and you get off with your best girl, both of you whole and unhurt."[44] Horror allows readers to experience terror and the semblance of death, and this tantalizing look into the world beyond is what keeps readers enthralled.

Stephen King is often associated with gothic, though the term "gothic" evokes images of vast castles haunted by tragic loss or heroines terrorized by blackguard villains, and King rarely uses any of these devices. However, the New American Gothic, which is "said to deal in landscapes of the mind, settings which are distorted by the pressure of the principal characters' psychological obsessions [where] we are given little or no access to an 'objective' world," seems more closely linked to King's style.[45] Though he rarely utilizes the first person narration such distortions may require, King does create worlds that seem at first very much like ours, and then after a few subtle interjections — a telepath here, a demonic car there — he has readers hoping that the initial resemblance to reality was not as close as they thought. After all, if the world seems so familiar, what is to stop the other events from happening to their town or their family? Readers may wonder if the world they are reading about is a mirror of reality, or if King has somehow given them the slip, substituting a world of dark magic and evil potential for the one they thought they recognized. King has a knack for interchanging the "real" world with his own creation so seamlessly that distinction between the two becomes difficult — King's world is both recognizably the America readers know and some disjointed vision of an America that readers recognize, much to their own horror. Readers are left wondering when their America became the horror landscape and when they lost track of the differences. This sleight of hand may make his work resemble the New American Gothic, where readers are never quite certain if the world is as the author portrays, or if it has been somehow infiltrated and fundamentally altered while they weren't paying attention.

King is sometimes credited with describing a "nightmare America" in his novels, a dark version of the country that readers want to believe and deny at the same time. Gary William Crawford considers King's status as a Gothic writer in "Stephen King's American Gothic," where he decides that King's work does relate to that of Irving, Hawthorne, Poe, and Melville, but that King shows the American Dream as it possibly may be — a nightmare. This inversion of that which is utterly American, the notion of the American Dream, marks King as a writer very much aware of his time period; King plays on modern questions about what it means to be American and to pursue the dream that literature has been dissecting for the last century. Though Crawford wonders if King's novels will stand the test of time, he cannot deny that King's success as a gothic writer has allowed other gothic writers to come onto the public stage, and he credits King for the return of the gothic novel (the short story having been the popular mode of gothic and horror for decades).

Despite his categorization as a horror or gothic writer, King has managed to transcend traditional genre boundaries, thereby earning himself a readership made up of a cross-section of American society. His work certainly has elements of the horrific and the gothic, but overall, it is the realism of his novels that have earned him so many devoted fans. Whether he is detailing the grueling work of a graveyard shift or narrating the internal monologue of a frustrated parent, King's ability to depict reality is a crucial ingredient in his storytelling capabilities.

King Criticism: Or Lack Thereof

Criticism of Stephen King is, to use Michael Collings's word, schizophrenic (in the misused modern sense of the word) at best. Critics vacillate between hedging approval and disparaging censure, often in the same essay. Typically, he is considered among fellow horror writers, and occasionally along with the American Gothic, but the number of complete books dedicated to his work is considerably less than fellow horror greats of American literature like Poe or Lovecraft. Stephen King's appeal for literary critics has grown with the rise of cultural studies, but in comparison to others in his genre, serious critiques of his work are lacking.

In fact, most of the reviews King's work has received by the critics echo the sentiments espoused by *The New York Times Book Review* in 1991, where the writer feels that *Needful Things* appeals only to readers with a stereotypical horror-novel-reading wardrobe (lots of black) because the work is "big, dumb, plodding, and obvious," and King's work is the "literary equivalent of heavy metal."[46] This review seems to overlook the

Introduction

specifics of the novel being reviewed to do what many King critiques do—evaluate King's work as a whole, as genre-specific texts with nothing to recommend them to serious study. It is unclear whether this reviewer (a seemingly bitter J. Queenan) is more aghast at the novel itself or the general culture of America. Apparently, baseball hats, black t-shirts, and an appreciation for heavy metal signify a lack of higher mental faculties because a person's wardrobe and musical tastes always indicate everything that is to be known about him, stereotypes be damned. Unfortunately, this kind of pigeonholed, cookie-cutter, knee-jerk response is typical of King criticism. In some cases, one begins to wonder if the reviewers actually read the books or just see the name on the cover and use the review as an excuse to vent their cultural observations. For instance, the ever-popular article in *Time Magazine*, "King of Horror," casually asserts that *IT* is filled with stereotypical characters, specifically as members of the Losers' Club: "a black, a homosexual, and — among others persecuted in adolescence and now called home to disinter a buried memory — a stutterer and an abused girl."[47] Perhaps some of the more serious subtext has been lost on this reader, but I did not realize that any member of the Losers' Club was gay. A quick skimming of the book might lead a careless reader to assume such about the effeminate hypochondriac Eddie Kasprak, but Eddie is a gentle person, not a man attracted to other men. Certainly King's work has its share of homosexual characters, but there is not one among the Losers, and such a casual comment brings the rest of the interpretations of the article into doubt. Just as Edmund Wilson revealed that he had not actually read *Lord of the Rings* when he continually misspelled Gandalf as "Gandalph" during his blistering review, King seems to have fallen prey to that old adage of judging a book by its cover.

Even those critics who embarrassingly admit that they enjoy King's work do so apologetically — take Ruth Franklin's evaluation from *The New Republic*. Franklin discusses her enjoyment of King's work the same way an alcoholic would describe her love of the drink, as though King is a dirty secret, a naughty pleasure, something that is bad for her health but somehow addictive. Like many pro–King critics, Franklin bestows some praise on King's later work, notably *Bag of Bones*, for some literary qualities, and even observes that King "does have an uncanny knack for seizing on the descriptive detail that makes you willing to suspend disbelief for even the most preposterous conceits."[48] Yet, even though she accepts that King does reveal serious issues, perhaps even literary matters in some of his work, the fact remains that being "true is not the same as being great," and in many critics' eyes, King will always remain a hack writer of horror novels.[49] Though some even praise his ability to tell good stories, apparently a lack of introspective characters and the unforgivable appearance of monsters disqualify King from the race of literary contenders. To anyone who claims that King's work lacks an inner focus, accept this challenge to read *The Stand* or *The Dark Tower* or *IT* or *Dreamcatcher* again, and this time pay attention to what is going on beyond the monsters and the gore. King's works teem with emotional inner lives—in fact, one of the criticisms of his work is that he spends too much time inside his characters, revealing too much of a person at the expense of the plot. Critics should not be able to discredit King for supposedly not doing something enough and then doing something too much at the same time. King's work may be filled with horror schlock, but there is depth to be found amid the blood spatter—should the critic be brave enough to really think seriously about (gasp!) a lowly Stephen King novel.

Yet even with such lukewarm critical responses to his work, King has been awarded the National Book Foundation's Medal for Distinguished Contribution to American Letters. Even so, there was such an outcry at the NBA's decision to bestow the award upon someone like Stephen King that the bitterness is reflected in King's acceptance speech: "What do you think, you get social or academic brownie points for staying out of touch with your own culture?"[50] Despite the outburst, though, King concluded on a positive note, hoping for a bridge between popular fiction and literary fiction to be built someday.

There have been other movements to reward King for his work; in fact, Frank McConnell explains how, when he served on the Pulitzer Prize Fiction Jury, he "made a 'silly'":

> I wrote, diffidently, to my two co-jurors and suggested that, while we might not want to award King the prize for that year, couldn't we maybe, like, mention him, and acknowledge that he was an American writer immersed in American culture and one hell of a good storyteller (those, by the way, being the announced optimal standards for the Pulitzer Prize)?[51]

The response he received for this preposterous suggestion left no room for debate. McConnell relates that he "may as well have suggested an orgy in a crack house" and explains how one of his co-jurors claimed that "nothing would induce him/her to sign anything praising Stephen King, and

Introduction

continued, 'I regard King as the chief cancer on our republic of letters—even more than Louis L'Amour or Danielle Steele.'"[52] Clearly, King is not a writer that the establishment is keen to acknowledge, even when notable critics humbly suggest the possibility.

Despite this, however, King has managed to earn the right to a Howard Bloom–edited collection of essays in 1998 — a rather surprising foray into the realm of serious scholarship. Before readers get excited about this apparent critical success, however, it is important to note that Bloom's introduction is devoted to a rather scathing theory of current fiction. In fact, Bloom baldly states that the fact that he must write the introduction to a collection of essays about the popular writer Stephen King marks the downfall of an entire generation of American readers, and that "King will be remembered as a sociological phenomenon, an image of the death of the Literate Reader."[53] He deplores the popularity of King's work, stating plainly, "The triumph of the genial King is a large emblem of the failures of American education."[54] And readers of his introduction might think that he connects anyone who dares to write of King critically with a tabloid celebrity squawking about the latest Hollywood gossip. In Bloom's eyes, King is entirely unworthy of criticism, and the fact that such a body of criticism exists marks the end of American literature as we know it. Bloom adds, after admitting to rereading *Carrie* and *The Shining* "with great effort," that "the prose is undistinguished, and there is nothing much that could be termed characterization or inwardness, or even vivid caricature."[55] Bloom does grudgingly admit that King has mastered the art of powerful images, though he believes that the images aren't themselves powerful but gain power as a result of his "heaping them up" until they "constitute giant or central images."[56] Bloom clearly dislikes King's work and goes out of his way to condescend to the writers whose critical works are included in his text with a number of "Ben P. Indick believes" or "Chelsea Quinn Yarbro claims" phrases. Essentially, the gist of Bloom's introduction is that King is a curious popular phenomenon, akin to jelly shoes or *American Idol*, and serious study of his work is an indulgence at best.

Though Bloom lambastes King in the introduction as a disgrace to literature, the authors and essays included in his book have become landmarks in King criticism. More recent criticism is still somewhat lacking (despite a small surge in theses and dissertations in the last few years), especially since the flurry in the 1980s, and full-length studies are negligible, but the collections that do exist are certainly insightful. Nineteen

Introduction

eighty-four marked the year of Douglas Winter's *Stephen King: The Art of Darkness*, and Tim Underwood and Chuck Miller's collection of essays under the title *Fear Itself*. These two works set the standard for King criticism with their evaluation of theme and style in each of his novels published to date. Both books devoted a section to each of King's novels, but neither delved into any one work with any real depth.

Michael Collings explains in his analysis *The Many Facets of Stephen King* the problem with much of the scholarship on Stephen King. Up until Collings' work in 1985, King criticism had addressed his novels from a chronological standpoint, a seemingly convenient but entirely impractical way to view King's work. After all, the order in which King's works were published does not reflect the order in which they were written. Collings organizes his critique topically, and, in doing so, takes the first few steps into serious King scholarship.[57]

As if Michael Collings had sounded the alarm for scholarly attentions, 1985 marked a year of much criticism. Still, most of these were collections of essays by various authors, each examining some aspect of King's work, but nothing too in-depth. Darrell Schweitzer, in his two volumes of *Discovering Modern Horror Fiction*, the first of which includes Ben P. Indick's "Stephen King as an Epic Writer" (the essay that compares *The Stand* to Tolkien's *Lord of the Rings*), explains that King's popularity is largely to thank for the existence of the collections at all: "King has attracted so much attention, and inspired so many books already, that it is useful to think of the *Discovering Modern Horror* series as typical volumes of Stephen King criticism — only about everybody else."[58] The swell of collections continued in 1985 with Darrell Schweitzer's *Discovering Stephen King*, an assortment of current King scholarship. Also in 1985, Michael Collings published *Stephen King as Richard Bachman*, a consideration of the works King penned under his alternate identity; and, with David Engebretson, *The Shorter Works of Stephen King*, a look at King's short stories.

Trends in King scholarship continued along these lines until 1987, when Michael Collings published *The Stephen King Phenomenon*— the first book to really address the collection of existing King criticism. Collings puts matters into perspective:

> At first, it was difficult to find neutral — to say nothing of favorable — criticism of King's novels; now, when critics have begun to take him seriously and to explore the complexities of the worlds he creates, they are themselves not taken quite seriously; the prevailing attitude seems to be that

> there must be something self-serving in someone who devotes this much time and effort to a writer who is himself "academically" suspect.[59]

Even two decades later, Stephen King is still not an accepted figure in American literature, and students are more likely to read J.K. Rowling's *Harry Potter* novels in class than King's; but there is something to this writer's work, for specialists and genre fans alike continue to find something compelling in his books.

In the late 1980s and 1990s, there were several book-length critiques of King's novels (though none examining a single novel), including Tony Magistrale's *Landscape of Fear: Stephen King's American Gothic* in 1988, Joseph Reino's *The First Decade:* Carrie *to* Pet Sematary, Tyson Blue's *The Unseen King* in 1989, and Jonathan P. Davis' *Stephen King's America* in 1994. More collections of essays appeared in the late 1990s, including an examination of King's depiction of women, edited by Kathleen Margaret Lant and Theresa Thompson; and both Stephen J. Spignesi and George Beahm have published several books of biographical criticism in the early 2000s. But the explosion of criticism in the 1980s has not been repeated since. Much of the recent work on King focuses on his *Dark Tower* series, likely because King recently completed the last installment in this seven-novel story.

So how does King deal with this kind of response to his work? As an author who is known for using public speaking engagements as a small soapbox to mock his critics, King is surprisingly humble in his reaction. If the critics do not approve of his work, he seems to say, then so be it. He isn't writing for them anyway. He will speak passionately about censorship of his work, particularly when it comes to teens, but as long as people have access to his books and can make their own judgments, King seems contented. To use his own words, King says, "I have become wealthy and well-known to a very real extent because I happen to be an average American of my time with some narrative ability and some visualization skills. To be well-paid for what I do is great; to be honestly enjoyed by so many readers is greater."[60] King admits that when he first writes a story, he has "zippo interest in theme, allegory, symbolism, politics, ethics, sexual roles, culture, or dramatic unity." Instead, King claims a secret desire to be Typhoid Stevie:

> I want to reach through the pages and grab the reader. I don't want to just mess with your head; I want to mess with your life. I want you to miss appointments, burn dinner, skip your homework. I want you to tell your

wife to take that moonlight stroll on the beach at Waikiki with the resort's tennis pro while you read a few more chapters.... I want you to be sorry you ever started the goddamned thing in the first place, and I still don't want you to be able to stop.[61]

This kind of visceral experience is one of the things that keeps King's readers turning pages long into the night, way beyond the point where they know they will have haunting dreams of clowns in sewers and cursed monkey toys. Still, even for King, that horrid blight on American literature, there can be more to a novel than a gripping story. Not to say that there has to be another level beyond the surface to a story — just that there is always room for such depth. According to King, a book which "lives only on an emotional spectrum is a disposable item — the mental equivalent of a stick of gum."[62] An avid gum chewer myself, it is clear that there is nothing wrong with a novel that works once to get the readers involved (consider the shelves at Walmart that are jammed with romance novels — the ultimate one trick pony). King just wants to allow for the possibility that just because it grabs readers emotionally and happens to be popular with the masses does not mean that it cannot have more literary qualities.

Despite what appears to be a mound of criticism for an author who is not taken too seriously, there is an obvious absence in King scholarship — an in-depth examination of just one text. Most King scholarship discusses connections between novels and stories, and settles for exploring common themes in King's life and work. Trying to find more than one chapter in a book devoted to the same novel is quite difficult. This is not to say that each novel has not been properly examined on different levels; instead, the intention here is to point out that a single novel has not been examined in-depth by one author in one fell swoop, nor have the echoes of a novel's themes been covered within that same study.

The intention here is to fill this absence — to make a thoroughly formalist examination of *The Stand*, a novel filled with so many themes and symbols that a book considering the whole picture could potentially be longer than the work itself. Hopefully, it is possible to evaluate this novel on strictly literary terms; by looking at things like setting and characterization, this analysis considers the text as a work of literature — inspecting the fine details in order to extract meaning on multiple levels. If the purpose of literature is, as Horace suggested, to entertain and educate, *The Stand* delivers on both counts. If the criteria for literature is to be Bloom's "arresting strangeness," this mysterious quality can be found in the work.

Introduction

At the very least, King's work possesses the "re-readability" that introductions to literary study often suggest is the key characteristic of literature. Readers of King's work get a glimpse of a world beyond the ordinary, beyond the known boundaries of their experience, and though the experience may be unsettling, it offers the opportunity for reflection — a chance to consider critical questions about the human condition that is the line of demarcation between classic works of literature and best-selling page-turners.

A Defense of Escapism

King's work may be worthwhile, yes, but it is still firmly stuck in the escapist category — an area not frequented by those scholars of academia. Certainly, many people read King as a way to escape from reality; in fact, many people read any books at all to escape from the everyday, or at least their everyday. Even those fans of true crime thrillers are trying to get away from the ordinary world they see every day — even though the works are based on true stories or real people, the readers can see and experience things they never could or would in their ordinary lives. Americans have a general disdain for the very idea of escaping, it seems, even while they engage in escapist activities. Who hasn't heard of a vacation spot advertising how it's the perfect time and place to escape the routine of the everyday? Yet, escaping suggests running away, hiding, fleeing the scene never to be seen again, and this flies in the face of the American value to stand and fight, to defend rights and Right even in the face of likely defeat. To read escapist fiction, then, is to be a coward of sorts, someone afraid to face the world or unable to reconcile with the harsh reality of life. This unfortunate connection between lexicon and literary term is partly to blame for the difficult relationship between critics and so-called escapist fiction.

However, as Tolkien so aptly demonstrates in his essay "Tree and Leaf," there is a difference between generic escapist fiction (i.e., bodice rippers and cheesy teen vampire romance, where there is no real depth beyond the story — not that there is anything wrong with those kinds of stories) and literary escapist fiction. The former are entertaining, to say the least, and enjoyable for what they are, but when engrossed in their pages, readers are not expecting to walk away with any sense of depth or renewed perceptions of life garnered from within their pages. Stories like these are the very definition of escapism — they take readers away from the ordinary, do not force them to think in any way, and deliver exactly what readers are hoping for. The characters may be engaging, the storyline fascinating, but as for insight into the human condition or re-readability after the last page, few readers will find answers to life's burning questions within their covers. Again, this is not to say that they have no value to society; if they did not, people wouldn't waste their time reading them.

Certainly there is a comfort in reading these works. In the midst of a crazy world, a hectic life, an unpredictable future, a constant sense of overload, and a near manic drive to get everything done that needs doing, a break from the daze of the everyday routine with a favorite cheesy romance may be just the thing to relieve stress. These books demand nothing from readers but time and the ability to read. Typically, there are no difficult passages to read, no confounding vocabulary to look up, and no tangential forays into symbolism to decipher. And yet, readers devour them whole. This suggests that Americans enjoy the opportunity to lose themselves in a book that will not give them anything but pure enjoyment. Most of the time, these stories work out precisely as readers expect them to, a quality that makes them even more equipped to fend off the stress of the everyday. In the real world, things rarely work out as planned. In cheesy escapist fiction, things are always going to work out as expected, and everyone is satisfied in the end — unless it's a murder mystery–type thing. In that case, there may be a shocking upset, but even this twist is expected of the genre, and readers are prepared for the moment of revelation (It really was the butler!).

These works are very different from literary escapist fiction. Though many authors, King among them, have been neatly filed away in the escapist category, not all of their fiction is so easily dismissed. As Tolkien explains, there is a marked difference between someone running away from reality for a moment to disappear into a good book — escapist fiction — and the escapist dreams of a prisoner. The former chooses to abandon reality for a time; the latter is forced to do something to occupy the time, and the dreams that come in those circumstances are typically far more engaged with the human condition than anything the former has to offer. When one has nothing else to do but dream, those dreams take on a deeper quality, an imitation of life as it is or as it ought to be, but always ringing with more reverberations of the eternal questions than any simple escapist novel can claim. Such escapist stories, then, are not an escape from life, as it were, but an escape into life — an attempt to reclaim that which has been lost along the journey. This quality, this deeper understanding of what it means to be human, is what distinguishes literary escapist fiction from something picked up in a bargain bin and devoured over a few mindless hours.

Like its poorer (in literary value, but certainly not in copies sold) cousins, literary escapist fiction often falls into the category of escapism due to genre or stigma, not because of the words that wait beneath the cover. Stephen King has written a few horror novels, critics assume; therefore, this newest work must also be a horror novel, and we can dismiss it without even really looking into it. Many popular authors suffer the same fate, ignored by academia because of their presumed content — or because that content is so quickly and greedily enjoyed by readers.

King's *The Stand* certainly asks readers to consider the deeper questions in life, to ponder what it means to be human at a time when humanity is in danger of extinction. In fact, King's survivors bear an even heavier burden — that of rebuilding society — and of deciding how much or how little the new world should resemble the old. What makes this foray into escapism even more relevant to most readers is that these big decisions are left in the hands of ordinary people, recognizable blue collar Americans, deadbeat rock stars, unwed pregnant girls, retired school teachers, and traumatized children. All have been deeply changed by the super flu, but they remain recognizable as Americans, as believable people in an extraordinary situation who must perform as best they can. Their story is an escape into the heart of living, of carrying on in the face of great odds, and even though the packaging of their tale may appear simplistic or escapist, what readers learn by following these characters on their journeys transcends genre and attains that elevated literary plain that scholars so value. Granted, King's story may arrive at the literary cocktail party wearing scuffed shoes and worn jeans, but it has traversed the same roads across the readers' consciousness to get there and deserves some consideration, even if it appears untraditional. In fact, it is by virtue of being escapist that King's story reaches so many readers; they pick it up expecting something simple to pass the time and end up learning more about the human condition than they ever expected — a very effective way of expanding literary influence across a broad spectrum of readers.

Some people who would probably never read Henry James can experience psychological realism through King's narration of characters' interior lives. Readers can absorb the tenets of Realism without having to read a manual on literary movements. The very draw of escapism is an easy way to teach an unsuspecting audience very literary matters; but what makes King's work truly brilliant, what makes him so unique in this field, is that readers do not *have* to imbibe literary values when reading him. They can enjoy the story first and foremost. If they absorb some insights along the way, all the better, but King does not require his audience to think so critically as some traditional literary works do. There is nothing wrong with using a traditionally escapist format to catch readers' attention, and for King, that unassuming appeal is how he hooks his readers before reeling them in by raising key questions in the back of their minds. Whether they choose to answer those issues or not is not King's concern; it is enough that the audience reads the story and has been given the choice of critical thought. This subtle schooling is the hallmark of literary escapist fiction, and *The Stand* is a perfect example of this technique.

The Stand

The Stand was originally published in 1978, an epic novel about a super flu that destroys 99.4 percent of the world's population. The real story, however, is not about the flu itself; rather, King focuses on the world after this modern (and much more vicious) Black Plague. The crux of the novel is the battle between the forces of good and evil, as each side is influenced by both Christian theology and outside forces of unnamed fate. King addresses serious issues of the human condition and human nature as he establishes the framework of his narrative, illustrating his ability to tell an engaging story while forcing readers to confront questions about the potential future of mankind.

The Stand begins with the flight of Thomas Campion and his family from a secure military installation. Though he managed to escape before the gates sealed the facility for good, Campion is not fast enough to escape a dose of a fatal super flu, and his flight allows the spread of this deadly virus to canvas the country. The narrative focuses on a large cast of characters as they experience and react to the super flu: Stu Redman, the good old boy from Arnette, Texas, who is inexplicably immune despite endless tests by government officials; Frannie Goldsmith, a pregnant girl from Ogunquit, Maine, who is one of two survivors in her entire town; Harold

Introduction

Lauder, an outcast boy from Ogunquit, Maine, who is tormented by aspirations of greatness (and obsessed with Frannie Goldsmith); Larry Underwood, a one-hit wonder who is patently "not a nice guy"; Glen Bateman, a retired sociologist who theorizes about mankind's future in the post-plague world; Nick Andros, a wandering deaf-mute who is used by divine powers beyond his control; Tom Cullen, a mentally challenged man who has an innocence that even the super flu cannot destroy; Nadine Cross, a woman tortured with indecision about the part she will play in the post-plague world; Lloyd Heinreid, a hardened criminal who willingly chooses to serve evil in the form of his master; and Trashcan Man, a pyromaniac whose obsession with fire manages to undermine the very cause he seeks to aid. Once the virus has taken its toll on most of the population, the survivors begin to group themselves into two main factions: the mostly good-hearted join Mother Abagail, a 108-year-old Christian woman in Nebraska; and the bad, though this is sometimes a matter of perspective, join Randall Flagg, King's embodiment of evil.

The narrative follows these characters as they converge in an epic showdown between good and evil. Some of the "good" characters betray their comrades as they try to rebuild society in Boulder, Colorado; some of the "bad" guys turn out to be bad news for their own people in Las Vegas, Nevada. At the end, four heroes set out from the "good" camp in Boulder, Colorado, at the behest of a dying Mother Abagail, to stand against their foes in Las Vegas, Nevada. Three of the heroes are apprehended by Flagg's people in Las Vegas (one falls along the way and cannot continue, but is rescued as an ironic result). Of the three heroes, one is brutally shot when he laughs in the face of his enemy, and the other two are paraded out for a public execution. Before things get too far underway, however, one of Randall Flagg's minions, the pyromaniac Trashcan Man, arrives with a nuclear bomb. Through a series of fortunate catastrophes — one of the "bad" people speaks out against the execution and is summarily electrocuted by a bolt of lightning — the bomb is detonated and everyone (except Flagg, of course, who manages to escape in spirit form at the last second) is blown up. The novel finishes with the tale of the lone hero's return to Boulder, only to find the new haven is quickly starting to resemble the America everyone remembers, problems intact. He and his family decide to find a place without so many people and potential pitfalls, and the novel ends with the unanswered question: "Do people ever really learn anything?"

Introduction

King's novels are known for their length, often several hundred pages, but *The Stand* is the only book that King had to considerably shorten in order to publish. When he first sent *The Stand* to his publisher, King was forced to remove close to 500 pages of text in order to make the book marketable. When he released a new and uncut version in 1990, after his popularity allowed him to publish as he wanted, King made several changes to the original story. First, he changed the date of the novel from 1980 to 1990. He added a new beginning and a new ending, along with restoring some 150,000 words. King also included a new preface to the expanded edition, explaining to readers that this rendition was not a new story but rather an expansion of the original. Though he insists that readers will not discover old characters doing new things, King does say that readers will find more information about old characters and even meet some new ones along the way.[63] When he considers the question of length (that is, why expand a book that was already over 800 pages), King gives an extended analogy. He summarizes Hansel and Gretel into a paragraph that captures the essentials of the tale, then explains how that version is like a stripped down Cadillac—the essence is intact, but the effect is lost without the finer details. The new version of *The Stand* is, in King's mind, a restored Cadillac with all of the bells and whistles—a car as it ought to be. King also adds as an afterthought to his preface that *The Stand* is his fans' favorite, and it is his intention to have this final version answer the thousands of fan letters asking, "What happened to so-and-so?"

At the end of his preface to the complete and uncut version of *The Stand* published in 1990, Stephen King refers to this story as a "long dark tale of Christianity."[64] The apocalyptic novel is not a new idea by any means, but King hasn't just written another end of the world tale. The curious thing about *The Stand* is that it is specifically about the end of America, and everything that the country stands for and encompasses, just as much as it is about the endless fight between good and evil as waged by a few memorable characters. Many apocalyptic novels focus on the destruction of humanity and the loss of modernization, and those forces are present in *The Stand*—perhaps not more clearly than the afternoon Frannie spends scrubbing clothes in a washtub and bemoaning the loss of her washing machine—but even more so, *The Stand* echoes with a thoroughly American consciousness. Perhaps this is because Americans are hard-wired into modernization, and they can imagine the loss of technological benefits more easily, as someone who relies on her computer can

Introduction

imagine a world without the internet during the hours when service is unavailable. King's work appeals to Americans because it is about the world in which they live — the brand names they recognize, the comforts they utilize, and the cars they drive appear in the novel.

The Stand introduces a theme common to the rest of King's work: the notion of the stand itself. Essentially, Standing Up in a King novel means to confront evil at all costs. When characters are forced to make their stand, they often do so without training, weapons, preparation, or expectation of survival. In fact, most of King's heroes do not survive their final stand, but what is important is that they do stand, for however long they can manage. King values the idea over the result of the idea.

However, *The Stand* poses certain problems for readers who want to know what to expect from the novel. First of all, it shifts from an apocalyptic end of the world set-up to an epic fantasy about good and evil expressed in Christian theology. Readers end up feeling as confused as the characters in the novel — not with the narrative but with their own expectations. Collings explains this uncertainty best when he says:

> In terms of genre, *The Stand* is problematical, since it lacks the monsters and creatures of traditional horror, except for Randall Flagg's occasional shape-shifting. It begins within a science-fictional framework, detailing with the care and precision of hard science fiction the consequences of an escaped super-flu virus; yet just as the characters begin to adjust to the new world technology has forced upon them, they must confront something essentially fantastic — their dreams of Mother Abagail and the Dark Man. Again and again, King shifts between dark fantasy and science fiction as the novel turns from the superflu to Randall Flagg. At the same time, its length and scope link it with the epic quest, as Ben Indick argued recently in "Stephen King as Epic Writer" when he points out a number of thematic and topical resemblances to Tolkien's *The Lord of the Rings*.[65]

What is one to do with such a mixture of purpose and genre? By blending modes, King manages to attract a wide variety of readers from all spectrums of interest, and he is also able to create a complete fabric out of variegated threads. *The Stand* is such a critical work because it is complete. As Tolkien explained in his essay "On Fairy Stories," any good fantasy needs to be believable according to the terms of the world in which it exists. According to these characteristics, King succeeds admirably in creating a viable Secondary Reality as believable to readers as their own lives, and this verisimilitude allows readers to get involved with the char-

Introduction

acters and events of the novel. When Larry and Nadine stare out at the deserted Maine coastline, Larry is conflicted by his emotions:

> Part of him clamored at their sad and blatant ugliness and at the ugliness of the minds that had turned this section of a magnificent, savage coastline into one long highway amusement park for families in station wagons. But there was a more subtle, deeper part of him that whispered of the people who had filled these places and this road during other summers. Ladies in sunhats and shorts too tight for their large behinds. College boys in red-and-black-striped rugby shirts. Girls in beach shifts and thong sandals. Small screaming children with ice cream spread over their faces. They were American people and there was a dirty, compelling romance about them whenever they were in groups—nevermind if the group was in an Aspen ski lodge or performing their prosaic rites of summer along U.S. 1 in Maine. And now all those Americans were gone.[66]

Larry understands what readers can only imagine—the loss of everything that identifies himself as a member of America. King illustrates this dislocation with handy images—most Americans will be able to picture such a summer vacation, even if the reader has never personally been to U.S. 1 in Maine. The people, quickly evoked with a few short lines, are familiar to readers, and King raises that familiarity only to destroy the tranquility of the readers' experience. These people, so easily imagined, are gone, victims of the super flu, and readers can only try to imagine a world without fun-filled vacation lands or, even worse, all of those empty vacation spots slowly being reclaimed by Nature. It seems a harsh judgment indeed on mankind. Scenes like this are typical of King's writing, evidence of his devotion to realism and his ability to capture the essence of the thing— the familiarity of Larry's recollection of U.S. 1 resonates in readers' imaginations, creating the sense that Bloom requires of literature, to feel strangely at home in the text.

One of the major questions raised by critics and readers alike on the subject of *The Stand* involves the overt Christianity of the tale. Like Tolkien before him, King's epic is sometimes considered an allegory; this is interesting in one facet, but such an interpretation ignores the multiple levels of meaning intertwined through the novel. When asked about the "Christian allegory" in *The Stand*, King replied:

> *The Stand* starts out with a plague that wipes out most of the world's population, and it develops into a titanic struggle that Christianity figures in. But it's not about God, like some of the reviews claimed. Stuart Redman isn't Christ, and the Dark Man isn't the Devil…. The important thing is

Introduction

that we are dealing with two elemental forces—White and Black—and I really do believe in the White force. Children are a part of that force, which is why I write about them the way I do. There are a lot of horror writers who deal with this struggle, but they tend to concentrate on the Black. Look at Tolkien and *The Lord of the Rings*; he's much better at evoking the horror and the dread of Mordor and the Dark Lord than he is at doing Gandalf.[67]

Allegorical readings are often too close to a child-like interpretation for comfort. Certainly, some things in *The Stand* can be read as allegorical (Stu Redman could be an image of the New American Indian—just look at his last name) but not as strictly allegorical (Stu is hardly a man who lives off the land and espouses a "back to nature" ideology). In other words, to focus on the one-to-one correlations between *The Stand* and Christianity seems to zoom in on one fraction of the work's potential and to ignore the whole picture entirely. It may enhance the reading experience to think of the Walkin' Dude (Randall Flagg) as the Devil, just as it may add to the overall believability of *Lord of the Rings* to see Sauron as Adolf Hitler, but this is only a sideline interpretation—one that makes it too easy for readers to disregard anything else.

The Stand offers readers a wide spectrum of American consciousness beyond the Christian overtones; from the small town of Ogunquit, Maine, to the backwoods of Arnette, Texas, readers are flooded with recognizable images and then forced to watch as their familiar country is ruthlessly destroyed by a deadly super flu. Of all of his novels, *The Stand* allowed King to delve the deepest into the backgrounds of many, many different characters. This is one of the complaints that some readers have of King. After all, they claim, do they need to know a man's entire history in order to grasp that he's the one who will spread the super flu to everyone at the movie theater? The answer to this question, on the surface, is no. Readers don't need to know the details of the character in order for him to perform his function in the plot. However, if one were to distill King's works into basic plot without detail, what would be the fun of reading him at all? Part of King's charm is his knack for creating believable characters for readers to identify with; his skill does not stop with main characters. He will devote several pages to the background and quirks of a character whom he will kill off in the next few pages. While some see this as excess information, others see that such devotion to detail is what makes a King novel work. Readers can't be expected to care about a random character who goes to the movies—not when so many other characters are well-developed—and yet King's readers find that they *do* care about that lone moviegoer despite themselves. For his few paragraphs or pages, he is just as vibrant to them as their next door neighbor, perhaps more so, and this resonance is what keeps readers engrossed after several hundred pages.

This attention to detail, this connection with the small behind-the-scenes characters in the novel, allows King to connect with his audience on another level. Most readers know that they will never be the hero of the story—most are ordinary people who will never stand up to the military or face down the Dark Man. Readers identify with the small people in the stories—the man who tries to take his family on vacation by car, the woman who plays bridge with her friends, the waitress in the small town. This is King's audience. When he mentions these ordinary Americans, even for a brief moment, the readers feel a connection, an appreciation, a consolation in the knowledge that someone somewhere may know their names, their history, and care, if only for a moment. It is a validation of the common man, a reminder that even the ordinary guy can have an effect on the world, and even if that effect is just to spread a deadly virus, someone is watching, and someone will remember.

The Tolkien Connection

King has been quoted as claiming his intention with *The Stand* was to create an epic akin to *Lord of the Rings* but for an American consciousness. It is curious how history repeats itself, as Tolkien himself claimed that he created *The Lord of the Rings* in order to give England a mythology to rival that of the already popular King Arthur and his knights. Though the longevity of King's American attempt remains to be seen, certainly Tolkien was successful in creating a legacy not only for his own country but for a worldwide readership. When considering *The Stand*, several critics have pointed out the similarities between King's epic battle and Tolkien's famous trilogy, but none so specifically as Ben P. Indick in "Stephen King as Epic Writer." In fact, most of the existing criticism on *The Stand* deals with the *Lord of the Rings* echoes in some fashion—it seems that King's work cannot be criticized without a comparison to Tolkien. Though this kind of examination does not encompass the complex tapestry that is *The Stand*, certainly there are obvious correlations between the two epics.

Introduction

For Tolkien scholars, the echoes are easy to see, even without Indick's essay. First, both stories concern themselves with a great battle between good and evil. For King's characters, the battle lines are between the Free Zone of Boulder, peopled with Mother Abagail's followers, and Randall Flagg's army making preparations in Las Vegas. For Tolkien, the Free Peoples of Middle Earth must stand fast against the darkness of Mordor and the elusive Sauron. Differences of time and place cease to matter once the bare components of the plot are revealed, but epic clashes between good and evil are by no means new to the realm of literature. In fact, most literary works deal with this conflict in some way, whether it is man vs. man, man vs. himself, man vs. Nature, or man vs. God; literature often displays such battles for control, and sometimes the battle lines are drawn along moral grounds. Both King and Tolkien have taken up this ancient tradition in their work.

Both stories revolve around the notion of a "party of heroes" who stand against darkness. Though King's party is made up of ordinary people from all walks of life, and most of his fellowship actually makes up the committee set up to rebuild life in Boulder—not the ideal image of heroes—King's characters still evoke images of Tolkien's intrepid travelers. The Free Zone Committee may not be entirely representative of the Free Peoples, but King's fellowship is thrown together by happenstance or fate, just as Tolkien's is chosen by Elrond—a god-like figure in Middle Earth. This is where the similarities end, however, as King's heroes are not happy about being in charge, nor do they see themselves as champions of good in the coming battle against evil. No one volunteers to help destroy the evil in King's work; there is no brave dwarf to step forward and offer his services to the greater good, no elf to show up in Rivendell and expect to be sent with the Fellowship. Even more so, the mission itself is unclear in King's work. The characters spend a great deal of time wondering what they ought to be doing and vacillating between believing that Mother Abagail is divinely inspired and speaks the Word of God, and convincing themselves that she's just an old woman and that such things don't happen in the real world. Perhaps this inability to accept the existence of forces beyond human control is a result of an American determination to separate the spiritual from the secular. Just as Americans divide church and state, so do they tend to divide the supernatural from everyday experience, and this split leads to a general uncertainty about both facets of the world.

This is King at his best again, creating believable situations with realistic characters. What American reader would not hesitate in such circumstances? Though many may think of the intrepid fellowship found in novels of epic quests, few would actually welcome the chance to endure such a journey in person. After all, it is far easier to suffer Frodo's pain in Mordor from the safe distance of a comfortable couch and words on a page than to imagine actually walking away from Boulder without even packing a bag. In *The Stand*, the heroes' journey to Las Vegas is not so far away and imaginary—readers know where in the country the men are walking; they know the familiar landscapes; and they probably have the slow realization that if it were up to them to march over to the evil camp and face down the Dark Man, they might decide that Mother Abagail is just a crazy old woman after all. It's easy to watch others torn out of their everyday, ordinary lives and hijacked into adventure; it is not so easy to consider such a journey for oneself. It is easier, perhaps, to justify seemingly supernatural events as coincidence, to ignore signs and symbols in favor of preserving the comforts of the known and the familiar. This is particularly true of those in *The Stand*—they have lost their familiarity once already in the aftermath of the super flu and only just gotten back into a routine, and now they must give up that newfound, and suddenly very much appreciated, security to face the unknown yet again, this time knowing that death is as likely an outcome as any other. It takes more courage than most Americans would want to muster, and King reminds them of that as they watch four ordinary Americans stride off into the darkness. Granted, the Americans are only characters, but readers have spent enough time with these people that their dilemma is not easily ignored, and questions of "What would I do?" inevitably echo in their minds.

Characters in Tolkien share no such ambivalence about their purpose. There is no question that Sauron is evil and that the Ring must be dealt with. Each character knows what he is expected to do. The question of certainty is a characteristic that often marks the difference between fantasy and horror fiction. In fantasy, heroes always know the quest before them. Frodo must destroy the Ring. Spenser's Red Cross Knight must rescue Lady Una. Peter S. Beagle's last Unicorn must free her brethren. In horror, characters spend a great deal of time trying to accept that crazy things really are happening. Nick never quite accepts the truth of Mother Abagail's God. In William Peter Blatty's *The Exorcist*, Reagan's mother tries every other alternative before accepting that her daughter is possessed. It is quite common for victims in horror tales to stand by as their death approaches—whether it be in the form of a monstrous beast or a deranged killer; true, characters in horror are frozen by the terror of what is happening, but they are even more paralyzed by their own inability to believe in what is happening to them. Characters in fantasy may suffer self-doubt or make poor choices during moments of stress, but they rarely doubt the very events that surround them; in horror, this uncertainty is a common issue. Still, both King and Tolkien have chosen a select group of characters to stand their ground against evil, and in this their works mirror one another.

The Stand and *Lord of the Rings* involve ambiguous characters who blur the battle lines but end up being crucial in the end. For King, the turncoats Harold Lauder and Nadine Cross plant the bomb that sends the four remaining heroes off to stand before darkness. Without their betrayal, Larry, Glen, Ralph, and Stu would never have left the safety of Boulder for Las Vegas, nor would they have confronted Flagg in his place of power. Indick is quick to point out that King also adds the odd character of the Trashcan Man, a tortured pyromaniac who would as soon serve his master as light him on fire—literally. For Tolkien, the entire idea of the Fellowship is to go into Mordor, but the presence of the ambiguous Gollum ends up becoming the most important thing in the end. Both King and Tolkien suggest that though evil may seem to cause only problems, sometimes such trouble is the only path towards victory. Occasionally, evil will serve the side of good at the crucial moment and tip the balance.

Both novels deal with excessively high stakes—the end of the world as the characters know it—and both end with a eucatastrophe of sorts. For King, evil turns on itself—a notion that Tolkien would have heartily agreed with—and Randall Flagg is destroyed ... for now. Through a series of happy coincidences (public execution, evocation of lightning, arrival of nuclear bomb, annihilation), evil is vanquished for a time, and though the sacrifices may seem severe, they are a necessary part of the battle. Even as events play out, readers may be uncertain about the outcome; after all, Flagg survives to the last page, but looking back, it is easy enough to see how each part came together in a fortunate catastrophe. If Larry and Ralph had not walked out to stand against Flagg, there would not have been a public execution, and though the bomb would still have arrived, Flagg would not have invoked his lightning anywhere near it. The chain of seemingly disastrous events culminates in the perfect scenario to destroy (or at least beat back) the force of evil. In the end, much life is lost, but it is for the greater good. For Tolkien, eucatastrophe is the heart of the story's climax. By combining the elements of Frodo's surrender with Gollum's greed and Aragorn's final stand, Tolkien was able to make a series of rather unfortunate events work themselves out in the end.

Even the villains of both works are similar. King's Randall Flagg is ambiguous; with his dreadful hilarity and his smooth palms, the dark man evokes horror through his terrible good joy. Flagg's horror is that he looks like an ordinary man, and his behavior is a mockery of humanity — a terrible insight into the human psyche. King suggests that the thing to fear the most is inside ourselves. Randall Flagg delights in evil for its own sake, and readers are shown little of his plans beyond the immediate future. The reasons why Flagg does what he does are as mysterious as Sauron's reasons for his evil nature. In Middle Earth, Sauron is merely a force of evil represented as a lidless eye ringed in fire. A big eye seems unlikely to pose a real threat as a villain, but Tolkien manages to use this simple device to make Sauron into more than just another bad guy. Sauron is beyond physical form, beyond the mind's comprehension, and therefore even more terrifying. He is beyond the scope of any character's experience. King also uses this idea of an Evil Eye, but it is less specific than Sauron's physical manifestation. Mother Abagail is aware of a great Eye that is sentient, searching for her as she waits for her supporters to arrive in Nebraska. When Harold first considers going West to Flagg, he too sees a Sauron-like eye in the distance that calls out to him, forcing him to acknowledge the darkness within himself. Clearly, King is influenced by Tolkien's imagery, for it appears in small strokes across the world of the novel, and specifically whenever Flagg is mentioned early in the story. In fact, before Flagg is introduced as a physical being, King hints at the existence of evil beyond the super flu with visions of eyes and fire, classic Tolkien symbols of darkness and evil. Each character senses the call of that Eye, and each must decide whether to heed the darkness or to stand against it. Ultimately, though, characters choose their fate, suggesting that though evil may call out to everyone, it is the decision to stand against it that makes one a good person. The evil is a reflection, then, a mirror of one's internal struggles. Where King suggests that true evil is internalized in humanity, Tolkien shows that real fear should be of that which lies beyond human experience.

Tolkien does explain Sauron's history in *The Silmarillion* and other stories, but readers must eventually accept that Sauron is evil because he is evil. Though this may seem a simple Manichean view of Middle Earth, there are shades of the Boethian as well. Characters in both stories are faced with a mostly faceless, mindless force of evil — the Manichean dualism expected in fantasy and horror. However, the characters in both stories are often given choices — a rather Boethian right. There are moments in *The Stand* and in *Lord of the Rings* where characters are robbed of their free will, but these usually occur after the character has been given a choice and has made his stand one way or the other. Nadine Cross can't help herself from going to Flagg in the end, but she had many chances to choose differently — the least of which is the night she throws herself at Larry and tries to have him make the choice for her. A person must choose, King suggests here, and trying to foist that decision onto someone else is a manifestation of weakness that will probably lead to a poor choice in the end anyway. For King, strength lies in making a decision; avoiding a choice is a sign of weakness in one's character and, more importantly, in one's soul. Apparently, Tolkien shares this viewpoint on free will as well, when he has Boromir eventually become obsessed with the Ring. There were many moments along the way where Boromir could have stayed true — Lothlorien's healing presence the most likely chance for his redemption — but Boromir chose his people before his quest; and in making that not-so-damning decision, he managed to fracture the Fellowship in one fell swoop. Both authors value the notion of free will in their novels, illustrating that making the choice is crucial for any character who hopes to someday triumph over evil.

The limited triumph over darkness that the characters in both *The Stand* and *The Lord of the Rings* enjoy is closely connected to the divine intervention in both stories. King's god is a Christian figure, a demanding deity from the Old Testament who tests his creations with quests and sacrifice, but more often with the act of faith itself. King's characters struggle with belief even as they are presented with cryptic images that both suggest and deny the existence of a supreme being. In Tolkien, the god is well known and accepted, if not mentioned in the popular story itself. Middle Earth has a "Bible" of its own, a series of tales compiled by the elves into the book known as *The Silmarillion*, a text published posthumously by Christopher Tolkien. The elves, as the "authors" of this history, are well aware of their creator, Iluvatar, and of the long history of the world before and after their Awakening into existence. Many have criticized Tolkien's world for its apparent lack of organized religion, but the absence of a traditional pattern of worship is actually a result of *knowledge*—the people of Middle Earth do not wonder if there is a supreme being. They simply have to read the old texts of the elves, immortal beings who know the truth, to learn about the world's origins. Galadriel, the Lady of Lothlorien, was among the elves who left Valinor, forsaking the land of the Valar (Tolkien's "angels") for a life in Middle Earth. She does not wonder if there is a supreme being; she knows there is one. She has seen his spirits create much of the world that she lives in.

Granted, the characters readers meet in *The Lord of the Rings* do not discuss such matters, and it is likely that the hobbits are not even aware of such histories, but the probable reason is that people who are intent on saving the world have other things to discuss beyond god. They may consider the purpose of saving the world for future generations, but they do not speculate too much on the past beyond the history of the One Ring. Again, Tolkien's heroes have the blessing of certainty—certain of their world, certain of their quest, and certain of the consequences of failure. King's heroes linger in the realm of possibility, of ambiguity, even at the very end of the story.

Despite the many similarities between these two stories, King's *The Stand* is not a carbon copy of *Lord of the Rings*. In fact, beyond these few characteristics of general scope (and certainly length—both stories pass the thousand page marker), King's story is one of an American idealism. His characters stand against evil, and though many are lost, they succeed well enough to secure their own futures. There is hope that when evil rises again it will be met with other heroes who will destroy it yet again. Tolkien's fantasy is less hopeful on that score. Evil is destroyed, that is true, but no one really dies (aside from Boromir, some horses, and a lot of orcs). Tolkien suggests that survival is somehow worse. Many critics have related this to his World War experience, but for Tolkien's characters, having survived the War of the Rings is not always a blessing. For Frodo, in particular, life is not the same, and he can never be truly whole again. Where Fran and Stu can look into the immediate future with hope for their family, Frodo can only hope for some release in the Undying Lands to the West, and he soon leaves the world to others. It does seem odd to accuse King of optimism—he is, after all, famous for killing his heroes rather brutally—but when compared to Tolkien's *Lord of the Rings*, Stephen King's *The Stand* does end on somewhat of a high note.

ONE
The Set-Up

The beginning of any novel is crucial to the story's development. Because *The Stand* shifts gears about a third of the way through — from an apocalyptic novel to an epic battle of good and evil — it is even more important to note the way that King begins his story. The start may be typical of the genre — the world ends with a whimper — but King subtly shifts the focus of the novel from this change of lifestyle to a poignant look at what has been lost. Through his depiction of the small town of Arnette, King evokes images of a dying America even before the super flu is released. After the stage is set, *The Stand* turns to more military matters, and readers are given an intimate look at the governmental response to the flu and the subsequent control of the media. Perhaps the most chilling portion of the preliminary chapters of *The Stand*, however, is the way in which the flu spreads from person to person across the country. King's subtly ironic tone as he describes the "most effective chain letter" ever created allows readers to feel the country's death throes as character after character is given a death sentence.

King's description of Arnette places readers on familiar territory. The America of the novel is recognizable, and this familiarity allows readers to believe in the world King has created. This believability in the Secondary Reality of the novel is only increased when King introduces the military. By playing on modern fears of military intentions and annihilation by weapons of mass destruction or germ warfare, King makes his America even more resonant with readers. Once King has the readers ensnared by his world, he allows them to feel the personal aspect of the super flu, quickly introducing utterly familiar people and then ruthlessly condemning them to death. As readers try to recover from the reeling sense of loss and betrayal (by their own government, military, and media), King sandbags them with a grim vision of reality. People die — horribly, quickly, and realistically. With this set-up, King guarantees that readers will not be able to walk away from the story unscathed.

King quietly establishes the themes that will resonate throughout the novel. First, there is desolation and loss, and then the notion of rebuilding. The entire start of the novel raises the question of the second half of the book—can people ever really learn anything? Is it worthwhile to rebuild America in the image of the old if it was that old way of life that doomed the country? What does it say about humanity when the loss of life so tragically depicted in the beginning suddenly inverts as survivors begin to feel that there are *too many people* left in the world? Questions like these are only the beginning of King's vision of the end of the world.

Small-Town America

The world that readers encounter at the start of *The Stand* is bitterly familiar. Life is hard in the small town of Arnette, Texas, where readers meet one of the novel's protagonists—Stu Redman. The calculator plant has cut shifts to a minimum, and there is no real work to be found. To pass the time, some of the town's residents spend their days and evenings at Hap's Texaco station. This is a quintessentially American venue—the idea of a small-town gas station filled with local good old boys is one that American readers can readily imagine, having probably seen such a place at some point in their life. If not in their own experience, Americans can fill in the scene with images from any number of Hollywood movies of travelers on the road as they pass through the middle of nowhere. Arnette, Texas, is literally the middle of nowhere, America. Vic Palfrey is actually referred to as a "good old boy" when questions arise about his character. The notion of the solid redneck is reassuring to the people of Arnette; it gives them the chance to set their expectations according to known behaviors. The mark of the "good old boy," typically a sign of disrespect in other parts of the country, is what marks one as trustworthy and dependable in Arnette. Even with this standby of caricature as a reference point, however, most of the residents of Arnette are uneducated, unemployed, and, for the most part, unadmirable.

Readers may wonder why King has chosen this small town in the middle of nowhere to begin his tale. The characters whom readers initially meet are not exactly awe-inspiring. As the good old boys linger at the gas station, Hap discusses the economy and politics from the limited perspective of an abbreviated high school education. The other members of his little crew are as intellectual as he is, debating the reasons for their economic situation without much understanding of the bigger picture, and even less influence on how their lives play out. Life in Arnette is frozen, King suggests, and if things do change at all, they certainly will not be for the better. In fact, having Charles Campion crash into their lives with his special gift that keeps on giving is perhaps the best thing that could happen to any of them. At the very least, Campion's introduction spurs some slight difference into their day-to-day existence. At the most, the arrival of the super flu in the form of a thoroughly American car, the Chevy, shows the residents of Arnette that, although their lives may have looked pretty pitiful at first, things really weren't all that bad. In true horror novel fashion, they could all be dead, and King seems to ask the question "What would be the difference? Some of them seem dead already."

King continues to build a sense of resonance with his readers as he describes the lives of the Texans. Norm Bruett, one of the Texaco crowd, wakes up into a typical middle American morning, complete with the sound of the arguing kids outside overshadowed by the country music on the radio in the kitchen. He is depressed at the state of his family's finances — his kids wear hand-me-down clothes, his wife is willing to babysit for a neighbor for a dollar — and yet he is also filled with an overwhelming anger that makes him want to beat the kids into silence. Norm is a character with whom American readers can relate. Contrary to the popular image of America as the place where anybody can live comfortably if he is willing to work hard enough, the Bruetts are struggling to survive. Work is scarce and getting scarcer with the factories closing down, they are reliant on donated commodities, and even the employment office can't offer any relief. Lila Bruett is willing to babysit for a dollar that won't even buy a gallon of gas at Hap's Texaco station. Another sign of the times is in Lila Bruett's note to her husband, where she misspells one word in four, including "dolar." The future does not promise any relief for their situation, either; they are like hundreds of families scattered across small towns in America, and that "familiar helpless anger" isn't going away.[1] King's depiction of life in small-town Arnette conjures Bloom's sense of "feeling at home" in the novel. In this time of economic recession, King's depiction of this family's trouble will echo with many readers, but even during times of plenty, Americans can still relate to the Bruett's plight. Readers can either remember a time when things were hard, or can imagine just how easy it would be to lose the security and dependability they enjoy. The Bruetts are a reminder of just how far the average family can fall in this country, and King subtly reminds readers that they are not too far from that precipice themselves. The characters that King evokes in these initial sections are familiar to American readers, and this resonance allows the world of the novel to become more believable.

The description of the Hodges' living room is even more resonant of American culture. As Lila Bruett watches their kids for her "dolar," she is struck by how nice the house is, decorated as it is with paint-by-number pictures of Christ. Lila sees the latest of these paintings as a real work of art because it took three months and sixty different oil colors. Lila's interpretation, or lack thereof, is a sad commentary on the lower-class understanding of painting. If Lila's idea of real art is a paint-by-number rendition of Christ, what would she make of Van Gogh? King doesn't answer this question, instead ending this slice of American life scene with the grim harbinger of death — a wracking cough by the infant, easily mistaken for the croup by the uninformed Lila, followed by a series of sniffles and a sneeze of her own. Of course, Lila doesn't understand the full implications of her cold as she sits smoking and watching her afternoon stories, nor does she have any inkling that her husband and children will soon be dead along with her.

King saturates the start of his novel with scenes like this one — images of comfort, or what comfort may be had during such hard times — but these moments are haunting for readers who know that disaster and destruction lurk in the next few pages. They do not want to identify with Lila but cannot help themselves; and knowing that she is doomed only makes her sad life more tragic, and yet, somehow more important in the grand scheme of things. Even though she is nobody special, or even anyone remotely interesting as a character, Lila captures the readers' attention with her very normalcy, and even though readers wouldn't want to follow her life for more than these few pages, the idea that her life ends so abruptly is disturbing, a jarring wake-up call that even the most routine existence is not safe from tragedy. Because she dies so ignominiously, readers want to remember Lila Bruett, and remember what her life was, and it is easy to forget that her life was nothing special. Death tends to alter perspective, impending doom stretches sympathy, and King has ensnared his readers without their even noticing the hook.

One : The Set-Up

There are some familiar and comforting practices to be found in Arnette despite a creeping sense that this is not what life in America ought to be like. For instance, Arnette is filled with people who know one another. There is a sense of camaraderie among the Texaco crowd, among their wives and families—they do stick together. Everybody in Arnette knows everybody else, a throwback to the short-term memory of American readers. While this is no longer so true in modern America, most readers will recognize that sense of community and cohesiveness. Stu personally knows the ambulance drivers that come to pick up Campion and his family. Joe Bob Brentwood, the cop that warns the men at the Texaco station of the impending quarantine, is a cousin. Such familiarity with one's neighbors hearkens back to an age that in the American consciousness was a simpler and more innocent time. The idea of small-town America, where everyone knows everyone else, and everyone behaves in an expected manner, is brought to life, even in a place as depressed and forlorn as Arnette. However, this comfort is short-lived, as King hints at the dark underbelly of such familiarity.

King illustrates the sense of entitlement some Americans feel while commenting on the tendency of citizens to disregard the orders of the military and government. Joe Bob Brentwood, Hap's cousin, is a police officer who warns the Texaco crowd of the impending quarantine. If the name alone doesn't convey the sense of quaintness, then the idea of Joe Bob as a cop who just wants to warn his friends and relatives of the approaching army presence will strike an even more familiar chord with readers. Warning friends is a time-honored small-town American tradition. On top of that recognition, Joe explains that he thought the good old boys at Texaco had a "right to know" of the coming quarantine since they had just tried to "lend a hand."[2] The idea of having a "right to know" something is definitely part of the American psyche; after all, if one does "lend a hand," that assumes going out of the way to offer aid, and in the American mind that favor should warrant something in return.

In this case, that idea of reciprocity, of deserving to know what's ahead, or what the plan is as a result of helping out some strangers, is the proverbial last straw for containing the flu; if everyone had done as he was told, the quarantine might have worked, and millions would not have died. Also, the Texaco crowd's reaction to Joe Bob's warning reveals more about their characters. For instance, readers must consider how much the crowd really went out of their way to offer help in the first place. They called the police, but that's no more than anyone else would have done. Their sense of entitlement to news about Campion and the impending quarantine shows that even this small gesture of aid has become a bargaining chip with the rest of the world—they expect something in return, as if their experience with hard times has made them more deserving of fairness than other normal people. Their belief in reciprocity suggests a sense of entitlement that life in America does not always warrant. The old saying "Life isn't fair" could hardly be more ably demonstrated than by the state of Arnette's people, and yet residents still believe that good things should and will happen to them. The "good things" may have been scaled back from a decent paying job and hope for a financial future to a sense of decency and the small feeling of importance being "in the know" lends them, but with things being what they are, the people of Arnette will take what they can get. In this case, Joe Bob's actions reflect what any reader would hope to do, and this reinforces the sense of security that King's rendition of Arnette conjures in the readers' minds, thereby securing the believability of the Secondary Reality that King has created.

King has established a false sense of security here, since the cop's well-intended warning ends up breaking the quarantine and allowing Captain Trips (as the super flu is eventually called) to spread across the country. Perhaps, King suggests, that long-lost comfort of togetherness is not always such a boon. After all, it was that connection that allowed the flu to wipe out the country. Had the cop not been related to those inside the quarantine, had he any respect for the authorities that were on their way, perhaps tragedy could have been averted. This lack of respect for authority is definitely an American point of view. As the ultimate underdog, the rebel, Americans often see themselves as individually smarter than any government agency. The cop doesn't really believe that there is anything to fear, and he sees the approach of the CDC as an annoyance of red tape and government interference more so than any response to a real threat. Perhaps part of this irreverent response to authority is a result of the government's tendency to assure Americans that everything is really all right and no harm could ever come to them. This line of defense is exactly the tactic that the government in the novel uses—they lie about the danger until it is too late for the truth to matter, assuring Americans in between coughing fits that all is well and there is no super flu at all.

The start of *The Stand* resonates with American culture and imagery, but the quality that makes this work worth studying is the subtlety that

One : The Set-Up

King displays in raising critical questions. His purpose in the novel is not to rail against the economy of America, and yet he has managed to critique the economy, prompting readers to ask questions of their own, a display of the purposeful purposelessness that Kant would have admired. In this opening, King has achieved Bloom's sense of "arresting strangeness"; readers know Arnette, no matter how much they may want to deny it. King has created a Secondary Reality that readers can recognize and believe. He continues enhancing the haunting familiarity of the novel with his description of the government and military.

The Military

The military in King's novel is a metaphor for the average American's lack of control over the larger issues. King is careful to construct the military machine in the novel realistically so that his Secondary Reality is not disturbed. The entire beginning portion of *The Stand* is concerned with the military response to the outbreak of Captain Trips, and readers will be quite familiar with the steps the military in the novel takes. First, there is containment, a plan that includes the murder of several insightful reporters and journalists, and when that fails, concealment in the form of flat-out denial. Though this may suggest a certain detachment from humanity, the novel's military machine is peopled with very real characters that try to do their best in a bad situation.

King gives the military a personal face in the form of life-time soldiers. Bill Starkey is the first military man in the story, and readers find him distraught over a folder filled with bad news. Along with the ordinary stresses of modern life, Starkey is faced with the knowledge that the super flu has not been contained, and things in the country he loves are only going to deteriorate. The thing that makes Starkey more believable than a stock military man who makes tough choices, however, is the stream of thoughts that King uses to introduce him. Instead of focusing on the massive snafu before him, Starkey is transfixed by the images on his monitors. His view of Project Blue, the government facility that produced Captain Trips and subsequently released it in a series of unfortunate accidents, includes camera feeds from the cafeteria, hallways, and labs. Instead of focusing his attention on the dead doctors who litter the scene, or even the pile of bad news on his desk, Starkey is fixated by a man in the cafeteria who has died

Respecting The Stand

with his face in a bowl of Campbell's Chunky Sirloin Soup. He is horrified by the notion of spending eternity with a face in a bowl of soup. Even the news that Vic Hammer, his son-in-law and the man in charge of Project Blue, has committed suicide doesn't quite break through his obsession. This behavior is a very human thing for Starkey to do; instead of being overwhelmed by the problems that threaten to drive him to suicide as well, his mind focuses on one small detail and allows only that one thing to bother him. He does wonder how to tell his daughter that her husband is dead, but even then his thoughts are still with the dead man from Project Blue—"I'm sorry, Cindy. Vic took a high dive into a bowl of blue soup today."[3] The soup has become Starkey's metaphor for death, and his obsession with it only continues to grow as the world around him deteriorates.

King suggests that the only way for a person to deal with what the military deems must be done is to focus attention elsewhere or risk madness. While the military takes its first steps towards covering up the outbreak, Starkey focuses all of his emotions on the man in the soup, whom he eventually identifies as Frank D. Bruce. He orders a very young voice to proceed with an operation coded "Troy," knowing that his orders will cause the deaths of several innocent people. Giving the orders doesn't bother Starkey, nor do the impending deaths that he knows Captain Trips will bring; in fact, the only thing that does bother Starkey is the death of Frank D. Bruce. As he stares at the dead man, he is able to recite his military mantra: "A regrettable incident has occurred," and he has to do something about it.[4] As his training decrees, Starkey chooses to cover up the incident by ordering the murder of several reporters who have stumbled onto the story of the spreading super flu. Despite his apparent coldness in ordering the execution of the journalists (whose death King relates in horrifying detail as they realize that even in America they can and will be silenced), Starkey remains a realistic person.

One of the difficulties of a novel with so many narrative threads is trying to involve readers with every event that happens. King manages to include the entire aspect of the military through Starkey's character. For readers, this man has become the face of the military, and though at times he is not to be admired, he is believable in his actions—and even justified. King has managed to put a human face on the mechanized institution of the military here, while simultaneously raising questions about the right to free speech.

King begins to introduce his concept of Standing very subtly in the

One : The Set-Up

novel, often choosing to emphasize the American right to free speech as his characters decide to rebel against the military and governmental decrees for silence. When the military comes to collect the few exposed citizens of Arnette, it is the babysitting Lila Bruett who becomes hysterical with her fear. As they are ushered onto a plane without any real explanations, she begins to scream, "What is all this? ... What's wrong with my man? Are we going to die? Are my babies going to die?" And afterwards, when she has made even her fellow citizens uncomfortable with the fuss she makes, she asks, "Why won't someone answer me? Isn't this America?"[5] Instead of the answers she seeks, however, the army men on board the plane simply force her to drink a glass full of presumably drugged milk, and she soon passes out. It is odd that King would choose to make this character, a woman uneducated and largely a symbol for the lower classes, the only one who speaks out against the military. She is the only one who questions what is happening. Everyone else, men and women alike, simply go along with the men and do as they are told. They may whisper quietly among themselves, but the full-out demands that Lila makes stand alone among her comrades. Her little rebellion is even a source of embarrassment to her fellow citizens; Chris Ortega grumbles to the others, wishing that Lila would just be quiet and submit meekly to what is happening. This entire scene is subtle criticism of the mob mentality that seems to happen when situations become complicated. No one is willing to step beyond the safety of the group; even Lila Bruett is only outspoken after she watches her husband collapse with illness and her children coughing more and more. Her situation is immediate and terrifying, and this gives her the strength to speak up. Her tirade has little effect, however, and she is soon forgotten among the many who fall prey to the super flu's ravages. Even while he is focusing on a military response to the spreading plague, King manages to guide readers into a specific interpretation of the army's actions. Anyone who witnesses Lila's outburst is simultaneously caught between admiration for her and a sinking sense of identification with her comrades — after all, what would anyone do in that situation? The military is just trying to save lives.

King is quite clear about the intentions of the military as a whole — to maintain order — but the actions of the individuals who represent the machine raise questions in the minds of readers. In direct opposition to the image of America as the lone rebel defending democracy where it can, the military decides that if America as a country is going to be destroyed, it will not go alone. In fact, the military (in the form of Starkey — the soup-obsessed man in charge of the clean-up) deliberately spreads Captain Trips around the world so that others will die as well. When Starkey is relieved of his command, his last order is "Rome Falls," a code for all agents around the world to release what they think are radioactive particles that will be mapped by Sky-Cruise satellites. Even as he damns the rest of humanity to death, Starkey believes he is rescuing his country. He quotes Yeats, whom he mispronounces "Yeets," to his underling, claiming that indeed the beast is on its way, and it is their job to hold the center together as long as possible. There is a terrible twist to a man who can simultaneously order the release of a deadly plague to millions and claim that he has been struggling to hold things together. What makes this situation even more difficult for readers, though, is that Starkey is a likeable character. Even when he goes to Project Blue to commit suicide, readers commend him for lifting Frank D. Bruce's head out of the infernal soup.

Still, most of the actions taken by the military echo as empty symbols. Lifting Bruce's head out of the soup is meaningless because, just as Starkey obsessed over the man's face in the soup, the man who takes over for him, Len Creighton, can't help but wonder why his old friend didn't wipe the soup from Frank D. Bruce's eyebrows before he shot himself. Just like his predecessor, who distanced himself from everything he did by focusing on soup, Creighton will focus on that one small image as a way to keep himself sane as long as possible. Perhaps King is saying that in the face of doom, a person has to focus on details in order to keep calm. Readers may be tempted to think of Creighton's wish for eyebrows free of soup as a last ditch attempt at human dignity, but this seems a flimsy excuse to justify the military's actions. It may seem like dignity to remove a dead man's face from a bowl of soup, but the action is meaningless if the man doing the removal has spent the afternoon condemning millions to die. The military in *The Stand* is filled with contradictions like this.

The military machine manages to control the panic as best it can, and it does have memorable characters working for it; yet it kills several innocents in order to maintain secrecy and then willingly spreads the flu to other countries. Readers are torn between respecting the institution for doing its best in a bad situation and being outraged as the military pretends to do the right thing while it really secures its own interests. At the very least, cleaning the soup out of a dead man's eyebrows is hardly enough to justify the "regrettable incident" of the super flu's release, and King seems

One : The Set-Up

to suggest that while military men may mean well, their actions are empty symbols that do more harm than good.

King's decision to make the super flu a man-made virus instead of a creation of Nature is worth noting as well. Though the novel does end on an emphatically religious note, the start of America's downfall is not through any outside means; instead, America destroys itself. Whether a result of the general paranoia regarding biological weapons or King's own preoccupations with governmental mishaps, the fact that America is destroyed by its own creation is terribly ironic. This apocalyptic ending is one way to resolve the rift between the "ideal cultural model of American government and the citizenry's views of the actual working government" that lingers in American readers' minds.[6] Americans have difficulty accepting a government that is both the epitome of democracy (or at least representative democracy) and totalitarian in the iron control it maintains over its citizens; it seems that the problem of determining at what point freedom becomes dangerous is never far away from American thoughts. *The Stand* is very much a novel of modern America and still resonates in the post–9/11 mindset where fear of the outsider has become part of everyday experience. The 1980 in which it was originally set, and the 1990 that King's revision related, are easily recognizable by the general mistrust and occasional fear that both characters and readers share about the government and the military.

From the frantic fears of the 1950s to the protests in the 1960s, America has long been a country of people worried about some form of nuclear fallout or biological destruction. King has taken that widespread notion and turned it into the metaphor by which his novel transforms from just another run-of-the-mill apocalypse to a very specific and recognizable possibility in American readers' minds. The military is more than a force in the novel — it is a symbol for the unknown people who actually make the decisions that run the country. The faceless machine of the military is capable of great inhumanity, and King exploits the fear of not being in control of one's own destiny when he has the military almost entirely controlling the way the country comes to an end. Of course, King reverses this as well by having several different episodes of resistance and uprising, but ultimately the military still retains the control and thus is worth fearing. By playing on this fear of mass destruction by some unknown military agency, King grabs hold of his readers' psyche and refuses to let go.

King's use of the military also demonstrates the anti-intellectualism that has run rampant in American culture since the 1950s. The highly educated individuals who work for the military at Project Blue have managed to destroy the population by accident — a sign of the incompetence of such individuals as well as an ironic twist to plans for self-preservation through biological warfare. If intellectuals continue to create viruses like Captain Trips to protect the country, King suggests, perhaps they shouldn't be trusted — after all, that protective intention does not matter when the super flu is released onto the public. It kills indiscriminately, just as it killed its creators. King is relying on an American distrust of intellectuals here, but he is also raising questions of responsibility. If intellectuals, or scientists in the case of the novel, are going to play with death, King suggests it is only a matter of time before death decides to return the favor. The military's failure to control the spread of the super flu compounds this sense of anti-intellectualism. In fact, even the gates at the facility malfunction, a sign that reliance on technology is sometimes just as damaging as reliance on human capability to control and contain dangerous substances. The super flu may act as the precursor to a showdown between good and evil, but the creation and subsequent distribution of the virus is a clear black mark on the face of intellectuals, a sign that questions how much trust Americans should put in these individuals.

Even with these misgivings, the recent panic over the Swine Flu is a real life example, perhaps, of why the government in the novel may not be so wrong in trying to keep the truth a secret as long as possible. If people did know for certain that the virus was decimating the population, the breakdown of society would happen very fast. If the knee-jerk reactions of school boards and government agencies to the perceived threat of the recent outbreak of Swine Flu is any indication of how people may react to a plague, then maybe King is right to have his military try to hold off the inevitable as long as it can. The Swine Flu wasn't fatal (by and large), most people recovered, and the communicability rate was far less than Captain Trip's astonishing 99.4 percent, and still Americans were panicking, stocking up foods, canceling classes, and imagining the worst. Some people even stopped buying pork for fear that any association with pigs may cause the virus — even though report after report explained how the name derived from the origin of the flu *among* pigs, not *from* them. The government even changed the name of the flu to keep pork sales from plummeting even farther than they had during the three- week flu scare. If this is any indication of how people react to such things, then readers can hardly fault the military for trying to hide the truth. Though it seems contradictory, they probably did save a few lives. Those who were immune to the ravages of the flu may have died in the civil unrest that could have started weeks before things actually fell apart. It seems odd to agree with the military's blatant abuse of the people's trust, but in light of recent events, King's readers may find themselves considering the terrifying idea that it might not have been such a bad plan after all.

However, just in case the notion of a government-created super flu wasn't enough to keep readers up at night, the casual way that King continues his tale of mass destruction is even more horrifying. It is one thing for government officials to release vials of flu to other countries; it is quite another to picture everyday Americans unknowingly passing a death sentence to their friends and neighbors. King has taken a distrust of government agencies and transformed it into a terror of fellow citizens as he uses ordinary people to facilitate the spread of the virus—a clever tactic that a simple hairy and clawed bogeyman could not accomplish. The fear here is not of the unknown entity but of all people (just think zombies). This is a brilliant device for the horror writer; readers can imagine an end to a specific threat (beast is destroyed, heroes live on, etc.), but a threat that exists within everyone around them is harder to defeat—and much harder to forget about even after the novel has been put away.

99.4 Percent Communicability

The Stand is not a typical horror novel, but it certainly has horrific features—vivid descriptions of corpses being the most prevalent, with mangling deaths a close second. Still, it seems like Stephen King has taken a break from the normal blood and gore that flavors his novels. Despite this seeming label of "horror lite," *The Stand* has elements more disturbing than most traditional horror novels. The most notable is the way King describes Captain Trips' journey from victim to victim across the country.

Part of the horror of the super flu is the speed with which it passes from one person to the next. Readers can learn that the virus has 99.4 percent communicability when Starkey reads the report on his desk, but they don't quite understand what that means right away. Stu Redman is perhaps the first character to realize the potential for disaster when he is en route to the airstrip in Braintree (after having been strong armed into custody by the military). Before the Arnette crew even arrives at the plane, the man driving them begins to sneeze. Though Stu is reluctant to believe it, wanting to believe instead that the driver simply has a regular cold, the evidence is clear that whatever is wrong with them, it is possible to pass it from person to person in the space of a short drive. From the ever helpful Joe Bob Brentwood to dozens of completely ordinary characters, readers will cringe as they watch the super flu spread from person to person. King flavors this deadly rundown with phrases like "He left the sweet thang that waited his table a dollar tip that was crawling with death" and "He also served him and his entire family death warrants."[7] Though seemingly trite, the simplicity of these observations combines with the short sketches King creates of each victim to make the reader actually feel the impending doom on a visceral level.

For instance, readers may recognize Edward M. Norris, who just wanted to show the guys back home that he could take his family on a vacation by car and have a good time. This ordinary man and his family are people readers know, and by having them spread the flu unknowingly to so many others, King makes readers imagine themselves in the same situation. The casual way that he traces the progress of the flu is enough to make any reader shudder. King introduces ordinary lives and damns them in the same paragraph with chilling efficiency. One might be tempted to think that such casual death may preclude readers from getting too attached to any one character, but here is where King weaves his most effective magic. Readers can't help but be drawn to his characters, even knowing that the person they are so involved with at the moment may be dead in the next paragraph or the next page. The people that wander into and out of the pages of *The Stand* are quite familiar to American readers. From small-town waitresses to older women who play bridge, King allows the readers to visualize someone they know or have seen in the new character, then abruptly reminds readers that these ordinary people are already going to die from the super flu, while still busily passing it around to everyone they get near. This double impact forces readers to accept the fact that Starkey could not quite grasp — 99.4 percent communicability is mind-blowing — but readers do not have a man face down in a bowl of soup to distract them from the truth.

The casual way that King allows the super flu to spread to supposedly protected military personnel is galling. When nurse Patty Greer begins to

One : The Set-Up

sneeze, she does not think anything of it, despite multiple warnings posted all over the military hospital. She is so focused on her next patient, and hoping that he won't be cranky, that she completely misses a significant detail. Her blasé attitude is compounded by her complete faith in her own safety; she is careless because she is absolutely certain that no germs can get inside her suit, and even when she displays obvious signs of the flu, she still continues as if nothing is wrong. Patty's reliance on technology and her own self-absorption allow her to spread her case of the super flu to everyone else working on her floor, and the deterioration of even military medical facilities begins. This is a sad commentary on American reliance on both technology and warranties, and King suggests that this dependency is both the agent of the country's undoing as well as the addiction that will spark the rebuilding of society. As Nick considers the future of Boulder, he keeps coming back to the same words: "Authority. Organization. Politics."[8] Once the people have been given a clear direction, they willingly jump in and help because they believe that such organization will lead them back to the way things were and the life they knew. Operations to rebuild in Boulder do not really coalesce until there is a plan to get the power back on — a sure sign that dependency on technology is the first addiction that must be assuaged.

King emphasizes his interpretation of human nature when, in perhaps the most unnerving part of *The Stand*, he gives brief snapshots of the people who die in the pause between the end of the super flu and the initial efforts to rebuild society. In these few vignettes, King demonstrates his ability to send chills down the spines of readers even without having to resort to the gross-out factor. From the boy who falls into a well and dies almost an entire day later, as much a victim of fear and misery as the physical factors of shock, hunger, and dehydration, to the paranoid woman who blows herself up when she fires an ancient gun, King showcases human fragility and stupidity in a shuddering slideshow of accidents, bad luck, and poor decision-making. Even with all of the death caused by the super flu, readers are more affected by this second wave of suffering because it is not due to circumstances beyond their control, but because of silly mistakes and thoughtlessness. Perhaps the most chilling statement of all, however, is the casual "No great loss" that King peppers throughout the chapter.[9] The people he describes, believable and familiar as they might be, are not important to the coming struggle, King suggests; but even more than that, they represent the people who die every day in America and are unnoticed by the masses. King seems to suggest that death, and life, only have meaning in connection with other people — what is the value of life when everyone they loved has died, or, even more, what is the value of death when there is no one around to witness and remember it? These kinds of philosophical speculations are subsumed into a single chapter amid many (78 in total), yet King's questions still manage to seep into readers' consciousness without overwhelming the narrative thread.

King is the master of understatement sometimes, and never more so than his chilling descriptions of public reaction to Captain Trips. When Stu watches the news from his Vermont hospital room/jail cell, he notes that as the newscaster smiles reassuringly into the camera and insists there is no danger to the few isolated cases of flu outbreak, someone sneezes off-camera. Even more disturbing is the transcription of the President's speech to reassure the country that there is no fatal super flu going around — a speech peppered by sneezes and coughs. The government feels that it is reassuring the people, albeit with empty words, but the manner of the speech's delivery does more to assure Americans of the super flu's seriousness and undermine governmental authority than to silence questions and assuage fears.

In a small twist, King manages to highlight the fast spread of the super flu through newscasts watched and heard by the main characters. Just as Stu and Nick watch the news for some mention of the flu, and are met with reassuring words, they cannot ignore the evidence before their eyes. As Nick watches the news in Shoyo, he hears a report that some public gatherings have been cancelled until the current crisis has passed; this is followed by the thought that "in Shoyo, the entire town had been cancelled. Who was kidding who?"[10] Even though both Stu and Nick realize that the news is not accurate, each character seeks out the news as a way to reassure himself, and when that is not possible, to gauge the spread of the super flu. The fact that the news is even still on is mildly reassuring, they think, but the cacophony of coughing in the background heralds darker times to come. This is an odd way to highlight the spread of the super flu while emphasizing the power of the media.

The Media

The news that the characters receive as the super flu ravages the country is completely controlled. Nick Andros notices that the newscasters

One : The Set-Up

behave as though someone else is in the room with them, someone perhaps threatening them to make sure nothing untoward is said on the air. This possibility is confirmed later on as the novel narrates events from WBZ-TV in Boston. Several newscasters and technicians stage a coup against the armed men and spend the next few hours broadcasting the real news. They are summarily executed for treason when the military blows up the building they are broadcasting from. The main newscaster, Bob Palmer, gives a small speech before diving into the real news, stating his regret that things have come to this end, but noting his pride that a rebellion of sorts has begun in Boston, the cradle of independence. Palmer's message is quite clear — Americans have always been known for their independence, their refusal to lie down quietly; and even if it means death, at least some of them are willing to stand up for the truth. Once the beacon of rebellion is lit, a series of small victories of truth are won — a man in West Virginia prints a small paper and hands it door to door to those left alive in his town. His only story explains the facts of the flu and includes the sad commentary that more than lives are at stake here — the very idea of government has lost its veneer of respectability. Mankind is on its own. Clearly, in King's America there are people willing to fight until the end, even if they can only manage to stagger across town handing out flyers before succumbing to the flu in the front seat of an old car. As each exercise of freedom appears, the government reprisal grows more extreme. The *L.A. Times* building is dynamited by the remnants of the FBI for printing a one-page extra with the truth.

King narrates the degenerating behavior of Americans with distressing skill as things start to fall apart. Just as there are those who would stand against the governmental and military lies, there are those who are determined to stay uninformed. In fact, in a few lines describing the brutal attack on a man wearing an end-of-the-world sign by four infected young men in motorcycle jackets, King manages to show just how desperate people can get, and readers are forced to reconsider their initial reactions to the military's plan of action. Had the truth been generally known earlier, readers wonder, perhaps the degeneration would have been worse. As things go, the last days of the super flu are quite nasty by themselves. In these brief sketches, King manages to undermine the attitude he has so carefully crafted in his readers (that of distrust and near disgust with the military response) and forces them to reevaluate their own opinions of events.

Respecting *The Stand*

The swift unraveling of the country is illustrated most clearly in the Ray Flowers episode. When the talk show host begins to take calls about the super flu, soldiers are dispatched to "take care of Ray Flowers." The first two soldiers to receive the orders refuse and are summarily executed, and the rest reluctantly head out to Springfield, Missouri, to do their duty. However, once Ray Flowers has been killed, the soldiers almost immediately turn on their sergeant, and a vicious fight ensues between the rest. This episode scares the rest of the (listening) populace into believing that things really are falling apart. When the military itself can't control its own soldiers, and career government men are refusing orders, it becomes clear that the entire system is collapsing.

King manages to raise a small amount of ambiguity with Ray Flowers. Does he continue his show because he truly believes in free speech and his democratic rights, or does he continue because, as an American, he simply does not believe that the government would really do anything to him? Though seemingly a small issue — Ray Flowers dies anyway — this is a crucial question of the stand itself. Does intention matter when one is fighting for freedom — or is it enough to simply be in the right place at the right time? King leaves the answer up to the readers. Flowers is a hero because he does try to get the truth out to his listeners, but at the same time, can he be heroic if he really didn't expect to die for his actions? Unlike the people at WBZ-TV, who had been surrounded by men with guns and knew that death was inevitable, Ray Flowers' rebellion may leave readers uncertain about the nature of heroism.

The student march at Kent State places readers back onto familiar ground. The notion of the military firing on unarmed students is not unheard of in the American psyche, and even as the unnamed military man screams, "Those aren't commie guerrillas out there! They're kids! American kids! They aren't armed!" readers can imagine the scene.[11] The subsequent bloodbath as those soldiers turn on one another for firing and/or not firing is not a surprise either, but readers are left with more solidarity than with Ray Flowers. As episode after episode of things falling apart is reported, readers grow more accustomed to the chaos, and by the time readers reach the silence at the end, they, like the surviving main characters, are open to just about anything that could follow.

TWO

The Players

Critics often dismiss King's work because some of his characters appear to be stereotypes. While some of his characters have stereotypical characteristics, to claim that they are simply walking caricatures is to ignore the subtleties that King employs when introducing them as symbols of deeper meaning that serve many functions in the subtext of the novel. Stu Redman represents the Everyman in all Americans, while Frannie Goldsmith's origins are a scathing commentary on New England small-town life. Larry Underwood raises questions about what it means to be a nice guy, and Nick Andros is a man used by forces beyond his control even as he tries to rationalize what he sees around him. Glen Bateman serves as King's commentary on the human condition, an intellectual put to good use, and Tom Cullen is an example of how innocence can overcome evil by virtue of being pure. Harold Lauder and Nadine Cross are intellectual characters who choose their own downfall willingly and with forethought, yet still remain somewhat sympathetic to readers. On the other side of the demarcation between good and evil lie Lloyd Henreid and Trashcan Man, each a different interpretation of human evil — one's sin is in knowingly serving a Devil, and the other's is simply self-destructive. All of these players are overseen by the devil incarnate in Randall Flagg and the White's champion, Mother Abagail, father and mother of the post–super flu world.

These characters may seem like stereotypes at first glance, and in some fashion they are. Stu can be classified as an ordinary, redneck, blue collar worker. Larry is the epitome of the rock star gone awry. King has not created these people entirely out of thin air; they are conglomerations of his own experience with people in different places and in varied stages of their lives. Like Eliot claimed good literature ought to do, King has borrowed from the literary tradition he has inherited. The notion of an

Everyman is older than King's Stu Redman, yet by associating his character with this convention, King adds another layer of meaning to his newest interpretation of an old ideal. In this cast of characters, King manages to both bring images of American personas to the page and revitalize them with freshly scrubbed faces and shiny new outlooks on life. Each King character has a distinct personality beyond his or her traditional traits, an individuality that allows readers to see them as more than walking caricatures.

Ordinary People Can Make a Difference

Stuart Redman is King's example of how an ordinary person can make a difference in the grand scheme of things. Stu is common, and yet even he can alter the course of the future by standing up when need arises. Stu serves as the Everyman in the novel, a representative of the ordinary man in everyone. His recollection of happy times includes hunting trips and poker games, and he reminisces about the people he knew in Arnette—Chris Ortega's endless ethnic jokes and Tony Leominster's Scout. He behaves in believable and familiar ways—he is calm under pressure, he is gentlemanly in his pursuit of Frannie, and he is fierce in protection of his newly discovered loved ones. His quiet Texan drawl allows readers to equate him with the Western heroes of old American novels—he is the Hemingway hero, the Western sheriff, and the canny underdog all at once, and he is an easy character to stand behind as a reader. Though it may seem like Stu is a walking stereotype, King gives his hero a force of personality that makes him stand out from the ranks of heroic protagonists. Stu is American; he is recognizable in his fears, in his failures, and in his occasional faithlessness. He is flawed, but not with the proverbial fatal flaw; Stu is troubled by simple human foibles—he gets annoyed by small things, he dislikes Harold's attitude towards Frannie, he struggles against the decrees of Mother Abagail and her God. Stu is a stereotype in that he is Everyman, but he still retains an individuality that most Texan characters in modern literature lose in the shadow of John Wayne or Shane.

King introduces his hero in the manner of the cautious and careful thinker. Initially described as "the quietest man in Arnette," Stuart Redman is clearly the hero of the novel from the start, and he is established early on as the man of thoughtful action.[1] When readers first meet Stu, he

Two : The Players

sits drinking Pabst at Hap's Texaco, the sign of an American blue collar worker for sure. To complete the image of a good old boy, readers learn that Stu almost had an athletic scholarship but had to work instead when his family got sick, a story that Americans can certainly relate to. Though he is often dismissed by townspeople as just another good old boy in a dying Texas town, it is Stu who acts when Campion's car comes crashing into the pumps. While the others stare dumbfounded at the Chevy heading for them, Stu stands up quite calmly and swiftly flicks off the switches to the pumps, saving the lives of everyone at the station with his fast thinking, but perhaps unknowingly dooming the rest of America by not allowing the super flu to be destroyed in a fiery explosion. He thinks things through, certainly, but when it becomes clear that something must be done, Stu is always willing to take the necessary steps.

King is careful not to turn Stu into a caricature of the strong silent type that predominates Westerns set in Texas. Instead, King allows Stu to show his emotions; he is not an unfeeling man or the image of the stoic Hemingway hero. When the Texaco crew stares at Campion and his family in the car, Stu is struck by the way the mother and child are still holding hands in death. Even though Stu has some military experience, having served in a nameless war (likely Vietnam before King's revision in the novel's setting, perhaps Korea or another conflict in the new version), he has never seen anything as disturbing as these two victims, still clinging to one another as they died. Stu is more affected by the scene than anyone else who stares into the car, and he is not afraid or embarrassed by his reaction. This empathy is a reassuring sign to readers that Stu is a trustworthy hero. He can accept his own emotional reaction to the scene without any objections; Stu is not plagued by expectations of masculine behavior. When something affects him, he says so; it just takes him a little while to actually say so— not out of fear or some secret shame, but because Stu rarely says anything that does not need to be said. He is careful with his words in the same way that some male characters are with their emotions, holding back until the time is right to speak. This taciturn quality makes other characters, and readers, pay attention when Stu does say something.

When the military takes him to the Atlanta Disease Control Center, Stu's tendency to watch and wait earns readers' respect. As the only one immune to the super flu, doctors and nurses continue to perform tests on him without telling him what is happening. Once Stu gets fed up, however, his stubbornness makes him a character that all readers can appreciate. He disregards the nurse's attempts to charm him into cooperation, instead refusing to go along with any more tests until they send him someone who can talk. Even more, he has no real problem with the actual tests; what bothers Stu in the facility is the way that no one will tell him anything, that he is being deliberately kept in the dark about what is going on, both with his particular condition and with the world beyond his isolated room. While not an intellectual by any means, Stu is not lacking in intelligence. As Gary Sinise says in the film version of *The Stand*, "East Texas don't mean dumb." When he finally does make his stand against his captors, it is final, but up until that point, he deliberately avoids asking questions. From his experience with his wife's death from cancer, Stu knows that not asking questions makes doctors and staff uncomfortable. They expect to be questioned, and those questions give them the authority to give unsatisfying or misleading answers. Stu's refusal to ask questions makes them take him all the more seriously when he finally does.

Stu also serves as King's commentary on the intelligence of the ordinary American. He may not be an educated intellectual, but Stu's knowledge comes from a lifetime of quiet observation. He knows people, and he understands how they behave. When the man finally does come to see him in Atlanta, Stu knows not to show fear. He notes that Denniger, the doctor who oversees his care, seems like a man who would lord it over his underlings but would easily turn subservient to his own superiors, the kind of man who holds civilians in contempt for their lack of knowledge, a vacuum that he himself has created. Denniger can't tell Stu any more about the situation, and his cajoling eventually breaks down to an argument where Denniger accuses Stu of disrespecting his country, to which Stu replies that it is his country that is currently disrespecting him. Stu could not be more right in this case. Though it takes him longer to react to his situation than Lila Bruett, Stu's reaction is just as familiar to readers. His threat to tear a hole in the doctor's germ-suit gives readers a chance to rejoice; finally, someone is going to stand up against those in charge. At this point in the novel, this small rebellion is the only recourse available to readers. With such rampant death all around, Stu's stand against Denniger reminds readers how important it is to fight for what is right. King also uses this altercation as a way for his readers to fight back against the death that surrounds the story — it isn't possible to rail against the super flu, but it is possible for readers to rally around Stu as he stands against

Denniger. King illustrates the reason for the dedication of his Constant Reader in this scene; he understands the needs of his readership and caters to those desires as he tells the story.

Stu's "tough guy" reaction also lets readers identify with Stu. At a time when they may become frustrated with the helplessness of watching the world fall apart, Stu's little threat takes on new meaning. He is willing to stand up to the man, in his small way, in order to get some answers. King has renewed his readers' faith in the ability of man to stand up to tyranny, even in a small way. King's other heroes are not so simply identified, nor are they so easy to appreciate.

Small-Town Maine: King's Specialty

Stephen King is known for his depiction of Maine in his novels, and the Goldsmiths of Ogunquit, Maine, are as average as they come, at least on the surface. Of course, like all families in King novels, they have their share of problems. Frannie's mother, for instance, is not about to win any mother-of-the-year awards, and her father is about as down-home blue collar as one can get. However, the relationship Frannie shares with her father resounds with believability, and this familiarity is what causes readers to immerse themselves in Frannie's life and situation more than any other character in the novel at this point. For all intents and purposes, Frannie serves as the novel's opening Every (wo)man. She has gotten herself in an awkward position, but she is a bastion of rationality. She makes her choices and sticks to them. If Hoppenstandt is correct in his assertion that King writes to women, then Frannie Goldsmith is sure to resonate with that core audience.

This resonance does not imply that Frannie is a stereotypical strong female. She has quirks and foibles that make her as believable as anyone the reader knew from school or the neighborhood. For instance, Frannie's way of ending her diary with a little "things to remember" list gives her a distinct personality. She wants to have some memories to share with her baby, and so she records random details about the ease of comfort foods that were once readily available in supermarket freezers. In her diary, Frannie also uses the word "sez" a lot to relate conversations, a girlish trait that makes Frannie more realistic to readers. In addition to her penchant for memory lists and slang words, Frannie is a sucker for the giggles. At odd times, like when she tells Jess she's pregnant, or at a solemn poetry reading, Frannie can't help herself. As her father puts it, "Sometimes King Laugh knocks and you're one of those people who can't keep him out."[2] The notion of a girl from Maine who gets the giggles is easy to imagine for the American reader, and the fact that she happens to be pregnant and poised for a great series of life changes only makes Frannie a character that American readers, male or female, young or old, can understand.

King's introduction of Frannie resonates with believability. When she finds herself in a family way, her strict New England upbringing forces her to compare herself to Hester Prynne, though there is no real adultery, and she is keenly disappointed to realize that her beau, Jess Rider, is no Dimmesdale. Far from the ideal of Puritan Americans, Jess is as confused as she is when he finds out she is pregnant. He gives no great impassioned speech, nor does he make any vows of love or devotion. Though she doesn't expect much more from him, she is still disheartened when she sees right through Jess's pseudo–Lord Byron, lonely but unafraid pose out by the water. Jess is the American poet, irresponsible and adorable but ultimately ineffective. He is not Lord Byron, just a copy of an ideal, like she is a copy of Hester. In contrast to the bastion of masculine strength Frannie hopes for, Jess is terrified when Frannie walks up behind him and taps his shoulder, even crying out with a very unmanly shriek. He considers offering her a handkerchief when she bites her tongue, but reconsiders when he realizes she will get blood on it — the image of the poetic ladies man but really a farce.

King suggests that Jess is the best thing America has to offer, or at least average or expected — a poor quality copy of a long-gone standard. Jess is not the reason for America's downfall, but he is a poor Modern substitute for the Romantic tragic hero. When confronted by Frannie's pregnancy, he panics, argues, sulks, and lashes out in turn. His romantic impulse of marriage, once denied by Frannie, turns into an adolescent temper tantrum that culminates in him slapping her, albeit lightly. This is not the reaction of an ideal gentleman, and his reaction to Frannie's situation only highlights the normalcy of his response. While Frannie doesn't really hope for much more than that from him, she has been conditioned by her American upbringing to dream of a better response, and when her own practicality brings him down to reality, she is doubly disappointed.

Not all of King's Maine characters prove false versions of old ideals though; Frannie's father, a machinist at the Sanford auto parts firm,

Two : The Players

resounds with genuine emotion. At first, Peter Goldsmith appears as a strong, revitalized version of the henpecked husband, but later on, he transitions into a model of modern fatherhood. He successfully balances a bitter wife with a beloved daughter, and his quiet voice rules the women in his family despite appearances otherwise. Like Stu, Peter only speaks his mind in family matters when he has something final to say — he may chat with his daughter of everyday things, but when he speaks before both wife and daughter, there is no doubt that he is in charge of the family, and the women obey his soft-spoken command. With this family, King manages to highlight a very loving father-daughter relationship while upholding a traditional Puritan notion of family life. Of all the parents in the novel, Peter Goldsmith remains the most developed, and his relationship with Frannie sets the example for Frannie's own standards of parenting. Even though he lives with a sharp-tongued, vicious harpy of a woman, Peter Goldsmith remains a low-voiced talkative man when it comes to his daughter. He tries to explain, though not to justify, his wife's behavior, claiming that Frannie's mother is simply unable to change. Even moreso, he elaborates, Frannie's mother has never been the same since Fred Goldsmith, her first and favorite child, was killed by a drunk driver. Such blatant favoritism among parents may not paint the most flattering picture of parenthood in America, but here King has enunciated a secret that most parents would not admit.

King shows his knack for capturing the essence of human behavior when he has Peter Goldsmith describe the changes that came over his wife after the death of her favorite child. Peter tells Frannie that Carla was a different person before her son, Frannie's brother Fred, died. She was hellfire and youth and everything that could be admired in a woman, but after Fred died, Peter explains, his wife just stopped growing, stopped living, stopped doing anything except going through the motions, a common response for parents who lose a favorite child. It was as if, Peter explains, "she slapped three coats of lacquer and one of quick-dry cement on her way of looking at things and called it good."[3] This is a very blue collar way of explaining a well known reaction to grief. When faced with disaster, some people just turn themselves off, and King has explained this in a way that readers can understand by using the imagery of a machinist. Essentially, Peter concludes, Frannie's mother was a lot like Frannie herself, and though it may be hard to see it now, there is a connection between them. King is addressing a very common human question here — how can children be so different from their parents? In this case, King explains, certain life events have made Carla the way she is now, and though Frannie may not see any resemblance, she can be reassured by her father's certainty that she and her mother are not so disconnected as they may think. It is in small insights into family relationships like these that King once again shows his capability as an author.

King also addresses the father-daughter connection with the Goldsmiths. As Peter puts it, he is an old man trying to relate to a young daughter, and he feels "like a monkey trying to teach table manners to a bear."[4] Still, despite this admission, Peter does his best to tell his daughter what he can, and in doing so, he serves as a model father in a novel that is severely lacking in family support. Once the super flu arrives, very few survivors actually have blood family, so the time spent on Peter and Frannie's relationship serves as a reminder of a past that is long gone. In the changes that engulf America after the super flu, the idea of family is largely lost, but Frannie's recollections of her father allow her to forge her own family in a new world.

King uses Frannie's position as a pregnant unwed woman to comment on New England perspectives. Frannie is very much aware of the small-town world in which she lives. She knows that even if she moves out of her parent's home to have the baby, she will still be the talk of the town. She may joke about a scarlet letter, but she is genuinely concerned about the gossip that will follow her as her pregnancy progresses. Here King has added a small critique of life in a resort town. The year-long residents will know her condition and publicly scorn her, but the visitors who makes the town thrive will not notice or care about Frannie's pregnancy. The people whose opinion her mother holds so highly are the same people that Frannie thinks about; for all that she claims to be different, she is not foolish enough to think that such things do not matter, especially when all of the visitors go back home. After all, she thinks, the town's permanent residents need something to distract them when the visitors leave for the year, and the shamefully unwed and pregnant daughter of another family will do just fine as fodder for much-needed gossip. Still, Frannie is a woman of action, and just as she worries about the future, she takes steps to ensure her place in it—confirming a new place to live and making her plans for the baby.

Frannie also serves as King's commentary on the place of women in the post–super flu world. Once she and Stu have sex, Frannie sets herself up as Stu's woman, and the title does not bother her as she thinks it ought to. After all, Frannie wonders, what good is feminist theory when biology has come around to a matter of physical strength? It may be all well and good to talk about equality when technology exists to make any physical difference unimportant, but in the absence of technology, the fact that women are physically weaker suddenly matters as it hadn't in many decades. Frannie is a thoroughly modern woman, and yet she does not feel constricted by her duties as Stu's woman, and she does not need any kind of formal ceremony (marriage) or name changing to show her position. Once they reach Boulder, Frannie notes that old systems of pair bonding seem to have broken down, and people are simply together as so-and-so's woman. This may seem degrading to a modern feminist perspective, but Frannie sees how precarious this new existence can be for women (she is part of a confrontation between a group of gun-toting men and their female sex slaves, and sees just how easy it is for men to subjugate women in this new world), and she is glad to have her man's protection.

Frannie is King's example of a modern Every(wo)Man, and she is an apt partner for Stu Redman as champions for the side of White in the coming battle. Even though she is fiercely loyal and a brave fighter, Frannie never loses the qualities that bring her to life for readers — she is a woman afraid for her man's safety and ever aware of the danger that Mother Abagail's God puts them in, but she also cannot help her bouts of the giggles, and it is this realism that allows readers to connect with her.

American Nice Guy

Not everyone on the side of good is as straightforward as Stu and Frannie; in fact, Larry Underwood is often described as a "not-so-nice guy." Larry admits this himself, though it does bother him when others keep bringing it up, especially when his mother tells him that there is strength in him but it would take a catastrophe to pull it out. Larry Underwood is a musician recovering from his first number-one hit. At the start of the novel, Larry is a symbol for the decadence of the music scene in California, as much as Stu is a symbol for the hard-working blue collar American good old boy. In his very first scene, Larry arrives back home in New York, where he has run back to his mother in an attempt to escape the massive debts his outrageous partying has racked up in Southern

Respecting *The Stand*

California. His very first sight on parking the Datsun Z in front of his mother's apartment building in New York is of a rat gnawing on the belly of a dead cat. Larry can't stop thinking about the image as he sits in his car, contemplating how to approach his mother after his double-edged success on the other coast. In this case, Larry has become the dead cat, or very near to it, had he stayed in California long enough for the drug dealers (to whom he now owes massive amounts of cash) to find him.

King uses the dead cat imagery as an extended metaphor for Larry's position in life. As soon as he became successful with his song, Larry's house became an unofficial party zone for anyone who happened to be nearby. He has already squandered the advance he received for the hit single, and keeping his guests happy has become more expensive than he realized. This is a typical scenario of the small-time musician who hits it big for the first time, or, even moreso, the American expectation of a rock star. Larry Underwood now has a song on the radio across the country; therefore, he should be able to host elaborate parties for his hangers-on. Except that in Larry's case, as in most cases, the people at the party aren't the friends that got him there; in fact, when Larry looks around, he realizes that he knows maybe one person in three. These strangers are the rats picking at Larry's guts, and when Larry has been emptied out, they will flock to the next free party for pizza and cocaine. It takes a serious talk from his keyboardist Wayne Stukey to wake Larry up, and with this talk, readers get a revealing glimpse into Larry's character. After Wayne has laid out the situation — Larry owes well over twelve grand, and he has less than a thousand left to his name — readers can see what kind of man Larry Underwood is, and it is not encouraging. Larry's first thoughts are to wonder what Wayne wants from him, then he is reluctant to actually hear his friend's words, and then, when everything does become clear to him, Larry hesitates on pulling the plug on his party because he doesn't want the strangers at his house to think poorly of him; in fact, when he even thinks of telling the hangers-on in his house to leave because the free ride is over, he feels physically ill. Larry is pathetically weak. Instead of listening to his last remaining friend, he is afraid of letting down complete strangers. This is like the dead cat hoping the rat feasting on his guts is satisfied with the menu.

King uses Larry to mock modern notions of success. Since he has "made it," Larry now has an image to uphold. He is the epitome of success in the American music business. He has a hit single. He has an album

Two : The Players

coming out. In a few short weeks, he has gone from the struggling musician everyone knows to the rock star everyone hopes to be. In that transition, Larry has also become the stereotypical overnight success — he is unable to deal with his fame in a reasonable manner; instead he throws wild parties and allows strangers to take advantage of him. Using the image of the dead cat that introduces Larry to the reader, King manages to offer a somewhat scathing commentary on the Hollywood success story without really breaking the pace of the narrative. King continues to build Larry's character in a way that leaves readers unsure if they've just met a possible hero or another villain.

King continues to keep his readers guessing about Larry's true nature when he relates Larry's reaction to his friends in California. When Wayne shakes some sense into him, Larry is at first annoyed, then embarrassed, then afraid. He wonders what all of those people will say about him, and then is torn between the hangers-on disapproval and the drug dealer Dewey Deck adding up the money Larry now owes him. Wayne admits that the partygoers will tell Larry that he has forgotten his old friends, but then reminds Larry that none of them actually are his friends. Larry's real friends, Wayne tells him, have left several days before, none willing to stick around to watch their friend drown in his own success. Larry's reaction to this news is somewhat disheartening to readers seeking any redeeming qualities in this character. Larry is angry, thinking that the reasons his friends gave for leaving seem lame. In other words, Larry faults his friends for leaving after he refused to hear what they said; he is indignant, when he is the one who has lost their respect — all marks of a weak man indeed. King seems determined to have readers see the worst in Larry. This depiction makes sense when, later on, King redeems Larry; the seemingly useless rock star manages to become a leader of his people, a man worthy of admiration, but only after intense struggle and hardship. King uses Larry to make a general comment about human nature — some people may begin poorly, but when tested, sometimes they reveal strengths that were not expected.

King does not make Larry's turnaround a miraculous event. With considerable foreshadowing, King notes that Larry does have something in him that allows readers to have hope. When Larry asks Wayne, with whom he has never been particularly friendly, why he has decided to warn him, Wayne explains: "Because there's a hard streak in you. There's something in you that's like biting on tin foil."[5] This hard streak continues to show itself more and more as Larry grows. Sometimes it allows him to survive where others would fail, and sometimes it lets him get away with terrible deeds. Of all the characters in *The Stand*, Larry Underwood is perhaps the most complex; he shifts between the dividing lines laid down after the super flu. Readers are left wondering which way Larry will turn — will he let that streak of hardness make him into a hero for good, or will he allow that streak to justify his cowardly support for evil? Stephen King does an admirable job in making Larry both lovable and detestable all at the same time. When describing himself, Larry remembers that he would always make stupid decisions that got him into trouble, and when it came down to it, he would abandon those foolish enough to follow him to their own devices, and use his own sense of toughness to survive unscathed and, more importantly, unchanged by the experience. Larry is definitely not a hero as one would hope for, but perhaps in the modern world, King suggests, Larry Underwood, like Jess Rider, is the best there is to offer. Or maybe, King hints, if a modern man like Larry can't get it together to do the right thing, then it doesn't much matter what happens to the rest of humanity. Certainly Larry is tested often throughout the novel, and even at the end, he is still ambivalent about his course, though he does choose to stand as best he can.

King points out that even a catastrophe as great as the super flu may not be enough to transform mediocrity into greatness. It turns out that his mother was right about him when she claimed there was something good in her son, something redeemable, but that it would take a great upheaval to bring that quality to the surface. The super flu may be the catastrophe she envisioned, but even it alone is not enough to bring out the steel in Larry's personality. When faced with her son's burning need for approval, Alice Underwood gives her own blunt appraisal of her son's character: "I think you're a taker. You've always been one. It's like God left some part of you out when he built you inside of me."[6] Larry isn't a bad person, she explains, but he is just a bit broken, and his condition is worse than expected because he knows he is broken but is unable to fix himself. Instead, Larry can only watch himself behave in ways that he knows aren't leading him to the moral high ground. He makes choices, and he does have free will, but he seems to lack the ability to make the right decisions, or at least the decisions that would help out anyone beyond himself. Then again, that self-interest is what allows Larry to survive in the harsh world after the super flu, so readers are forced to wonder which is more important—moral high ground or a devotion to self-preservation. To make matters even more pointed, King has named Larry's hit single "Baby, Can You Dig Your Man?" with the refrain of "He's a righteous man." Larry constantly asks that question as he seeks approval from anyone, but he is not so righteous. Whether he is explaining to his mom why he hasn't called her as often as he ought to or fleeing from a one-night stand, Larry, in the words of the spatula-wielding oral hygienist of his short-lived fling, "ain't no nice guy!"[7] The question of whether or not Larry is a nice guy continues to crop up throughout the novel, and readers are never quite sure which way to answer.

The manner of Larry's introduction showcases King's ability to capture American landscapes. The city of New York is brought to life in these few pages through the eyes of Larry Underwood, a clear example of King's ability to render the world of his novel believable and recognizable. In his dejection, as he sits outside his mother's apartment, Larry decides that the city resembles a dead whore. The neighborhood has degenerated since he grew up there, as many city streets have, and American readers will recognize both the loss of boyhood innocence and the idea that John Updike put so baldly: "You really can't go home again." As far as Larry is concerned, his home is somewhat embarrassing; though, in truth, the embarrassment is his own for having to flee back under his mother's skirts—the city itself may have degraded some, but not nearly as much as Larry sees. He is externalizing his own emotions onto the surroundings, and in such a state of mind, even dead cats and rats start to reflect on his own ill-lived life. When his mother wakes him up in the car, Larry is shocked to see how unchanged she is. He expects her to seem smaller, less confident than the woman he remembers, and he is oddly emotional when she tells him to come inside and have some breakfast. For a second, Larry fears that she will simply turn away from him, abandoning him as she ignores his presence and goes inside alone. This is an old fear of Larry's, some sense that he is not worth the effort, and, at least partly, he is right. Still, blood rings true, and his mother takes him in: she sighs like someone lifting a heavy burden, but when she speaks to him, she sounds pleased, and Larry quickly forgets the sound of her reluctance. He is a mixture of gratitude and expectation at this point. On the one hand, Larry is nearly in tears when he hugs his mother (a hug that she flinches from at first before receiving and giving back her own embrace); on the other hand, he is smugly sure that his return means more to her than it does to him.

Yet when he does enter the building of his youth, Larry is curiously caught off guard by the combination of things missing (like the pair of stone dogs that once stood guard on the end of the stone steps leading inside) and things remembered. For a moment, he has to reassure himself that he hasn't somehow regressed to a child, reminding himself that the last ten years have really happened. Larry is a man afraid of his past and uncertain about his future, and his initial prospects as a hero for the cause of good are dubious. He is a man at war with himself, and this struggle is both internal, as he debates which course to take, and external, as the world around him starts to resemble his interior split. In the foreground, Larry embraces his mother and the hope for yet another chance to do the right thing; in the background, however, is the dead cat with the rat still gnawing at its guts. In true gruesome detail, King has managed to juxtapose the idea of home and family with the grit and grisly beat of the city, and these twin concepts continue to revolve around one another as mankind slowly falls apart.

King continues the theme of coming home as Larry wanders through the city of his youth. He expects Times Square to be different, almost magical, and he imagines that things would seem smaller to his world-weary perspective and yet still special in some small way. Instead, "it all looked just the same — more than it should have because some things really had changed."[8] Larry wants the outside world to change, as he feels that he has changed, and yet he wants it to remain as he remembers it — a simultaneous need to affirm his difference and confirm his similarity that marks the essential split in his personality. Throughout the novel, Larry struggles to walk the thin line between the side of him that "ain't no nice guy" and the person he wishes to be — a man who will stand when the time comes. Larry does not immediately shift into hero mode with the onset of the plague. In fact, it takes him much longer than most to make his decision. When things do first get difficult in New York, readers are sorely tempted to agree with the spatula-wielding oral hygienist. After all, a man who can wonder how badly his mother's sickness will screw up his plans isn't worth much sympathy. Even the villains in the novel seem more worthwhile at times than Larry does at first.

King uses Larry as a test for his readers' sense of outrage. He has created a self-centered character with few redeeming qualities, and yet, when readers find Larry alone in Central Park, trying to deal with the remains of New York City, they find it hard not to be sympathetic. King is fast to

Two : The Players

temper that newfound sympathy with speculation, however, as Larry reminisces about an old friendship that he abandoned over a matter of twenty-five dollars, and a failed relationship that he took for granted. Every time Larry seems to gain ground with readers as a respectable character, he backpedals just as quickly. King also uses Larry's relationship with Yvonne as an image for the perfect American day — sitting on the couch watching the World Series — and readers can relate to Larry as he longs for that lost perfection.

King stretches out that feeling of connection between readers as he relates how Larry reacts to Rita's suicide. Like any normal person, Larry is torn between disgust (he was waking her up so he could have sex with her) and guilt (he was semi-responsible for her survival) when he discovers her body, yet it is hard to accept his justification for leaving her body in the tent they had shared instead of burying her. Larry candidly admits that his actions aren't what a "nice guy" would do, but he also realizes that watching the dirt fall onto Rita's dead body if he buried her would break the small hold he still has on sanity. He calls it cowardice, but it is a fear that most readers can understand — almost. Again, though, Larry manages to make readers shake their heads as he thinks about the event. He shifts from guilt to a sort of ruthless rationalization; Rita wasn't a survivor-type, and she would not have made it as long as she did without him. In fact, Larry rationalizes, she probably killed herself to set him free, and he is glad to be rid of her. The initial guilt he feels on finding her body quickly fades as he moves away from her remains, and soon he is determined to keep going. Still, leaving her dead body behind in a tent is somehow sacrilegious, and it's hard for readers to forget how easily he abandoned this first responsibility, and, more so, how happy he was to be relieved of his burden. King is really stretching the boundaries of "nice guyness" here.

Larry does have a moment of clarity, though, and King marks his first steps towards change with a surprisingly self-aware experience. After endless days of running away from the memory of Rita and the significance of her suicide, Larry is forced to either face his situation or die. He doesn't consciously choose to survive, but he does realize the moment that something has changed within himself. As he stares at Nadine Cross and the savage boy Joe, Larry realizes that he wants to be with other people and that he doesn't want to disappear into the dreams that haunt him every night. He admits that he doesn't understand the change within him: "There are no maps of the change. You just...come out the other side."[9] By the end of the novel, Larry has a woman of his own in Lucy Swann, and a pseudo-son in Joe, and it is these things that he must give up when he goes on his spiritual journey with Stu, Glen, and Ralph. Larry finally becomes a man on his own terms, and by the end he has earned the title of hero, if not really a "nice guy" type of a hero.

A Pawn in the Hands of Providence

The world of the novel may be infused with spirituality, but some characters are especially resistant to the notion of a metaphysical reality. King is careful to keep his world realistic as he builds towards his divine climax; he accomplishes this verisimilitude by adding details about people that readers can recognize. Not all of the "good old boys" in the novel are as noble as Stu Redman. When readers are introduced to Nick Andros, the deaf-mute is being attacked by some self-appointed "good old boys," and he is lucky to escape with his life. King is trading on readers' recognition of this stereotype here, and he uses the standard as a double comparison between Stu, whom readers already identify with, and other people often associated with someone like Stu. King is shattering stereotypes even as he upholds them. King's introduction of a wanderer, another stereotype, also challenges preconceived notions of what kind of person matters in America. Nick seems an unlikely character for a hero, never mind a protagonist, but he soon becomes one of the central players in the battle between good and evil. The part that Nick plays in the conflict between Mother Abagail and Randall Flagg, or God and the Devil, as it were, is curious because Nick himself is an avowed atheist. He does not believe in God, he tells Mother Abagail, who replies with the cryptic "He believes in you."[10] Nick has the hardest time believing that there are forces at work beyond his comprehension. When he is on the road with Tom Cullen to see Mother Abagail, he can't believe it; after all, he is a skeptic, a man confident that things like precognition and visions simply do not happen in the real world. Even when he is faced with the truth of Mother Abagail in the flesh, Nick still tries to rationalize his experience. What if, he asks, the Dark Man is just the fear everyone carries inside, and that the dreams are only projections of that fear, the fear of what will happen in this strange new world? Nick is trying to be rational about things, a quality that may go far in his role in the Boulder Free Zone but will not earn him points

Two : The Players

with Mother Abagail. As Nick tries to give a psychological interpretation of his dreams of Randall Flagg, he is cut down when Mother Abagail asks, "You dreamed of me. Ain't I real?"[11] Nick grudgingly accepts this logic, but inside he is extremely uncomfortable with the very notion of her existence. It suggests that there is more to the world than he knows or expects in his experience, and, given the limits to his sensory perception, such knowledge makes him wonder just what else might exist in the wide world that he doesn't know about. The possibility of a metaphysical reality scares him even more than the dreams of the Dark Man.

King introduces the metaphysical aspect of his novel in cryptic bits at first. While readers are still watching as emerging main characters fight their way through the last days of the super flu and the chaos that precedes the emptiness, King subtly weaves in the deeper issues of his story. The super flu, it turns out, is merely to set the stage for the real conflict, but characters have a hard time coming to grips with the new world around them. Nick, in particular, is exposed to the new reality early on; in fact, he has his first vision of the future before the super flu has even managed to kill everyone. After his dream, Nick wonders if "the normal world had skewed into a place where babies were sacrificed behind closed blinds and stupendous black machines roared on and on in locked basements."[12] In other words, Nick has stumbled into the world of horror. Everything that he fears is suddenly possible, and in the wake of his first glimpse of the cornfield and Mother Abagail, Nick is forced to reevaluate his understanding of reality. Nick's experience with the clear sense of good and evil in his dream makes him consider these two forces as more than abstract notions. Very soon, Nick realizes, he will have to make a choice between them, and that decision will be more than a lifestyle preference — it will define his place in the new world that will follow the super flu.

Christian allegorical interpretations of *The Stand* often focus on Nick Andros as a Christ figure. Nick is tempted by Flagg in dreams when the Dark Man offers to restore Nick's hearing and speech if only Nick will get on his knees and worship him. Nick refuses, as any hero ought, but he is sorely tempted. Curiously, though, what tempts Nick are not the usual things that Flagg offers — cities, women, treasure, power — but rather the "entrancing sound his fingernails made on his shirt, the tick of a clock in an empty house after midnight, and the secret sound of rain."[13] Nick longs for the ordinary things in life, and because Flagg cannot quite understand this, he fails to ensnare Nick's loyalties. Nick doesn't refuse Flagg because of any moral or spiritual qualms—he refuses because Flagg's offer is too big for him, too impossible to imagine, though fear of the dark man also plays a part in his decision. Where others are cowed or amazed by Flagg's dark aura, Nick turns away from the coldness, consciously choosing to stay as he is rather than embrace the evil that Flagg represents. As soon as he does refuse Flagg, however, Nick is rewarded in his dreams with sound and speech, but this time it is the music of Mother Abagail's guitar he can hear, and he accepts the noises as the gifts they are. Mother Abagail does not demand that he bow down before her, but she is nearly as commanding when she suggests that Nick stop by and see her anytime. Instead of trying to scare Nick into submission, Mother Abagail wins his heart with a few comments. It is intriguing that both representatives of good and evil tempt Nick with sound, and the fact that he chooses to seek out Mother Abagail is as much a result of her good singing voice as of any conscious decision to value good over evil.

King develops Nick as a man surrounded by forces beyond his control. However, Nick tries to logically justify his beliefs as he is carried along with the force of Mother Abagail's faith. For reasons that appear to Nick as a bad joke, he is elected the leader of the first group that comes to Mother Abagail's farm in Nebraska. He accepts the responsibility reluctantly, but he is more eager to believe in it than he is in Abby Freemantle's God. He justifies things in small pieces, thinking at first to let Mother Abagail have her God and her visions, while he promises to focus on one thing at a time, just surviving the moments as they arrive. Still, even with his resolution to take things slowly, Nick can't help his skepticism any more than he can help his innermost feelings—in his heart, he believes everything Mother Abagail says, and that belief frightens him even more than thoughts of a mysterious and evil Dark Man setting up camp out west. When Mother Abagail declares that her faith is in the Lord, Nick can only think, "I wish mine was."[14] Abagail is shielded by her faith; it gives her something to cling to, and though her God expects difficult things from her, she can find strength in her belief. Nick has no such relief. He can see how strong her faith is and only wish that he had a belief that could carry him or give him encouragement.

Nick plays his part in the divine battle despite his status as a nonbeliever. Even though he dies in the explosion of Harold and Nadine's bomb, and remains a bastion of rationality (and helpful thoughts for the day-to-day running of the committee), Nick's spiritual role happens after

Two : The Players

his death when he serves as a ghostly guide to Tom in the days after the destruction of Las Vegas. Nick comes to Tom in dreams and tells him how to care for the ailing Stu, and is largely responsible for saving Stu's life. Despite his reluctance, Nick manages to serve Mother Abagail's God with his death, a blow that cripples the first Free Zone Committee and leaves Boulder open for new government. Still, the loss of Nick weighs most heavily on the heroes who head West, and it is his loss more than anything else that lets them accept Mother Abagail's edict that they head out at all. Though he never believed in her God, apparently Mother Abagail was right when she said that God believed in him, for he certainly plays his part in the dramatic struggle.

Nick represents the classic American division between reality and spirituality. In a country that values the separation between church and state, Nick is a solid depiction of many Americans' moral outlook. He is fascinated by others' belief in something beyond themselves, longing for that kind of surety, that sense of knowing that permeates the faithful, but he cannot bring himself to believe wholeheartedly in what he cannot perceive. For all that he may want to share such a sense of certainty, the thought of something beyond the visible world terrifies him, not because of what it says about the nature of the universe but because of what it says about him. For a man already deaf and mute, to accept that there is yet another aspect of the world that he cannot perceive is devastating, and to even contemplate that such a layer of existence may be there is too much. Nick is far more comfortable with what he knows—the real world, filled with real people, who commit very real acts of real evil. Nick has seen enough human evil in his life, much of it pointed in his direction; he does not need a supreme being like the Dark Man to stand forth as a symbol for Evil. In fact, when he first meets the Dark Man in his dream, the very existence of such a creature is nearly enough to drive him mad. He immediately begins to dismiss what happened, focusing on Mother Abagail instead, though even her existence is frightening. Even still, while the reality of Randall Flagg suggests that there is more evil in the world than Nick thought possible, the fact that Mother Abagail is also real suggests that maybe there is some force for good as well, and something beyond the human decency that Nick has associated with Good. While he is not thrilled about these lurking suggestions of things beyond his control, Nick is satisfied that his life after the plague has a reason, a purpose; and however reluctantly he takes on his new duties, he is still pleased to find that the new world suits him. Despite the growing evidence around him, though, Nick stubbornly clings to his beliefs, a faith in himself and his reason that seems even stronger than the faith of those he envies.

Nick faces the classic conundrum of spirituality. He does not choose to believe in god, but in the context of the story, surrounded by some very strong beliefs and confounded by some suggestive evidence, he must decide for himself. The problem with choice, however, is the secret that Nick realizes—if there is a god, that being created him as he is, and the doubt he feels is a result of that being's creation. In other words, Nick has been engineered with his doubt, and so the creator, if there is such a being, must value, or at the very least accept, that kind of ambivalence. This is the problem any atheist faces when considering the transition to faith: If he has been created, then his internal conflict is also divinely inspired and as such cannot just be cast aside. To put it into Tolkien's terms, Iluvatar (the Creator of Tolkien's world) created everything, even the rebellious Melkor, and so everything that creature does is only done with the consent of the Creator. Just as the Christian God made Satan a rebel, designed him with rebellion in mind, that same god has created Nick with his doubt, and so cannot truly be displeased when Nick uses the gifts he has been given. To believe in Mother Abagail's god, for Nick, is to surrender a part of who he is, and Nick is not a man who gives in easily. Even surrounded by evidence of Flagg and Mother Abagail and hints of the fight ahead, Nick clings to his skepticism, unable to take the leap required by faith. Nick is certainly not alone in this respect. Many readers can sympathize with this kind of spiritual split, and the character of Nick Andros echoes in the memory long after he opens that closet door to find Harold's nasty surprise.

Human Nature

King espouses many theories about human nature throughout the novel, and the mouthpiece of these varying interpretations is an aged intellectual. Glen Bateman was an associate professor of sociology at a community college before the super flu, and his commentary about human nature is perhaps the most influential among the characters who form the new government in Boulder. When Stu Redman first encounters Glen after the superflu, the old man is standing in the middle of a road in New

Two : The Players

Hampshire painting a rather poor rendition of the roadside foliage. Of the main characters in the novel, Glen seems to have the least trouble accepting the new world; a world without people means that he can retire and paint full-time, something he had always wanted to do anyway. Glen doesn't lose anyone in the super flu; his wife has been dead for a decade when the virus arrives. He had no real friends at the college — he tells Stu at their first meeting that his colleagues thought he was crazy, and he admits that they may have been right. For all of his jokes, though, Glen is perhaps the sanest of Mother Abagail's stolid crew. As a sociologist, he has considerable knowledge about human behavior, and his ability to abstractly critique and predict how people will act gives the survivors some much needed insight into the future they all face.

Glen is the first person to claim that the super flu has given Western Man the high colonic, a purge of sorts that each new century requires, so that Man can start the next century unburdened, as it were, by the excrement of the last hundred years. He introduces King's theme that the super flu, though man made, has served humanity in a divine sense by offering the clean slate that seems necessary for a fresh start. Over beers with Stu, Glen also admits to being almost happy that humanity has been decimated, a grim way of dancing on the grave of the world, but the sociologist is careful to qualify his feelings with overtly historical references or sociological theories. When Stu asks him about the super flu, Glen candidly admits that he feels it has done America a favor. He explains that he suffers from an end-of-the-century malaise: the idea that the world has gone quickly downhill, and that it would be better if the last few years had not happened. Such a negative view of society and civilization gives Glen distance from the world, and it is this detachment from the world that allows Glen to accept his fate calmly. He wasn't too fond of the world anyway; in fact, Glen isn't fond of much at all. That is not to say that he is a cynical, bitter man. Quite the contrary, Glen still sees the best potential in people — he just expects them to behave as his sociological training has taught him to predict.

King also uses Glen Bateman to comment on Modern Man's interpretation of science. For instance, Glen Bateman is the new owner of one of the few dogs to survive the flu. He speculates that Kojak is the only survivor, but Stu assures him that if there is one dog alive there must be others. Glen is quick to tell him that Stu is not being very scientific about his dog theory: "What kind of American are you? Show me a second dog — preferably a bitch — and I'll accept your thesis that somewhere there is a third. But don't show me one and posit a second. It won't do."[15] King raises the question of intellectualism here — Glen is clearly an educated man, but he puts his knowledge to good use. He knows how Americans typically react to things, and he uses this knowledge to help create a new government and make the world a better place — he does not use his intellect to build weapons to fight against imagined foes. Even with the knowledge that Flagg is a real enemy, not some figment of the community's imagination or fears, Glen still chooses to use his mental prowess for the advancement of Boulder in practical ways instead of focusing on ways to defeat the enemy. He is a thoughtful teacher, a chatty philosopher, and his theories about humanity contribute a great deal to the new society that Mother Abagail's people build in Boulder. Though readers may at first be thrown off by Bateman's lecture hall tendencies, it does not take King long to make Glen one of the most endearing characters among the heroes. Of everyone who Stands, Glen is the only one who does not let emotions take over; he never loses control of himself. Whether this is a positive quality or not (Hemingway would certainly have approved), Glen's stoicism allows him to survive quite easily in the world after the super flu. True, many of the main characters are stoic in some sense, but Glen is the only one who does not have any chinks in his armor — Stu falters when it comes to Frannie, Larry wavers when it comes to his responsibilities, and Nick hovers on the edge between emotional explosion and calm acceptance. King's understanding of human nature as depicted in this novel is both intensely pessimistic and ultimately optimistic at the same time, a divided outlook reminiscent of the modern world, where many issues are seen in different ways at the same time. King describes the worst behavior of people as sociological facts, and yet he extols the potential of all people to overcome such tendencies and rise to the best behavior, an outlook similar to Orwellian doublethink.

Glen Bateman serves as King's mouthpiece on human nature. As he travels with Stu, Glen shares much of his sociological information about how societies form and what they might be able to expect from their fellow survivors. More importantly, though, Glen is the first character to mention the fact that while America may be empty of people, the country is still filled with stockpiles of weapons. The people may be gone, Glen notes, but all of the weaponry society had made is just lying around waiting to be picked up by a willing hand. As he imagines how communities may develop in the post-flu world, Glen gives Stu, along with readers — most of whom are still reeling from the staggering notion of so much death — their first glimpse of the future. People will rebuild society, but Glen speculates that such a new beginning may not be the peace and perfection that survivors are hoping for. There is likely to be a great deal of bloodshed and confusion before things get going again, and even when they do, Glen isn't so positive about making the new society a mirror of the old one. He points out, "They won't remember — or won't choose to remember — the corner we had painted ourselves into. The dirty rivers, the hole in the ozone layer, the atomic bomb, the atmospheric pollution. All they'll remember is that once upon a time they could keep warm at night without expending much effort to do it."[16] Glen's words serve as a harsh reminder of things to come and foreshadow the novel's central question — do people ever learn anything? Glen gives a number of speeches throughout the novel, but none is so relevant to the plot than his explanation of what sociology says about the human race:

> I'll give it to you in a nutshell. Show me a man or woman alone and I'll show you a saint. Give me two and they'll fall in love. Give me three and they'll invent the charming thing we call "society." Give me four and they'll build a pyramid. Give me five and they'll make one an outcast. Give me six and they'll reinvent prejudice. Give me seven and in seven years they'll reinvent warfare. Man may have been made in the image of God, but human society was made in the image of His opposite number, and is always trying to get back home.[17]

This example is almost exactly what happens to the survivors as they begin to form new groups. King uses sociology to explain the actions of the superflu's survivors as they rebuild society.

Glen Bateman is also the first one to point out essential changes in the economy of the post-superflu world. He tells Stu that technological knowledge will be the new currency, replacing gold as the standard of exchange. Gold and money will not buy food nor get the lights working again. Those who can use the technology are the new aristocrats, easily able to get the best houses, the best food, the best of what is available, because their expertise is now in high demand. This concept is played out in the novel, as Boulder struggles to get the power back on, and Flagg's followers in Las Vegas are already doing training runs with the leftover jets. Glen raises one of King's main themes in the novel — is technological superiority something to be proud of, or is the ultimate end of any technological pursuit going to end in destruction? The citizens of Boulder may focus on getting the power station up and running for now, but how far are they from setting up an army base of their own? If one judges by the end of the novel, then King seems to believe that humanity can only begin the same cycle over again. Life may be simplistic for a few years, maybe even an entire generation, but before long, humanity will pursue technology again to make life easier, or to increase safety, and the same weapons will appear as the destructive cycle inches back around towards another super flu or nuclear bomb.

In the end, Glen serves as powerful commentary on Flagg's faltering powers when he faces the Dark Man in Las Vegas, and on the nature of evil's power over men. Because he has willingly walked into the enemy's camp, Glen knows what fate awaits him, but he is not afraid. His casual dismissal of Flagg does more to undermine the villain than anything else in the novel. When Glen laughs at Flagg, he is laughing at his own foolishness as much as he is mocking the Dark Man. Glen realizes that the real fear has been that of the unknown. Once he faces Flagg in the flesh, the Dark Man of his nightmares is, after all, only a man. Yes, Glen knows, Flagg can kill him with a word, but he is still just another man, and that realization lowers the readers' perception of this villain as well. All evil, ultimately, is embodied in the flesh, and that body is never so terrible as our minds make it out to be. The fact that Flagg does not kill Glen himself but repeatedly asks Lloyd to shoot him raises a question about Flagg's capabilities. Glen knows that Flagg has otherworldly powers, and yet the old man seems invulnerable to them. King suggests that Flagg, or any evil, requires belief in order to hold power, and Glen's belief in the Dark Man has receded to comical proportions. To Glen, Flagg is an ordinary man whom he, and everyone in Boulder, had made into a bogeyman in their minds. They had willingly given him power over them through their fear, but now that Glen has seen the Man and realized that he is just a man, any control Flagg had is gone. This is intriguing commentary on evil in general and the horror novel in particular — most of the villain's power comes from the acquiescence of his victims. They agree that he is a formidable force, and so he becomes one. Leave it to Glen, the sociologist and student of human nature, to recognize this flaw in Flagg's armor. Even with his realization, Glen's stand doesn't end with his dismissal of Flagg and the evil he represents. Glen goes a step further and attacks Lloyd in the only way that he knows will work. When logic doesn't work, and Lloyd

Two : The Players

shoots him, Glen tells him that it is all right, since Lloyd just doesn't know any better, and these words haunt Lloyd as he continues to serve his master (even as Flagg's empire begins to unravel). Of all of the heroes, Glen manages to give Flagg the worst wound — he raises doubts about Flagg's capabilities in the minds of readers and, more importantly for the flow of the novel, in the minds of his own followers.

The Sanctity of Innocence

King has a tendency to idolize innocence in his novels. *The Stand* is no exception, except that the innocence in this tale is not that of a preteen boy or girl, but that of a forty-something retarded man named Tom Cullen. When Nick first meets Tom Cullen, the initial result is a bit of a cosmic joke — Nick communicates by writing notes on a small pad; Tom can't read. Still, Nick is quick to attach himself to Tom, both for the sake of some human company and the instant connection the two men share. Even though they can't really talk to one another, Nick sees something in Tom's innocence that draws them quickly together.

The introduction of Tom Cullen allows King to delve into one of his favorite issues — innocence — and address the potential for good such innocents possess. Tom Cullen experiences moments of clarity despite being feeble-minded. When Nick first stumbles onto him, Tom has been drinking whiskey, something his mother never allowed him to do, and Nick waits for cognition to creep back into the man; he looks a little like a robot without a charge, a machine that isn't plugged in, and it takes a few moments for life to come back into his face. Nick later realizes that Tom's little moments of blankness are not a manifestation of his retardation but rather moments of what could be considered almost normal thinking. When Tom feels close to comprehending an idea, he tunes into himself and feels around for the root of it, a notion that King compares to a man crawling around on the floor of a dark room trying to plug in a lamp cord. Sometimes Tom is able to find that connection, and he sees the idea wholly, and sometimes he continues to stumble around in the dark; but this ability to reach into himself to find the answer makes him a sounding board of sorts—Tom can't have many ideas by himself, but he can reach into some sort of universal set of knowledge like a man rifling through a desk drawer. Tom's character is not the commentary on human nature that Glen Bateman extols, but his ability to somehow tap into a universal unconscious shows that he too is an example of what human nature can accomplish when it is pushed to the limit. In order to survive at all, Tom needs these moments of insight, but overall, it is his innocent awareness of the world around him that makes him a key player in the fight between good and evil.

Tom Cullen is King's symbol for innocence, and the way that characters react to him reveals their deepest tendencies; to be kind to Tom shows a good-hearted streak, and to make fun of him marks a tainted soul. It is immediately clear to Nick that Tom Cullen is going to slow him down and make his traveling harder. Unlike Larry Underwood, however, Nick almost welcomes the challenge that Tom poses, and he certainly appreciates the company, however little they can communicate with one another. Where Larry viewed Rita's company as an albatross that the fates had dealt him, Nick willingly chooses to take Tom with him, and he accepts everything that encompasses. Clearly, Nick is a much better person than Larry at this point, but even with his good intentions, Nick's nerves are a bit frayed by the minor challenges that Tom brings. Even when taken on willingly, someone like Tom is a serious burden, especially in a world so drastically altered from what he knows. Unlike Larry, who abandoned Rita's body in a tent because he couldn't face the notion of burial, Nick watches Tom Cullen's eager face and realizes that one thing is certain — he just can't leave him alone. Nick is also quick to defend Tom when others threaten or mock Tom's retardation. King suggests that innocence ought to be protected, no matter what shape it comes in, and it is up to good people everywhere to step in and Stand when the situation calls for it.

The way that some people react to Tom's appearance — by mocking him or yelling at him — reveals their character flaws. In a world so diminished, where human life has become so sacred, showing contempt for someone like Tom displays a complete lack of human decency and understanding. One would assume that anyone still alive should be cherished and appreciated, but the encounter with Julie Lawry shows right away that this is not the case. Julie delights in mocking Tom, in teasing him and tormenting him, lying to him just for the sheer joy of watching his confusion grow. Her reaction to Tom's innocence is vulgar by the standards of the pre-plague world, but in a world so changed, her continuation of this kind of taunting shows a complete disrespect for humanity. For someone like Julie Lawry, the super flu was just the thing she needed in order to release her inner wickedness; and though her treatment Tom is the first

Two : The Players

time readers see her true colors revealed, they are not surprised to find her solidly entrenched in Flagg's camp later on in the story. People like Julie Lawry cannot appreciate the sanctity of innocence, and by virtue of this fatal flaw, they illustrate that even in a world where everyone should be appreciated, some people just are not worthy. Julie can only earn readers' scorn and contempt, as she gains Nick's when he forces her to leave at gunpoint. In a world so devastated by death, it is disheartening to meet a character so devoid of human empathy. When so many better people have been lost, readers may wonder why someone like Julie Lawry has managed to survive. Surely there were more worthwhile human beings in the world. This is more of King's commentary on human nature—the wicked survive just as the innocent do—but in this tale of good vs. evil, right and innocence will win... for a moment. Part of that victory is a result of Tom Cullen—the fact that Flagg can't perceive such innocence distracts the Dark Man enough to allow for his undoing.

Tom winds up playing an important role at the end of the novel, particularly in the survival of Stu, and it is his retardation that allows him to survive as he does. When the Free Zone Committee sends him as a spy into Flagg's territory, they hypnotize him so that he knows to return when the moon is full. This subconscious image is what protects Tom from detection by Flagg, as the Dark Man seeks the third spy and is confounded by images of the moon. Were he a normal person, Tom would have been easily discovered by Flagg, and Stu would have been left alone by the roadside to die of exposure and (ordinary) flu. Tom's retardation also makes him more susceptible to prophetic dreams, long after the others have forgotten them, and he readily accepts Nick's nightly advice for how to care for the dying Stu. Tom plays a pivotal role in Stu's rescue and symbolically serves as God's hands in the matter of Stu's survival. King often uses retarded adults or young children to exemplify innocence in his novels, and *The Stand* is no exception. Tom Cullen is one of the more memorable characters in this large cast, and his endearing manner makes readers smile when he says, "M-O-O-N, that spells [insert word here]."

Tom is not the only innocent in the novel—the savage mute boy Joe (later known as Leo Rockway) also has the ability to see things more clearly than everyone else. He has abilities that border on precognition and telepathy, and yet his behavior is wild and untamed. He is soothed by music and actually turns out to be quite the musical prodigy, but essentially he is an uncontrollable creature. When he senses that his Nadine-mom is succumbing to the Dark Man's pull, he draws away from her, clinging to Lucy instead. Of everyone in the novel, Joe manages to hold on to his psychic abilities long after others have forgotten they ever had prophetic dreams. King seems to suggest that such abilities may be more commonplace in the post–super flu world, but even so, only certain people will be able to hold on to them in the face of a rationality left over from the old world. Those who are innocent are somehow more susceptible to such metaphysical capabilities and, because of this, are to be valued by the newly forming society.

Intellect Gone Awry

Harold Lauder is the man that most readers have been trained to react to in one of two ways—either they will idolize him for his abilities and his knowledge, the epitome of the useful intellectual, or they will despise him for his inability to be socially acceptable. Throughout the novel, it is hard to feel a certain way about Harold—he is too variable. One moment he is essentially useful and helpful and insightful, and the next he is a spoiled brat complaining about his lot in life. This constant battle between his abilities and his inabilities causes Harold to shift quite easily into the Dark Man's power. Tempted by power and women and respect, Harold is a prime candidate for corruption, and yet his intelligence forces him to realize that he does have a choice in things. When he contemplates reading Frannie's diary, he has a moment of revelation. He can stop, he thinks; he can put her diary away and accept his role in a new world, a world that may not remember his past as the gross, fat nerd in the neighborhood. In a world that has a new respect for technical know-how, Harold is in a good position to benefit, even if it does mean that he does not get the girl he wants. Harold has a choice here, a real chance to become a better person.

Instead, though, Harold acknowledges his responsibility in choosing to snoop into Frannie's private thoughts, but he tries to excuse himself from the blame, claiming that somehow it was already too late. At this point, though, it is far from too late. Harold has many, many chances for redemption, but he casts each one aside with increasingly convoluted logic. He uses his considerable intellect to logically damn himself. In fact, the very night that he steals and reads Frannie's diary, Harold has a prophetic

Two : The Players

dream where he lies dying at the bottom of a ravine in the desert, a nightmare complete with cruising buzzards and pain. This is exactly the way that Harold dies, and the fact that he is given a glimpse of it here suggests that he has taken the first few halting steps towards that end, but there is still a chance for him to choose another way. Harold remains torn between his potential in the post–super flu world and his memories of the injustice he suffered in the old world. His ambivalent nature is clear despite his usefulness to his fellow travelers: At times Harold is compared to a low-rate god, ultimately capable of awesome deeds by the post–super flu standards, but just as likely to fall into an emotional mess that renders him more than useless, or even a burden to his fellow travelers. Harold is unable to embrace his future because he cannot let go of his past, and this conflict makes him very contradictory. Harold's instability is a key element in his vulnerability to evil.

Harold has the potential for good in him, despite his many flaws. In an ironic twist, King has the originally flawed Larry explain that potential to Frannie when he tells her how he followed Harold's signs across the country; he describes how he had reached the point where he started wondering what Harold would do in a situation in order to help him get through it. Harold became a rallying cry in Larry's mind, a capable guy who had answers and plans. This is a glimpse of the person Harold could become if only he could let go of the anger and resentment inside of him. The post–super flu world is a brand new one for him — all of the people who treated him poorly are dead, and he is surrounded by people willing to see the potential in him — and yet Harold still chooses to serve Flagg because he cannot get rid of the hatred inside of him. He cannot forget the past and move on, even though he actually sees what his new life could be like. When he spends time in the Free Zone and others begin calling him Hawk, Harold realizes that this is his new life calling to him, and yet he still chooses to reject the possibility.

King illustrates how evil seduces its followers. When the notion of possibly belonging to Boulder as a useful citizen does threaten to change Harold's path, Flagg responds in the best way he can. How should one reorient a wavering servant? Send him a woman to serve his physical needs. That is exactly what Flagg does to secure Harold's loyalty; when Nadine Cross shows up on his doorstep, claiming that they could do anything except that one tiny thing of altering her physical virginity, Harold is lost. He still justifies his behavior to himself as he has throughout the novel, but readers become hardened against him. As if the introduction of Nadine into his life as His Woman obliterates any possibility of redemption for him, Harold begins to first abuse and then neglect Nadine, so much so that even readers unsympathetic to her will begin to feel some pity.

Harold's own theories of redemption and personal responsibility are King's way of mocking those who willingly choose to follow evil. It is slightly ironic that Harold's final confession, that he acts of his own free will, is only "heard" by the deaf Nick Andros as he pulls the shoebox from the closet seconds before it explodes. This is fitting, though, since Harold's statement is a false one, a justification that should not be heard because it is not worthy — Harold may think he is exercising free will at the last moment, but any freedom he had is long gone by this point. Now he is only an agent of Flagg, someone convenient to do some necessary dirty work on site. And once Harold's duty is done, Flagg is quick to discard him with a motorcycle accident. Readers may be tempted to pity Harold as he lies dying in the ditch, as King's prose is quite touching, but it is too easy to remember everything that Harold has done; and in the end his death is justified to readers, a symbol of intellectual corruption. Harold is doubly damned because he was intelligent enough to know better and yet willingly chose to serve evil.

The Self-Fulfilling Prophecy

Nadine Cross seems at first like the virgin sacrifice to the dark god, but this image is really a careful construction of her own design, not King's. The former schoolteacher makes choice after choice that propels her down the path to her own undoing, and it is hard for readers to really sympathize with her. For a woman who claims that taking life in a world where so many have died is the one unforgivable sin, Nadine slides quite easily into the darkness. Even when she still has a possible bright future, Nadine fears that all of her words about the sanctity of life would someday come back to mock her. For all that she talks and thinks about doing the right things, an intellectual mind at work, her actions rarely mirror such pure intentions, and every little thing she does sends her even further down the path of damnation. Her rebellion against what she has decided is her "fate" is more of a show, an act she performs to fool herself, than any true desire to reject evil.

Two : The Players

Nadine is King's example of a self-fulfilling prophecy. Despite all of her opportunities to choose the side of good, Nadine allows herself to give in to evil because she believes that it is inevitable. She begins with an act of kindness in taking in the boy Joe, and his innocent savagery does protect her for a time, but she quickly becomes unworthy of his affection. Just as she allows herself to entertain ideas of her demon lover, Joe begins to slip away from her into the care of a more "worthy" mother in Lucy. Nadine chooses to ignore this divine judgment, even though she knows that Joe is connected to the metaphysical world in ways she can only glimpse; Joe's dismissal of her is a clear indication that she is falling from the right path, and yet Nadine does not waver in her direction. Nadine is also warned quite plainly by Mother Abagail in her dreams when the old woman looks at her with pity, saying, "Your trip will be longer than ours, if'n you don't fight off his power. ... You'll go straight to hell if you don't watch close, daughter of Eve. And when you get there, you are gonna find that hell is cold."[18] Nadine tries to ignore what is happening to her instead of fighting, though, putting her faith in the things of the real world instead of the nightly visions that haunt her. Nadine tries to think her way through things, as she has done her entire life, but her refuge in rationality is foolish when the world around her has become infused with the metaphysical. Still, Nadine refuses to give up her need to think things over logically and do what feels right. When logic doesn't work, and she accepts that her fate is to be the Dark Man's woman instead of going completely mad with the dreams he sends her and the fear that he uses to keep her under his control, Nadine can still be saved by others — namely, Mother Abagail and Larry, both of whom miss their chances to rescue her. Still, readers must wonder if Nadine deserves salvation if she can only rely on others to save her. Nadine only makes one last-ditch effort to save herself when she throws herself at Larry, but by then it is too late, and any rescue that Larry might have been is lost to her.

For all of her intellectual debating, Nadine refuses to acknowledge any sort of personal responsibility for her plight. She blames Joe for leaving her and Larry for abandoning her, but the truth is that everything that happens is her own doing. Yet, Nadine refuses to see this, claiming, "So, you see, none of this is my fault. *None of it!*"[19] Even when she plants the bomb in the closet, Nadine refuses to take responsibility for her actions. She does what she has to in order to hold on to her sanity, she justifies, and this is an ironic excuse, since she loses her mind as soon as she goes to Flagg. Nadine Cross is not exactly like the scientists who created the super flu, but she certainly stands as an example of the dangers such a devotion to rationality can lead to. If Nadine had considered her feelings, and her inner sense of rightness, she may have been redeemed, but her dogged determination in clinging to logic is what dooms her entirely. Thus is the fate of the intellectual in America, and especially in King's work.

For Every Villain a Right-Hand Man

Lloyd Henreid is the quintessential "bad" guy — he is the Walkin' Dude's right hand man, a murdering criminal without much of a conscience; but even with such stereotypical characteristics, Lloyd is still very much a creature worth studying. When readers first encounter Lloyd, he is participating in an interstate crime spree where he imagines himself as an old-time criminal using phrases like "you dirty rat" and "ya lousy copper."[20] However, Lloyd and his erstwhile companion Poke are hardly big-time criminals worthy of the black and white screen. They are small-time crooks from the start, but the moment they turn on Gorgeous George, the man who set them up with a pseudo-robbery, readers realize that King is introducing more than just a few flat characters to kill time. Lloyd and Poke's actions set up a running theme in the novel, one that readers will recognize as lines between good and evil are clearly marked.

Evil, King suggests here, will always turn on itself. This idea, one that Tolkien would certainly have agreed with, is shown again and again in *The Stand*, each time increasing in intensity and importance. The betrayal of Gorgeous George is hardly an event worth crying over — he wasn't a wonderful guy himself, and readers aren't too sad to see him go. But when readers watch as Poke and Lloyd, though he's mostly along for the ride, tear through a store full of people, sympathies shift sides. Lloyd is no longer a pathetic wannabe criminal; he is a murderer, and the fact that he blames Poke for the entire episode, refusing to ever take responsibility for his actions, makes him even more solidly a villain. Despite the evidence of Lloyd's damnation, however, readers can't help but be moved by his plight when he nearly starves to death in prison. Lloyd isn't a nice guy by any means, but when King describes his struggle, readers are tempted to pity him; after all, no one, no matter how bad his crimes, should be forced to eat the man in the cell next door to stay alive. Lloyd recognizes that he should have been locked up for his crimes, but once the guards die from the super flu and he slowly begins to starve to death, he stays alive by feeding on his hatred; he is tortured by the knowledge that they had left him there to die when they could have, quite easily in Lloyd's mind, set him free. The idea that he has been purposely abandoned torments Lloyd, just as he is haunted by images of the pet rabbit he had forgotten as a child (and the rabbit's corpse after it starved to death). He bemoans his fate, lamenting that just because someone has THE KEY, he does not possess the right to abandon Lloyd and make him choose to eat another prisoner's decaying body to stay alive. Lloyd's outrage and indignation allow him to keep trying to stay alive, if only to spite those who have left him for dead. Even in such dire circumstances, though, Lloyd continues to blame others for his plight. When Randall Flagg shows up and offers him release, Lloyd's first words completely avoid responsibility, blaming the already dead Poke for his troubles. When Flagg forces him to actually look at his face, Lloyd's terror causes him to scream that it is Poke who should be there, not him. Despite his tendency to avoid responsibility, Lloyd recognizes Flagg for what he is: "Mister, if you're real, you're the devil."[21] He has a moment where he can choose not to serve him. True, his alternative is to starve to death, and given those choices, most people would choose to survive, but Lloyd's mind is not clouded on exactly what he is doing. He knows that serving Flagg means damnation, and he chooses to live and to serve.

King couches Lloyd's decision to serve Flagg in religious terms. Lloyd justifies his choice and even feels special in a way; he feels an almost religious ecstasy, a sense of special pleasure because he has been *chosen*. This is a complete mockery of a proper religious moment, something that Flagg makes quite clear when he tells Lloyd that he will make the prisoner his right-hand man, akin to Saint Peter. Lloyd is a far cry from a saint, and he is the polar opposite of a disciple, yet in a strange way his devotion to Flagg is just as viable as any of Jesus' followers. The difference lies in the reason for the loyalty, perhaps, because Lloyd follows Flagg out of desperation and fear, while the disciples followed Jesus out of love and admiration. The religious imagery continues as the two leave the prison — when Lloyd stumbles from weakness and delirium, Flagg helps him walk, bears him up as a leader ought — and Flagg is rewarded by a look that contains something like love. To someone like Lloyd, Flagg would be deserving of worship and love. The Walkin' Dude has offered freedom, food, and a position of considerable power all in one fell swoop — much more than anyone else had ever offered Lloyd, and at no real cost to Lloyd either. In fact, Flagg wants Lloyd to continue to serve as he has served his whole life. Flagg wants Lloyd to assume the position he has always assumed — a subservient place of no responsibility or decision making.

Lloyd Henreid is King's illustration of mankind's willful evil. Flagg is evil incarnate, but he lies beyond humanity; Lloyd is a man, and though he may be damned by his position as Flagg's right-hand servant, he is doomed long before the novel ends in a fiery blaze. Lloyd's major failing is in his inability to make any choices for himself, and in the post–super flu world, such lax behavior will be met with consequences — divine punishment, in fact. Lloyd is King's example of how not to live, not only because he is a prisoner but because he is a man who cannot choose anything, and it would never even occur to him to stand in any capacity. In King's mind, Lloyd is a terrible waste of a human being. He has the potential to *do* things, good or bad, and instead he decides not to do anything of his own accord, but lives to serve the whims of others.

Lloyd suffers from the same need for approval that haunts Larry Underwood. When he arrives in prison, Lloyd sees the comments of his fellow prisoners as accolades because he has become a real "heavy hitter"; in fact, Lloyd imagines that his walk into his cell is similar to the way Tom Cruise (pre–Oprah couch jumping incident) must feel when he enters a world premier of his newest movie. Lloyd cannot distinguish between the praise heaped on an actor for a job well done and the admiration of other villains — to him, either form of praise is acceptable, and he develops a small swagger as he feels himself a big man around the prison. Even with his small burst of pride, though, Lloyd is a character quickly cowed by those around him. Even his defense attorney manages to make Lloyd shut up and listen with a small order. Lloyd functions best as a right-hand man and is particularly good at following orders. He is loyal, almost to a fault, but he always chooses a perfectly villainous man to follow. Lloyd is what Larry Underwood could have been if Larry had chosen not to make any choices. His easy acquiescence is what makes Lloyd excel as an underling. Lloyd is uncomfortable making decisions and taking responsibility for himself, but he can execute orders with brutal efficiency. Ironically, when Lloyd is first in jail and faced with the hard truth of his execution, he is furious — raging against any kind of quick trial and judgment — and yet it is exactly that kind of system that he embraces in Las Vegas under Flagg's rule. Lloyd is unable to even grasp the connection between his former situation as an Arizona-condemned prisoner and any of those he condemns to crucifixion according to Flagg's brand of justice.

What is curious about Lloyd, however, is his likability. Even as he serves as the right-hand of the devil, Lloyd is a hard character to condemn entirely. He is not evil in himself, but he does serve great evil. Though that may seem enough to write him off as a lost cause, Lloyd's sad devotion to his master, even when things begin to unravel quite obviously, makes him a character worth some admiration. He is the only "evil" character in the novel who does not turn on his master. He remains loyal even after he realizes that Flagg's reign is ending and his own death is near, choosing to stay with the one person who had given him anything in life. As things spiral out of control in Las Vegas, Lloyd shifts only slightly; instead of turning in his compatriots for their plans to desert Flagg, he lets them go without warning his leader — a choice that shows he still retains some humanity — even if those he allows to escape get caught anyway. Unlike what Glen Bateman decides about him — that Lloyd doesn't know any better — Lloyd does actually know better, but he chooses the age-old plan of standing at the right hand of the devil rather than being in the devil's path. Even as an agent of evil, though, Lloyd remains a fascinating character for readers, a curious glimpse into the mindset of the follower.

Evil Always Undoes Itself

Trashcan Man, King's pyromaniac, is an odd character to judge in the novel. Though clearly psychotic, Trash has moments of curious clarity that make him frighteningly believable. When he is threatened by the Kid, readers actually worry for his safety, and King is careful to build Trash up as a weakling deserving of pity, not derision. Trash has spent his life as a whipping boy for the townspeople. From his earliest childhood, he has been ridiculed and battered. So when Randall Flagg shows up with promises of friendship, and not just camaraderie but actual authority in the new world order, Trash is helpless to resist. The pyromaniac is not a strong man, and having been the subject of abuse his entire life, he quickly latches onto the first person who does not treat him with disgust, pouring all of his twisted love into the relationship as a dog will to a hand that feeds it. Even if that hand does occasionally beat him, the dog will still love unconditionally and eternally. He just can't help himself, King seems to say, and yet, just as readers are warming up to a grudging understanding of Trash, King throws the entire thing off balance as Trash blows up one thing after another — regardless of who or what is nearby.

Trash serves as King's commentary on the nature of evil. The man is mentally unstable, clearly, and Flagg's choice to make him one of his special followers with free reign of the military base turns out to be the Dark Man's undoing. When Trash does turn on Flagg's men, planting explosives on trucks and planes, he doesn't quite know the reason why. Certainly he imagines that the men had made fun of him in some way, but even this justification pales in comparison to the one thing he does understand — fire. By chaining him up as a pet weapon-finder, Flagg forgets the most important thing about having a pyromaniac for a servant — pyromaniacs need explosions, and after a while it won't matter whose trucks are being blown up as long as there is a big bang and lots of flames. Trash sabotages the base's equipment out of boredom, a sign that evil turns on itself for arbitrary reasons and sometimes without any planning at all. Trash doesn't set out to hurt his master, but when he realizes that he has done so — his little bomb party kills the only men who know how to fly the planes left at the base — he tries to atone by finding an even bigger weapon. The moment of his arrival in Las Vegas with the nuclear bomb as a gift for his master could not have been more poorly chosen, and the careful series of events in which Trash plays a key role makes readers wonder just how much influence good and evil have on people's actions.

Is Trash subject to God's orders, however subconsciously, or is he simply a loose cannon? Does he turn on Flagg as a result of God's intervention — the very embodiment of a eucatastrophe — or is it mere happenstance that he arrives when he does? Trash seems to be a wild card throughout the novel, so this would support the random event theory, but the careful way that King has crafted the events in the novel, and the metaphysical influence experienced by most of the characters, suggest that more than random chance is at work here. Perhaps the answer lies in Trash's free will, which would always revert back to a need for fiery explosions, and in Flagg's choice in making him one of his followers. Flagg knows that Trash is unreliable and dangerous, but he assumes that those qualities will make him a great ally and supporter — it does not occur to Flagg that the unpredictability might turn around and harm him. This is the nature of Evil as well, King suggests — it rarely assumes that people like Trash will turn on it; rather, it seeks to use Trash as a weapon against his enemies, not realizing that any kind of weapon can easily turn self-destructive.

In the Hands of a Demanding God

For a novel that is centered on a religious climax, King is not always so kind to the so-called "good guys" on the side of White. The God of the novel is demanding, according to his mouthpiece, and sacrifice is a requirement of survival. Even Mother Abagail admits that serving the Lord is sometimes not the easiest thing to do: "I have harbored hate of the Lord in my heart. Every man or woman who loves Him, they hate Him too, because He's a hard God, a jealous God. He Is what He Is, and in this world He's apt to repay service with pain while those who do evil ride over the roads in Cadillac cars."[22] Such words reveal a curious view of the God to whom she has dedicated her life. Mother Abagail's God is very Old Testament, filled with vengeance and fury and hardness, and the redeeming loving God of Christ and the New Testament is hardly seen in the novel. Characters are expected to first give up the world they know, then the people they knew, and then, at the end, the world they have struggled to rebuild. When she sends the four heroes on their road toward Las Vegas, Mother Abagail (and her God) insists that the men go with nothing but the clothes on their backs, a spiritual journey that requires a shedding of material goods and cares as a way of preparing for enlightenment.

Mother Abagail has several stereotypical qualities of a religious leader. She sees herself as touched by God, and she is firm in her belief that God has plans for all of them. Her stalwart faith sometimes throws off the less faithful members of her following, and her constant commentary about her God makes almost everyone uncomfortable. After all, the characters are modern Americans. They may have some sense of faith, but to believe in God as an active force in their lives is a step beyond what they have been raised to comprehend. Only Mother Abagail, 108 years old and raised through and through on a Christian grounding, can have the sheer belief. Her followers are tormented by a modern sensibility, a doubt that such a metaphysical reality is even possible, despite the evidence of the prophetic dreams that everyone shares. In this sense, Mother Abagail is a throwback to the deep-seated faithfulness that characterized the earlier part of the twentieth century but seems to have been lost in more recent times. Sure, some Americans are believers, but those with the faith of Mother Abagail are often regarded as fanatics, and their warnings often go unheeded. Mother Abagail only wields the power that she has because America has undergone such a devastating change. Once things in Boulder get back on track, people forget about her as anything more than a figurehead or a spiritual symbol for their new life. They don't even start going to a church on a regular basis as a nod to her faith.

Mother Abagail definitely parallels Christ in her journey — she consciously puts herself in the position of savior and punishes herself for the sin of pride with her own walk into the wilderness. She gains some clarity from this episode, realizing that God wants her to send her heroes out to face Flagg, but the result of exposure on her body takes its toll, and she dies. Mother Abagail is so caught up in the spiritual world that she often loses sight of the ordinary one. Mother Abagail serves a dual role in the novel. She serves as the spiritual symbol for the White, and yet she is at heart an old black woman from Nebraska. She has all of the quirks and foibles of an old woman who has been living according to her own rules for some time, and King is not above making his symbol for the good side a bit foolish in her set ways, much as any old person may be viewed as foolish by a younger generation. Mother Abagail has her reasons for acting as she does, but King is careful to make her a realistic old woman for all of her theological importance. Abby Freemantle is still a fragile woman with arthritis and sore hips. She is as real as any reader's grandmother, and her stubbornness makes a character who could be inflated to gigantic proportions as a symbol into a sometimes cranky old woman. King manages to blend the spiritual and the physical in Mother Abagail — she is both a symbol of the coming battle between good and evil and also just another old person trying to come to terms with the eager youngsters who surround her.

American Evil

Readers do not get their first glimpse of *The Stand*'s devil until nearly 200 pages into the novel, but they certainly see enough ordinary evil before then. By the time Randall Flagg is introduced, readers are ready to accept that Flagg knows America — his kind of evil resonates in the landscape of a country that has long been home to dastardly deeds. King's physical

Two : The Players

description of Flagg is curious. Flagg looks like a country western star — from his denim jacket to his cowboy boots, readers may be tempted to dismiss him as a fashion victim. However, it is the "dark hilarity" of his face that sets him apart from any kind of cheap joke. This "hatefully happy man" is not to be taken lightly, King suggests, even with his Boy Scout backpack and his cutesy little buttons (a yellow smiley face and a pig wearing a policeman's cap). In fact, King states, Flagg's was "a face guaranteed to make barroom arguments over batting averages turn bloody."[23] Like an evil creature, Flagg travels the roads at night and sleeps by day, and his passage disturbs those he passes; even the evil-hearted are made uncomfortable when he is near, as even madmen can only look at his hideously grinning face from an angle. Flagg is introduced as an instigator, a man who easily turns small unrests into civil wars, and he sometimes thinks that he may have been born during the unrest of the civil rights movement — but then he also recalls days of school with Charles Starkweather and reading pamphlets with Lee Harvey Oswald. It seems that though Flagg has no real memory of how he moves through space and time, he has vivid recollections of the darkest moments in American history, and King very clearly places him at the scene of nearly every crime. If the American psyche did have a devil, then Randall Flagg is that force personified; but even with all of his dark history, Flagg is still very much at the mercy of forces beyond even his control. He appears in the novel because he feels his time is at hand, but he is not privy to any knowledge beyond that. This doesn't seem a very big detriment to him, however, since Flagg is a mostly instinctual creature, but his lack of true comprehension is the quality that makes him equally human and terrible.

Flagg's lack of intellect relegates him to a creature of passion, and he is often ruled by his emotions, such as they are. Flagg suffers from his outbursts of anger; often he will lash out in anger without thinking things through, and his extreme behavior somehow undoes a little more of his plans. When he allows Nadine to goad him into killing her, Flagg manages to destroy his hope of an heir, along with his woman, and the loss of that security undermines his authority among his own people. He cannot control himself and so manages to undermine his own cause as much as the forces gathering against him. Again, King suggests that evil does enough to destroy itself on its own. Even so, Flagg manages to survive the destruction of Las Vegas, and his evil is certain to return again. This cycle of evil's rise and fall is crucial to the world of King's novel.

Evil is a given in King's creation. It will always exist, whether it is in the form of Flagg or in other people whose agendas involve death or subjugation; it is not something that people will ever really destroy. The knowledge that evil has only been beaten back for a short time makes the people in King's world value the peace they have earned even more—because it is temporary. Flagg may have been undone for now, but he will return, and King can only hope that worthy heroes will stand against him in the future as they have in the past.

Constant Readers of King's work will recognize Randall Flagg from other novels, particularly as the evil court magician from *The Eyes of the Dragon* and, even more famously, the man in black from King's *Dark Tower* series. The infamous R.F. is King's signature for evil in his multiverse, and whether the man wears robes or a denim jacket, he is always equally dangerous, often representing chaos and disorder with a grinning face. Flagg is King's explanation of evil in his works. He resembles a man, though he sometimes possesses powers beyond those of the other humans in the story. Mostly, though, Flagg's power lies in his ability to goad others into action, often saying just the right thing to spark events in the direction he chooses. When he wants to get rid of Roland, the hero of *The Dark Tower* series, he engineers an untimely meeting between the young gunslinger and his mother—an encounter that reveals the affair she had been having with Flagg, this time disguised as Walter, a magician living in Gilead and working with Roland's father (and, as it turns out, the agents of evil in Mid-World). Flagg is quite good at provoking people to do his will. Rarely does he have to do anything more than make suggestions, though occasionally he has to flex his terrifying muscles, scaring those few reluctant followers into obeying; but usually the people in King's novels are more than happy to obey him. King suggests that human nature itself is destructive, and it takes but a few well-placed words to unravel the entire fabric of society.

Randall Flagg is the embodiment of that destructive force within all humanity, and whether he is poisoning a king and framing the prince, or inspiring bloody, society-ending revolutions, this evil is always at work in the society of King's novels. Even so, despite what appear to be soul-sucking odds of good's eventual triumph over evil, King doesn't allow Flagg to run amuck forever. The Dark Man meets his end in the final installment of King's *Dark Tower* series, and his undoing proves to be his own sense of superiority, a theme well in keeping with King's overall depiction of evil. It doesn't even occur to Flagg that he can be outwitted or out

Two : The Players

manipulated; he has always been the smartest man in the room, or, at the very least, the man with the most weapons at his disposal — even if some of those weapons are just people he has coerced to his side of things. Flagg has no loyalty to anyone but himself, and in the end it is his very nature, his evilness, that leads to his downfall. When a new beacon of evil rises in Mid-World, King's setting for part of the *Dark Tower* series, Flagg is quick to swear fealty to that new power; but like all villains, his oath isn't to the new embodiment of destruction but to the very idea of destruction. Therefore, when the time comes, Flagg is eager to dispatch the newest dark leader and replace that force with himself.

Unfortunately for him, facing Mordred, the half-spider offspring of the Crimson King, doesn't go quite as he had planned. Though Mordred is still a mostly helpless infant during their encounter, Flagg is so caught up in finally getting his revenge on Roland, the gunslinger who has eluded him for so many long years, that he forgets that evil can use him just as easily as he has used those who have fallen before him in the past. Flagg is momentarily deceived by Mordred's seeming helplessness — just as he had been deceived by Nadine's apparent malleability right before she leapt to her death, taking Flagg's unborn child with her — and he forgets that he is facing the spawn of the greatest evil the world has ever known. Even though the Crimson King himself may have run mad, Flagg fails to realize that the King's heir is still quite sane — relatively speaking. This failure to recognize the power of other evil entities allows Flagg to overestimate his odds of survival, and when Mordred easily overtakes Flagg's mind, causing him first to blind himself and then to cut out his own tongue, the only thing Flagg can think of is his own stupidity. Even though Flagg has been responsible for the downfall of nations, he is undone by a baby, overcome by his own sense of superiority; and in typical King fashion, evil undoes itself once again.

In destroying Flagg, Mordred has actually done more for the cause of good than even he suspects; yet King's Constant Readers know that this is a temporary reprieve. Randall Flagg may have been destroyed, but who knows what great monster King will create to take his place? Evil will always exist in a King novel, so readers know that something must appear to fill the gap, and it is horrifying to realize that some of them may find themselves longing for old R.F. — scary as he was, at least Flagg's brand of terror was recognizable. The unknown entity that will eventually rise up in his place is even more terrifying, and in killing his great devil, King has only made his readers even more worried about the future of their beloved characters.

THREE

The Big Picture

The Stand has several main themes trailing through its thousand-plus pages. The first of these is the issue of the dreams shared by the survivors and what these prophetic visions mean to the world after the superflu. King questions notions of free will and predetermination, settling for a curiously Old English view of human choices, and then considers what is worth standing up for and the sacrifices that epic battles sometimes demand. King also raises questions about government and who has the right to rule over others, and then ends the novel with an unexpected hope, despite the despairing knowledge that evil will return.

Thematically, *The Stand* resonates with literary tradition. Issues of a metaphysical reality are old questions in literature, as are considerations of fate and free will. King is drawing on the vast tradition behind him in these areas, but he also manages to add his own twists to each of these old concerns. Where traditional literature considers the human condition, King considers the potential greatness in ordinary humans.

Good vs. Evil: Dream a Little Dream

Most of the events in the second half of *The Stand* are sparked by the occurrence of prophetic dreams. Charles Fisher said, "Dreaming permits each and every one of us to be quietly and safely insane every night of our lives."[1] It is during the dreaming episodes that King's main characters are able to accept the notion that they are playing a part in a metaphysical drama — the unreality of dreams allows them to accept the inherent insanity (as in the opposite of the sane rationalism they are accustomed to in the pre-flu world) of a world not only imbued with spirituality but practically drowning in it. Dreams are also an easy way to see into the true

Three : The Big Picture

natures of the main characters; there is no need to lie or dissemble in dreams, so the divvying up of survivors into separate camps is quite a simple process. Those who are drawn to Mother Abagail's quaint Nebraska home have little doubt that the "other fella" in Las Vegas plans general harm to anyone who disagrees with his plan. Even so, King does not allow his lines to be drawn so easily. For instance, Detective Second Dorgan decides to stand with Flagg because he had seen the worst of what the pre–super flu society had been capable of, and he feels that the only way to save humanity is with strict rules and regulations. He tells Glen that he remembers what the old world was like, and he chooses Flagg over reliving that state of affairs, that potential future that is a copy of the previous society. At this, Glen snappily replies, "Young man, your experiences with a few battered babies and drug abusers does not justify your embrace of a monster."[2] Dorgan does make an interesting point, though — he appreciates order, and even Glen has to admit that in Las Vegas the trains are running on time. Still, Glen observes that Dorgan will not last long in Flagg's new world; after all, he tells him, "There doesn't seem to be quite enough Nazi in you."[3] When the end eventually comes, it turns out that Glen's prediction is somewhat correct — even among Flagg's followers there are those who will balk at certain actions. Consider Angie Hirschfield, who cringes at the sight of the stage they erect for the public execution of Larry and Ralph because she harbors a secret fear in her heart, sensing that something even worse than the super flu is about to happen. In small details like this, King manages to rekindle hope in readers' hearts about the future of the human race.

The plot device of the dreams may seem at first a flimsy way to draw battle lines between good and evil, but King manages to imbue these omens with symbols rich in American resonance. The good dreams involve Mother Abagail in her 108-year-old reassuring glory, her sagging porch, her worn rocker, and her familiar guitar chords and hymnals— all signs associated with Middle American Christianity. Music plays an integral part in Mother Abagail's appeal. The songs she sings remind Stu of his childhood. It is Abagail's musical talent that she is most proud of, especially the moment when she played in 1902 on a stage that had only been home to white people. Though some of her memories are failing her now, Abagail's recollection of that experience is still quite clear, and the Dark Man tries to use this memory to trap her. Just as everyone else in the novel dreams of her or Flagg, Abagail herself dreams of the Dark Man; he twists her memories of that triumphant moment, and tries to sway her with doubts and haunted promises of failure. Still, Abagail's faith in God is strong, and she clings to that belief in order to hold steady her course—even though at times even she does not know where the path may lead her.

King uses common literary and religious symbols to describe Mother Abagail's experience; she is surrounded by more symbols than she herself gives to her followers. She is attacked by weasels in the corn, animals known for viciousness and rabies—*his* animals, as she comes to think of it; and she is hounded by the crow-shape that Flagg sometimes uses when watching his enemies. Crows and weasels have long been symbols in the American mindset for trouble, especially among farmers in the Midwest, and it is this Middle America mind set that King manages to recapture as he develops Abagail's understanding of Christianity. For the survivors who flock to her side, Abagail's faith is sometimes a thing of simplicity that mirrors their own beliefs, but more often it is a symbol for the hope that the members of Boulder desperately need. If the survivors cannot truly put their faith in God, they can put their faith into the person of Mother Abagail—a woman whom they dreamed about who turned out to be real—and this empirical evidence makes them more likely to believe in what she says, even if they try to ignore the bigger picture of why she says anything. In other words, the survivors succumb to a sort of idol worship instead of more traditional Christianity, and Mother Abagail decides to take a spiritual journey of her own to make up for her imagined sin in accepting the people's adoration; she has committed the sin of pride, and for that she must redeem both herself and her followers—a rather Christ-like idea. So in trying to atone for her sins, Abagail actually manages to place herself even more into her role as savior; the people worship her even more after she returns, but by this point, she has become an icon to them, an idea and not a real person at all, and certainly not a representative of any God. Still, Abagail's duty is to call the good-hearted to her, and this she does, in dreams, with the aid of very familiar American symbols of life and faith—corn, guitar music, and hymnals.

Evil symbols are fairly universal as well—King uses the image of a creature in the corn, two red eyes back in the shadows, to signify the Dark Man and his influence on the survivors. Even before the super flu has gotten well underway, Nick Andros dreams of endless rows of green corn as he looks for something before him and flees something unknown behind him. Corn has long been a symbol of the American Midwest, and many horror movies have played on the fear of getting lost in endless rows. But if the corn is vast enough to get lost in, it is also a place to hide away from things, and King uses both sides of the double-edged symbol in the dreams. As Nick searches for something he cannot name, he uses the corn to hide himself from the Walkin' Dude, as yet an unnamed force when he first begins to dream.

The demarcation between good and evil is quickly established in the dreams as well. On one side there is the cornfield and that safe sense of growing things; this feeling quickly fades as the dreamers realize that someone very dark is in the corn watching them. As Nick puts it, "Ma, weasel's got in the henhouse!"[4] People are quickly drawn to one side or the other, though the method of choice for Flagg's dreams seems to be terror rather than Christian overtones. He tends to arrive with a fanfare of fear and offers the dreamers what he imagines they want; sometimes this is effective, as his followers are cowed into servitude, and sometimes this backfires, as when he offers the wrong thing to a person and practically propels that person into the other camp. Once the dreams have arrived, however, and survivors have accepted them as a form of truth—something that does not happen so easily—people are quick to avoid them altogether, and sleeping drugs to prevent dreams become commonplace as they head to their respective cities.

The fact that the survivors in *The Stand* move west is more than an arbitrary choice of direction. Douglas Winter explains that "these stories enact the recurrent American nightmare—the terror-trip experienced by Edgar Allan Poe's Arthur Gordon Pym, Herman Melville's Ishmael, and a host of fellow journeyers: the search for a utopia of meaning while glancing backward in idyllic reverie to lost innocence."[5] The eastern United States is traditionally the side of the country associated with the founding, development, and government of America. Pilgrims settled in New England, Washington, D.C., is the seat of the capital, and the first colonies were all along the Eastern seaboard. The West has long been a source of romance and mysticism for Americans, from stories of the Wild West to notions of manifest destiny, the untouchable, uncontrollable unknown is in the West, and it is fitting that King sets his epic battle between mountains and deserts in what was once the last frontier of the modern imagination. Still, while the places have resonance for American readers, the cross-section of society that King chooses to represent good in his fight may seem odd to some readers. Why these people? The question is one that both readers and characters are constantly asking.

The only thing medical science can discern about Stu to explain his resistance to infection is the fact that he dreams a lot more than the average person. King is ambiguous as to why certain people are immune to the flu — beyond simply needing to have his main characters survive the apocalypse in order to stand against the coming evil — but certainly there is a metaphysical aspect to their survival. Though ordinary people, they all experience a spiritual awakening of sorts through the dreams. However, the dreams only serve as a beacon to call both sides to order; once the people have reached their respective camps, the dreams cease and most people are quick to forget they ever happened. It seems as though the survivors were chosen specifically, according to a plan; and yet at the same time, it seems like survival is arbitrary. King keeps readers guessing if there is a rhyme and reason to events, or if it is just a random series of happenstance.

The Problem of Choice: Predestination or Poor Judgment?

King begins the novel with predestination in mind — the immunity to the super flu is an individual quality of the survivor and has nothing to do with personality — but once the stage is cleared for the coming battle, it seems that free will begins to take precedence. Characters are given many chances to choose their paths. Yet the pendulum swings back the other way at the end of the novel, when the four heroes are sent out by Mother Abagail to stand — here they have no choice, but it's as if all of their previous choices have led them to this point of requirement.

King's philosophy mimics the Germanic code of courage under fire exhibited in *Beowulf*. Certain events are fixed, as wyrd or fate would have them, and no choices can turn them aside. This type of event would include Stu, Larry, Ralph, and Glen heading off to Las Vegas to face Flagg's minions, or the main characters arriving in Mother Abagail's camp. Other events seem up for debate, as the individual actions of those involved determine the outcome. As Glen posits about the dreams, the main players are being given a preview of the future, a choice along with a glimpse of what may be. For instance, if Nadine had chosen to be with Larry when she had the chance (and she knew the moment when it would have

Three : The Big Picture

mattered), her life could have been spared, and Flagg's plans would have proceeded anyway — her death only enhances the downward spiral that Flagg faces in Las Vegas, but she is not pivotal in any way. She could have easily gone down a different path without drastically altering the outcome of the story.

King suggests that certain events are part of the design, whether it be a plan of Mother Abagail's God or some other divine providence, while others have multiple possibilities determined by individual choice. Even the mad Trashcan Man has a chance to reject evil and refuse to join Flagg; when Lloyd offers him the pendant that marks all of Flagg's followers, Trash consciously realizes that he has a last chance, a final opportunity to just be Donald Merwin Elbert and abandon the moniker Trashcan Man and all that goes with it, but then the pyromaniac chooses to stand with Flagg because, as he says, "In for a penny, in for a pound."[6] Even someone as damned as Trash has the chance to choose his fate, and he does so willingly and knowingly. This curious interpretation of free will raises essential questions about the characters' control, though; for instance, if certain events are pre-planned, then it stands to reason that others are guided. Can characters be sure that they do have free will at all, or are they simply given the illusion of free will while really behaving according to some mapped out path?

Characters in the story never really work out the answer to this question, but, more importantly, most of them decide that it doesn't matter in the end. Larry feels this most keenly; as the character who struggled the most with his fate, Larry decides at the end that he has chosen to be where he is, and that choice is his alone. Nick too becomes a semi-believer, but only in death when he serves as a spiritual guide for his friend Tom Cullen; his transformation is because he has died and presumably knows the answer to his questions about God. Larry is still alive, and his acceptance of his fate illustrates a combination of faith and free will — two themes that King sets up in opposition but that wind up complementing each other.

The Stand: It's the Journey That Counts

King is known for his penchant for killing his main characters just as they Stand up to some form of evil. Typically, evil is only temporarily beaten in King's world, even with great sacrifice. As Collings explains, "Since evil is frequently external to characters, coming in its own time and through its own will, it cannot be destroyed; the best King's characters can hope for is a temporary victory in a single, isolated skirmish."[7] This Manichean view of evil gives the force a mind and a will, along with a serious agenda. Evil is not just a turning away from good but a vital source in and of itself, and though King's characters may stave off the darkness by Standing true, in whatever fashion they can muster, there is always the nagging knowledge that such a Stand is only effective for the time being, and that eventually evil will swing back around to threaten them again. Therefore, readers expecting a complete resolution and a hopeful future may be disappointed.

Love is a key element in *The Stand*, and not only because some of the characters pair up. Perhaps Jane Baker puts it best in her death raving: "Love is what moves the world, I've always thought...it is the only thing which allows men and women to stand in a world where gravity always seems to want to pull them down...bring them low...and make them crawl...we were...so much in love."[8] Jane is not the only one who thinks this way. Even Larry Underwood, that not-so-nice guy, finds love in the end—a love that proves his redemption when it gives him the chance to refuse Nadine. Many other characters reflect that the only real reason to stand against evil at all is because of love, or to protect that which is beloved.

The notion of standing up, or the Stand, has a number of components, but one of the easiest to spot is that of necessity. Many of King's heroes are heroes because when the time came, they happened to be in the right place (or the wrong place, depending on how the stand went down). Nick realizes this when he stares down at Jane Baker's corpse and contemplates her burial; she isn't his responsibility, not really, but he is the only one left alive to bury her, and so he must do it. The novel is filled with people who do their duty because they are the only ones left to do it, and they know it must be done.

For King, the individual journey towards the moment of the stand is the defining quality of the good person. The hero—for the one who stands is always heroic for that moment—must understand the reason for his stand and accept the consequences, knowing that he may not even make a difference in the end. Larry and Ralph find themselves in this situation when they face Flagg in Las Vegas. The novel's ending may leave some readers wondering about the purpose of the stand. Why send Larry, Ralph, and Glen off to die? Their deaths aren't significant in and of themselves—they do not fight the evil hand to hand and prove that good is stronger. Yet their journey is the important thing. As the four travel towards Las Vegas, they become aware of a change within themselves. Glen analyzes the difference, explaining that they are "emptying out the vessel."[9] What Glen refers to here is an ancient custom of mankind, from manhood rites, to Biblical journeys—the foursome are embarking on their own journey into the desert, and the fact that they go without any supplies, choosing to walk instead of drive, shows their dedication to the purification ritual. They are aware of the effect this journey has on them in different ways. Stu asks if they are changing, and Ralph, ever pragmatic, replies, "We've dropped some weight," a line filled with symbolic overtones that are lost on him.[10] Clearly they've dropped physical weight, a sign of increased health and vitality, but they have also dropped their physical possessions and their need for worldly things. They have also dropped their disbelief in things beyond their experience. Even though they may not believe in Mother Abagail's God, they certainly believe in her enough to undertake the journey, and as they get closer to the Dark Man's territory, each man has his own insights into the purpose of his journey.

Divine interference becomes more and more obvious as the novel continues, though some characters are reluctant to see events as such. When Stu falls in the gulley and can no longer travel, the others are certain (along with the reader) that he will die there, another victim of something like chance; but this catastrophe actually turns out to be the accident that spares his life—a eucatastrophe that is only completed by the arrival of Tom Cullen just in time to care for Stu as he battles sickness and injury. The others are not so keen to see this as divine intervention—as Larry says, "It wasn't God's will that Stu fell down here; it wasn't even the dark man's doing. It was just loose dirt, that's all."[11] Larry hasn't yet reached his moment of illumination; but for the others, Stu's fall is a sign in a series of signs, and it means they must leave their friend behind. Though they think they are walking to their deaths, the idea of abandoning Stu bothers them; but they do not falter for long—each secretly hoping that this apparent tragedy may somehow work itself out. King suggests that sometimes things may seem like the end of the world, but they are not always so, and certainly they can't be understood by bystanders. Yet Stu's survival is divinely guided, as Tom is told which medicines to give Stu by the spirit of Nick. Obviously the ambiguity about the existence of God throughout the novel is clarified in this series of events. It seems that once God shows His hand in Las Vegas, He can't keep from tying up loose ends, one of which turns out to be saving the life of Stu Redman and sending him safely home to his family.

The actual appearance of a Godly hand above Las Vegas has many readers speculating about where King stands on the issue of religion. Clearly the novel spins on a Christian base, with a Christian mouthpiece and a Devil stand-in, but up until the annihilation of Las Vegas, the existence of God is still a debatable issue — everything can still be explained as the ravings of an old woman and stress-related mass hallucinations. Once things come together in Las Vegas, however, the existence of God becomes clear. Though it can debated how much control God had over the events that occurred there — did God make Whitney Hogan stand up and rebel against Flagg? When Hogan does push his way through the crowd, he is pale-faced with fear and shaking with emotion, but he still manages to stand as best he can, shouting, "We was Americans once! This ain't how Americans act. ... You wanna watch these two guys ripped in two right in front of you, huh? You think that's the right way to start a new life? You think a thing like that can ever be right?"[12] Flagg's response to Hogan's speech is almost mechanical — he conjures a ball of lightning and fries him — but that small speech has set a series of events into motion that even Flagg cannot understand.

King's ending leaves readers perplexed about the ultimate nature of fate. When Trashcan Man arrives with his nuclear warhead in tow, readers are forced to wonder how much of the events are ordained by God — after all, were it not for the presence of Ralph and Larry, the people would not have gathered for a public execution, and Hogan wouldn't have had his outburst. Without Hogan, Flagg had no need of a lightning ball, and the subsequent explosion between the lightning and the bomb would not have happened. Still, even with a belief in arbitrary events, readers cannot ignore Ralph's shout as he looks into the sky: "The Hand of God!" Still, Ralph was always a believer, and his interpretation holds the same weight as Mother Abagail's words. It is when Larry looks into the sky — Larry the unbeliever, who even so has reached a kind of peace in his heart — and sees something that really did look like a hand, that readers can begin to believe with him. Surely King has many forces at work in his eucatastrophe, but the appearance of God is an extra that he could have omitted, leaving readers without the certainty of divine intervention. Yet, even with mostly clear evidence of God's existence (and more to follow when Tom saves Stu using Nick's aid from beyond the grave), the message here is not to believe in God but to believe that Good can Stand against Evil, even when things do not appear to lay in a straight line and ultimate outcomes are hidden in shadow.

The Right to Govern

The question of government is central to the novel's theme. The survivors of the super flu find themselves both in need of new authority and distrustful of rebuilding any of the old systems that so drastically failed them (in the sense that the government led to the current predicament). Frannie's father, Peter Goldsmith, puts it best when, on the outbreak of the super flu, he tells her not to trust the princes of this world, for they will only cause problems for the normal people, and that Frannie can only rely on herself and her own judgment. His live-and-let-live philosophy seems a great idea until survivors are faced with big decisions about how to live and get along in the Boulder Free Zone. Several of the main characters are quick to establish a committee, and it isn't long before they are scheming to stay in charge of things just like the old government — an irony that is not lost on them. Still, they all realize that someone has to make some kind of rules, especially after the incident with the teenage boy who gets drunk and nearly kills a few people with a car. Everyone in Boulder saw him and disapproved, but no one felt they had the right to do anything. That kind of apathy shows a serious need for an authority figure, and the Free Zone Committee sets itself up to fill that demand.

King is quick to show how even the best intentions are corrupted by the responsibilities of control. No one really disputes the need for a governing body, but some of the choices the committee makes raise curious questions about their true intentions. First of all, Nick unilaterally disqualifies Harold as a member of their committee just because he doesn't trust him. True, this kind of insight turns out to be the right point of view in the end (as Harold does turn on the Free Zone and head West to Flagg's people), but it does raise the question of responsibility. How much tragedy could have been averted had Harold been allowed on the committee and made to feel an important member of the new society in Boulder? It is even more curious that the decision to block Harold is made by a deaf-mute, a man who should be used to snap judgments about his character and who should be willing to give people more credit, and yet Nick damns Harold simply because he doesn't trust his smile. For a man who claims to be thoroughly rational, Nick's reasons for excluding Harold seem awfully personal and arbitrary, and this illustrates the fundamental problem with forming a new government.

Some people must be excluded in order for any government to work, and though the majority may be kept happy, there are always going to be malcontents on the fringes of society, no matter how small the society may be. King's description of events in Boulder shows that even people who have experienced great loss still manage to create outcasts. In a world where every person ought to be valued just by virtue of being alive (even if only to be a viable person for procreation and the survival of the species), human nature still demands a scapegoat, and nowhere will that process be more clear than in the formation of a government.

The Stand does state quite clearly that people need a government, regardless of what kind. Even the totalitarian dictatorship that Flagg creates in Las Vegas manages to keep his people contented. For modern readers it is hard to accept that Flagg's type of government could actually work out for the people, especially Americans, but when considering the type of people that Flagg has on his side, the no-second-chance rule seems the only way to keep control. Even with the harsh penalties in Las Vegas (crucifixion is the popular method of execution), Flagg's policies on drug use of any kind and even alcohol abuse don't seem like totally bad ideas. Though he can be cruel, he does manage to keep his people in line, mostly contented and working as useful members of his society. Still, King seems to raise the question here — is it acceptable to use Flagg's methods if it means controlling a dangerous section of society? Readers may find themselves torn between horror at Flagg's methods and grudging approval of his results, a conflict that causes readers to question how much of Flagg is inside them — how far would they go to maintain control? As Hogan observes at the end of Flagg's ill-fated public execution, the people were Americans once, and he asks how they can bear witness to such a spectacle. This throwback to the days when public executions were common strikes a chord with readers who may find themselves wondering what it would take to bring those days back — and if such a resurrection would be such a bad thing. Flagg may have the worst kind of people on his side, but, as

Glen noted, he certainly does have the trains running on time. To keep society in line, he has established a totalitarian government that may chafe the sense of inherent freedom most Americans have, but ultimately this system works. This is a haunting possibility for American readers to consider; the potential for such strict regulations to be effective is enough to remind readers of just how precious their freedom is and how easily it can be usurped (or even willingly handed over to someone who promises the right things).

Still, it is easy at first to disregard the notion of government. After all, if 99.4 percent of the country is gone, why can't the remaining people just work things out among themselves? This is something that King addresses early in the novel. Once the super flu has wiped out the existing government, the survivors begin to feel the absence almost immediately. Frannie feels that loss quite keenly when she emerges as one of two survivors from Ogunquit, Maine. She doesn't exactly seek out the company of Harold Lauder, but when he approaches her with plans for a picnic, she does not refuse. Part of Harold's appeal for Frannie at this point is his tendency to plan things. Harold is motivated and has ideas for the future; Frannie is barely managing to keep moving, though this feeling ebbs as she begins to travel with a purpose again. When Harold suggests going to Stovington, Vermont, to check out the Disease Control Center there, Frannie is delighted with the idea because it soothes her need for structure and authority. This is the same need that the Boulder Free Zone Committee will exploit when establishing a new government. As Glen would explain, people need someone to tell them what they can and cannot do, and if they (Stu, Larry, Glen, etc.) don't tell them, then someone else will, and who knows what kind of system those other people may come up with? The desire to have a ruling body in place reveals an "inability to break the mind-forged manacles of the past [that] results in a repetition of the same political system which created the dystopia in the first place."[13] Glen's idea is to act quickly, before things in Boulder get too crowded and anyone else can get organized, and the sociology professor turns out to be right — people need structure, and they will turn to anyone who seems to have a plan, especially if the plan is comfortingly familiar. Unfortunately, King seems to feel that "any government system, however beneficent in origin, will eventually deconstruct because abuse of power is inherent and inevitable."[14] The only way to escape this cycle is to live where there are few other people, King suggests, and this pessimistic theory about the capability of mankind explains why he ends the novel with his hero choosing exile from society. It is ironic that King can see such negativity in humanity when he stresses the capability of mankind to stand when the time comes; perhaps King feels that people are only redeemable in an individual or small group sense — once the numbers get too high, people are reduced to mob mentality and subject to a degeneration of morality.

People need people: The axiom may seem trite, but King pounds it into his readers' heads. People need other humans, even if those others are not so wonderful. The survivors of the flu share prophetic dreams, but, more importantly, they also all experience the need to regroup. The figures in their dreams give them a direction to head, and that impetus is what keeps them from losing their minds in the absence of any other structure. Even so, Nick notices that his journey to see what is probably a figment of his imagination is really just a manifestation of a deeper human need for a clear-cut goal. Even going to Nebraska to see if Mother Abagail is real is too hazy for him. He compares it to a quest without a clear-cut goal in mind — no holy grail, no sword in the stone, no magical pendant to make everything better. In his hopes for more human contact, Nick imagines a man with sunburned elbows driving a regular American car who would pull over and tell them, in a Texan drawl, to hop in. Sadly, before Nick runs into a fellow goodhearted survivor, he meets the wicked Julie Lawry, who delights in tormenting the retarded Tom just because she can. With all of the death around the survivors, any kind of human contact is appreciated, so the fact that Nick very quickly wishes that he hadn't met Julie Lawry is significant. He'd rather face the emptiness of the world than listen to her jabber on about her small life; and when this becomes clear to her, she retaliates with gunshots, a sharp reminder to Nick that not all of the survivors will be worth finding. Nick's reaction to her is just as shocking when he first hits and then threatens her after she taunts Tom. Though Nick is generally a peaceful man, he can be violent when necessary, a quality that many survivors suddenly find emerging in themselves.

As Larry observes, "If we don't have each other, we go crazy with loneliness. When we do, we go crazy with togetherness. When we get together we build miles of summer cottages and kill each other in the bars on Saturday night."[15] King may leave readers uncertain about the need for government, but he is certainly clear about human nature and the need for some kind of direction.

Three : The Big Picture

Hope vs. Despair: "Do People Ever Really Learn Anything?"

The Stand ends on a curious note for many readers. After the mostly symbolic deaths of Larry, Ralph, and Glen, readers are left feeling empty. What was the point of everything if life will just continue down the same path as before? Frannie and Stu are faced with this question as they stare down at baby Peter. There is hope in the child, and in the fact that he is one of the first post-plague babies to survive, but even the small community of Boulder is too much for them.

Just as Glen Bateman predicted, society has rebuilt itself in an image of what it once was, and though the lessons of Captain Trips and Las Vegas are still fairly fresh, it is easy to forget them under contemplation of the everyday in Boulder. After all, people decide, sheriffs do need guns to protect themselves, and once guns are expected again, then it is only too easy to see the path that lies ahead. Just as sheriffs protect themselves from unknown citizens, maybe the Boulder Free Zone should look into protecting itself from other communities who may seek to do it harm. After all, people think, there are all of those weapons out there, just lying around, waiting for someone to pick them up. Why shouldn't it be them? And with that mindset, Stu and Frannie see, things pick up right where they left off. With such a sad chain of events to ponder, it is no wonder that the answer to the fundamental question of "Do people ever learn anything?" is a solid "I don't know."

King suggests that there is hope for the future, at least in the immediate sense. Evil has been vanquished this time around, and though King is sure that it will return again, there is hope that there will be those to stand true when the time comes. The world has been saved for those who survived this battle, and that is no small matter. The notion that evil will inevitably be back may seem like a terrible dark cloud that can ruin any contemplation of the future, but King does not end his novel on such an apprehensive note. The end of the novel has Frannie and Stu watching children play — a sure symbol of innocence and hope. The epilogue that ends that novel — that of Flagg's return — only serves to reinforce the resolve that has tempered Stu and Frannie, and others like them. The world is a place worth saving, and they will stand whenever they need to, just as others after them will do. Humanity has a chance, and with that possibility, King eliminates the despair that the notion of an endless battle between good and evil may bring. The knowledge that Flagg returns only strengthens the hope that the survivors, and readers, feel. Evil will return, and good people will be ready.

This ending is King's ironic twist on human nature — a theme which he has not been very kind to throughout his novel. King seems to say that although mankind can be awful, can be cruel, and can self-destruct at the smallest provocation, there will always be people willing to stand against the darkness, and they will win in whatever fashion is possible. Certainly good people will die, and sometimes for what appears to be no reason at all, but there is reassurance in the idea that their deaths somehow contributed to the victory of the moment, and that is — somehow — enough.

FOUR

The Nitty Gritty

Joyce Carol Oates once said there were three aspects of King that could be examined: the man, the writing, and the phenomenon. Considerations of biography may be left to others, but certainly a closer look at a few things would not be unseemly — notably, the writing style that Harold Bloom condemned, the genre that made academics squirm, and the popular appeal that made it acceptable for literary critics to dismiss King as a pop culture fad instead of a writer worth studying.

Writing Style: "The Prose Is Indistinguishable"

According to Harold Bloom, King's "prose is indistinguishable."[1] This phrase is up for debate, for the things that distinguish prose in Harold Bloom's mind are very different from those that ordinary readers expect and enjoy. Harold Bloom views Stephen King as a child who has somehow stumbled onto an adult playing-ground, and he doesn't understand why everyone who comes into contact with this newcomer is so intrigued by his work. This is largely to do with the schism between literature and popular culture. The novels that are studied in school rarely mirror the stories that students would choose to read on their own. Those which are considered classics are so for very specific reasons — one of which being that they have been studied for some time, and that in itself suggests that they shall continue to be studied, a view that treads dangerously close to tradition for tradition's sake. Certainly the classics contain valuable insights into the human condition and offer readers life lessons as well as stylistic examples, but rarely do books like *The Canterbury Tales* or *The Grapes of*

Wrath top a student's pleasure reading list. Even students who enjoy reading do not willingly pull out their Dante or *Beowulf*. This reluctance does not suggest that these texts do not have meaning and worth — they do, but it is sometimes hard to make high school and college students understand the themes and underlying meaning in them. Part of this difficulty has to do with the way that some of the classics are written — the writing style that Bloom finds lacking in King's work.

This disapproval stems from a popular practice in academics today — that is, the proliferation of essays whose writing style is so convoluted and overtly academic that meaning has been reduced to a contest of vocabulary flexing. Harold Bloom comes from a school of thought that expects writing to require deciphering; indeed, for Bloom, not having to figure out what a text is about means that the text is too simply crafted or too easily grasped, and the fact that the ordinary public can understand and actually enjoy reading something must mean that it operates on a lower level of comprehension and is not worthy of study. This is the problem that Bloom has with Stephen King — his simplicity, his lack of grandstanding, his quiet unassuming way of just telling a story and leaving other questions of academic prose and literary criticism to the experts. King does not set out to write a masterpiece of American literature; he sets out to tell a story, because at heart he is a storyteller. Bloom doesn't know what to do with a man like this, who uses his writing to entertain people without any overt agenda or sublimated meaning that is revealed after much digging. For Bloom, the clarity of King's work is its fatal flaw. For if everything is clear, then what is left for literary critics to illuminate? This examination may serve as a possible answer to that question; even with a fairly straightforward story there is much in King to consider, from the basics of theme to the subtleties of symbol and hidden references. The difference here is that an average reader can enjoy King without understanding the subtext, and that seeing the entire picture only enhances the reading experience but is not a requirement of comprehension. King delivers the same sense of satisfaction that readers receive from classic works of literature but without the effort (and reader's guides) often required to appreciate such overtly academic texts, a quality that makes his work an accessible literature for the masses to devour.

King's later works have occasionally been taken more seriously by the academic world, especially *Bag of Bones*, the novel considered to be King's "literary work," but this is not because King's prose has changed all that much. Certainly he has grown as a writer, and his later novels may have some clever word play or beautiful turns of phrase within, but King's work has never been poetry. His words do not typically sing across the room in haunting melodies that linger in the mind. King's power is not in the way he strings words together; rather, his gift lies in the effect of his words — the way his easy-to-follow sentence structure and vocabulary allow readers to visualize what is happening. In other words, King is a great storyteller, someone who can wrap readers up with the plot and the characters. This is not to say that King's writing style is simple or boring; on the contrary, his sentences are easy to understand as they convey complex images and situations. King doesn't need to rely on fancy word play or overly complex sentences to make his work seem "literary"— his themes and images stand, despite their simple clothing. It is this ability to consider serious literary questions without the grandstanding that Bloom detests. Perhaps this dislike of seemingly "simplistic literature" stems from a rather curious question: If King can address these same issues in the plain English my students long for, then what is the benefit of serious literature written in a way that requires a companion guide? If the true purpose of literature is to share insight into the human condition with the unschooled masses, and King has done that (quite simply and easily), then what can be said about the entire tapestry of "literature" that has come before? Should the so-called great works be considered great because they require more effort to understand? Is literature only a test of reading comprehension? Questions like these make literary critics squirm, and not only because if the answers lean a certain way it could put those same literary critics out of the work they know and love. It may seem so; after all, who needs elucidation when the story is so clear? But elucidation is always a benefit because, by and large, King doesn't force the literary aspects of his work on readers. Often they do not even realize that such qualities exist in his work. They need trained scholars and critics to point them out, even scholars like Bloom who refuse to see the qualities in anything less than those genre-shattering literary giants who have changed the face of literature as they confounded the reading public.

Genre Choice: Today Is a Good Day to End the World?

King's choice to make *The Stand* an apocalyptic novel reflects the time period in which he lives. During the last few decades, Americans have learned to fear the secrets of their government, and death by annihilation has become a common enough worry. Whether it be fears of terrorism or biological warfare, Americans are very open to the idea that in some secret place, the government and the military are working on weapons that could just as easily be turned on the American people as some foreign enemy. King is very aware of this fear, having grown up in the Cold War era of hiding under his desk for air raid practice. Fear of the military's plans is part of the American psyche today, and King manages to exploit that emotion in his novel, where he shows not only a military's biological weapon gone awry, but a military willing to go to extreme lengths to secure its interests in the last days of the country.

King's choice of initial genre also allows him to address other issues traditionally associated with the apocalyptic novel — loss of technology, human responsibility and culpability, survival of mankind. Because he begins with these themes, King is able to secure a readership among those interested in the plight of Modern Man, a creature defined by the trappings of technology, by playing on modern fears and exploiting them — as any good horror writer ought to do. Curiously, though, apocalyptic novels often focus on the new world after the old one is destroyed — typically a utopian vision of sorts where people try to avoid the perils of the last civilization — but King patently avoids this direction. The new world that arrives after the super flu very quickly resembles the old world, a twist on the genre's expectations that allows a broader audience to appreciate the story. King's vision of the future is more realistic, some readers feel, because he shows what most people would crave after such an apocalypse — normality, routine, the expected, and to get the power back on as quickly as possible.

Popular Appeal: The Kiss of Death?

There has long been a divide between what is considered literature and what is considered popular culture. If the definition of literature includes a sense of re-readability — that is, the text reveals more and more each time the reader begins anew — then the canon of works considered literature and taught in classrooms is negligently brief. So, literature must be something more — as Horace said, it must entertain and educate. As later critics, with whom Bloom would agree, have said, it must illuminate the human condition in an academic or cerebral way. With this somewhat basic list of criteria in mind, readers may still wonder why there is such a stigma against certain authors who display these characteristics—genre writers in particular are easily dismissed for writing escapist stories generally lacking in depth.

Popular culture, on the other hand, is known for lacking depth—that's what the experts claim make it "pop culture." Still, even with this apparent missing ingredient, people still clamor for the newest Danielle Steel romance or John Grisham thriller, so one has to ask the question—does something need to be literary in order to have value? Academics answer with a resounding "yes," claiming that Steel and Grisham novels are time-wasters or fluff-filled snacks empty of any real substance, but why then do these popular novelists have such a dedicated following? Surely there must be something to them if so many find enjoyment in their pages. Academics would claim that ordinary people are entertained by these pop culture novels because the pages are easy to digest, raise no questions about the human condition, and leave readers reassured about the world around them instead of forcing them to ask difficult questions about what it means to be human. For the most part, such academics would be right—most of pop culture reaffirms the status quo instead of challenging it, but does literature always have to break standards and destroy traditions? Could these pop culture novels have value in the same way that some literature does—in showing how people of the time lived and what the readers of the time sought in the pages of a book? Perhaps the debate between literature and pop culture is not so much a question of depth but a reflection of a mindset that is not as interested in deeper meanings as some feel it ought to be. Does this make contemporary America akin to the Roaring Twenties, where people focused on song and drink to escape the problems of the world around them? Does the public read pop culture novels because they need reassurance of something in a world filled with uncertainty?

Stephen King may describe worlds that are familiar to readers and somewhat comforting in their resonance, but King's tendency to fragment that ordinary world with horrific events of supernatural occurrences often serves to disorient readers more than reassure them. Perhaps King's popularity is due to his ability to make the real world seem dependable in comparison. When people are uncertain about the world around them, they can turn to King's novels, where the ordinary world they know will soon fall prey to any number of catastrophes, and suddenly the oddities of the real world pale in comparison to the possibilities King can envision. In this sense, King reaffirms Aristotle's notion of catharsis, a feeling that most pop culture reading will not evoke. Certainly such a fearful resonance is not required for audiences to appreciate a well-told story, though, and King's popularity in the world of pop culture may simply be a reflection of his ability to tell an engaging story that can be appreciated "as is." Pop culture often does not require interpretation in order to be entertaining, but King's ability to be criticized as a serious writer puts him in a category that straddles popular and literary fiction.

FIVE

The Dark Tower Connections

Much has been written about Stephen King's opus *The Dark Tower*, and more is being said even as I write this. No one, it seems, critic or fan, can agree on whether King's final chapter to this long tale is a satisfying and appropriate finale or the cheap cop-out of an author who is simply done with a story and wants to hit "print" and get out of there. Either way, for the purposes of this study, it is not particularly relevant whether King's last installment is fitting (and, just for the record, in the eyes of this Constant Reader, it is very dreadfully apt indeed) or not; instead, we will focus on the earlier parts of this epic tale — specifically, those sections where the intrepid ka-tet wanders, at least for a brief time, into the world King brought so vividly to life in *The Stand*.

For a story set in Mid-World and concerned with the fate of the Tower that stands at the lynchpin of the universe, King spends a great deal of time in America — notably New York City, but also the backwoods of Maine. Readers expecting Roland to stay in his fantasy world will be surprised to find door after door connecting his world to ours, and then to worlds beyond even his imagining. The world in the mind of the writer is vast, and he allows readers a glimpse into these multiple realities. Yet, often times readers are surprised to find themselves back on comfortable ground. After all, when the door leads to a period in American history, how can readers not be comfortable? This is their country, their America, and despite the lens of fantasy and multiple realities, readers know and connect to what they see.

Stephen King's opus may focus on rescuing a world that has moved on, but the story spends a great deal of time on familiar ground in American territory. Readers will recognize the New York of Eddie Dean, Odetta Holmes/Detta Walker/Susannah Dean, and Jake Chambers, despite distances in time or place. Even readers who have never been east of the Rocky Mountains will know the world King describes; and whether the author is taking liberties with geography or faithfully detailing minor statues in Central Park, readers connect to the place, the feel of the city, even as King allows them to see it through new eyes—the eyes of the ka-tet. Even Eddie, who craves the city almost as much as he craves his drugs, starts to see the city as a stranger—reintroducing readers to his hometown just as he starts to see it in different ways. As with many other things, the old saying is true: One cannot go home again, or, at the very least, Home is never the same as when one left it. Of course, mature readers know the secret to that magical transition; it is not the place that has changed but the person. Still, for a place that is iconic in the American psyche, King brings the city to life anew for readers who can hear the horns honking and the horses clopping along the streets outside their windows as they read along just as easily as he presents a believable whole for those who have never been any closer to the Big Apple than a movie screen. King does not hold himself to the wonders of New York City, however, and is often describing other, less mythic places in America, but each time readers of *The Dark Tower* slip into their own world again, they are reassured by the familiarity of the place.

King doesn't explicitly mention America in the first installment of the Dark Tower series, but *The Gunslinger* is filled with pop culture references that will resonate with readers. Everything from "Hey Jude" to Citgo rings true to readers, and though Roland's Mid-World is not their world, it is a place filled with leftover images from the Old People—a mysterious group who begin very quickly to remind readers of themselves. King brings to life the echo of American consciousness in his tale, using imagery from the idealized American West and the demonized oil corporations as easily as he invokes a medieval Gilead reminiscent of Arthur's Camelot, blending the concepts together and blurring the lines between the worlds—a theme that sets the foundation for the entire story. Beginning with King's second Dark Tower novel, *The Drawing of the Three*, readers are introduced to their own America through the eyes of a stranger, a technique that makes the ordinary seem extraordinary and revitalizes the idea of America in readers' minds.

Some New American Heroes

When Roland first looks through the door on the endless Western Beach, he is shocked to see that he is miles above the ground, looking

Five : The Dark Tower Connections

down on the clouds as if a bird or a god. To readers, this jarring entry into the familiar world of airplanes forces a reevaluation of their own perceptions when it comes to technology and modern travel. Consider the fact that this is a moment of weakness for the ever-strong gunslinger — he actually screams when he sees the clouds streaking out below his field of vision, uttering what is the first scream of his adult life. Following this abrupt shift in the main character's expected behaviors, readers are then treated to a scathing commentary on modern Americans — well, modern in the 1980s. America and Americans seen through Roland's eyes make it new for the readers: On his first glance around the plane, he notes that no one carries weapons and thinks, "What kind of trusting sheep were these?"[1] Americans are not likely to think of themselves as sheep, not to mention trusting one another, but King raises intriguing questions about American society by this observation. Do Americans not carry weapons because they trust one another, or do they not carry weapons because it is against the law? Obviously, readers know that guns are not allowed on airplanes, never mind any kind of blade or weapon — even in the 1980s, before the increase in airline security that followed 9/11, airline passengers were relieved of their nail clippers — but Roland's casual comment brings to mind memories of a time when weapons were expected on every man's hip. America wasn't always so tame, readers may think, reminiscing about Westerns and notions of a Wild West filled with cowboys and exemplified by John Wayne. Those thoughts bring them back around to the idea of gunslingers and what those men of spaghetti westerns would make of modern society; and suddenly Roland isn't just a gunslinger in a foreign world glancing in on the world readers know — he is a member of a well-respected class of fighters that remain a large part of America's romantic memories of a time before civilization made it all the way across the desert. Even in an airplane far above the landscape, King is able to reign in his readers' concepts of gunslingers and the Wild West, correlate those ideas with his own rendition of a gunslinger (thereby making his own creation more viable than ever before), and make a comment about modern man — all by asking a simple question. Talk about understatement.

This ability to make America new and familiar at the same time continues when Roland considers the notion of Customs. To Eddie Dean, cocaine mule and heroin junkie, clearing Customs is a ceremony of sorts. He must pass inspection in order to first deliver the goods to Balazar, more importantly to collect his idol of a big brother, and most importantly, according to Eddie himself, so that he can get more of the heroin his body needs. When Roland describes this passage through the airport security in terms of a religious rite, he reminds readers how easily simple processes—for those law-abiding citizens, that is—can reach epic proportions in the mind. For Eddie, getting through security actually is a Rite of Passage, an idea that Roland picks up from his host's subconscious and applies to his own knowledge of the way the world works. He assumes that Eddie is going to profane the ritual and sets to work to stop not the ruin of a ritual—Roland has little use for such frivolities as spirituality—but to stop his Prisoner from getting caught. This is a curious perspective for American readers who may be forced to reconsider their own views of law. After all, who doesn't want Eddie to succeed in his task, even though he is a junkie smuggling drugs into the country? King manages to get audiences to like Eddie, to root for him because of what he represents to Roland—a chance to survive his lobstrosity-caused infections. Since Roland needs Eddie to succeed, audiences are on the young criminal's side.

It is interesting to see that King does have some kind of standards when it comes to characters worthy of sympathy and reader identification. When the gunslinger later inhabits the body of Jack Mort, serial pusher and brick dropper, Roland has no doubts about the man's fate. He cannot use such a creature as a companion in his quest, so he chooses to use Jack as a means to unite the split personalities of the Lady of Shadows. Where Eddie, broken as he is, can be salvaged, the brutal insanity of Jack Mort makes Roland uncomfortable. King seems to suggest that people like Eddie, addicts and whiners though they may be, deserve a chance at redemption. If someone like Larry Underwood can be put to good use after some swift kicks to his conscience, then certainly the young Dean brother can be utilized for some good cause. Even after knowing that Eddie seems nothing more than a street kid with a huge monkey on his back, Roland (and readers with him) remains convinced that there is steel in the junkie somewhere, and though it is deeply buried when readers first meet the addict, Roland believes he can draw it forth. For a man without imagination, Roland is very modern in his feelings towards what most readers would consider a screw-up. Still, Eddie's mistakes stem from a difficult childhood and a wayward older brother, and though he makes poor choices, he is not damned. Jack Mort, on the other hand, with his penchant for dropping bricks on unsuspecting passersby, is beyond

Five : The Dark Tower Connections

salvation. Even in this early work King is already establishing characters according to American sensibilities. Readers can forgive Eddie his addiction and his youth, but they cannot forgive Jack's murderous assaults. King is tapped into the American conscience in this novel, and he seems to instinctively choose characters that American readers will embrace. Readers will be surprised by just how much of their sensibilities and their familiar world appears in this novel of Mid-World.

King swiftly moves from the "faces of spoiled and cosseted children" Roland sees on the airplane, and notions of the romantic Wild West, to the gritty realism of the Mafia gangsters found on the streets of New York City.[2] These men are not sheep, readers realize right away, and Jack Andolini and Enrico Balazar come swiftly to life as characters worthy of caution. Certainly King does his share of setting them up as massive roadblocks in Eddie's way to his brother's side. From Andolini's too-smart face and Balazar's left-hand desk drawer, readers are left without any questions regarding the lethality of these men. And yet King is drawing on yet another undercurrent of American culture to underscore his creations and force them to resonate with readers. Andolini is a classic right-hand man, the character Americans can recognize again and again from *The Godfather* to *Goodfellas*. He is smart, yes, but ultimately restricted under the rule of the Don, the Boss Man, and his warnings may go unheeded when the hero needs some luck. The Boss is a classic stereotype, and whether he disdains breaking his word or shooting people himself, readers know what to expect from him. Even the goons surrounding Balazar who participate in the gunfight are recognizable — some dumb, some funny, some scared — and each will spark instant recognition with readers and remind them that this is New York, this is America.

This is not to say that King's characters are solid stereotypes. Enrico Balazar has the added quirk of building card towers and a curiosity that gets him killed. Jack Andolini may appear to be a simple right-hand man, but he's sly — not that his craftiness can prepare him for a doorway through worlds or the gunslinger's deadly aim — and he is onto Eddie's game long before the rest of Balazar's crew. Even the game of Trivial Pursuit gives each of Balazar's henchmen a name and a personality, even as King brings readers back to the America they know and love. With Henry's constant answer of "Johnny Cash," readers can remember the man in black who caused riots, and they realize that in Henry's heroin-addled brain he thinks he is Johnny Cash, cool and collected, when in reality he is an addict about to take his last trip. While he is developing characters and establishing personalities, King also takes a moment to reinforce his world, herding readers into familiar territory and making his characters echo with believability.

The story even goes so far as to blend Hollywood notions of masculinity with Mafia gangster fighting styles. When Balazar's men bring out the Amazing Rambo Machine in the shootout with Roland and Eddie, readers imagine Sylvester Stallone in his classic role as John Rambo, facing down lines of enemies with this marvel of military destruction. Of course, Balazar's men are not Rambo, not heroes, and so King uses this weapon to destroy them. When they start shooting each other instead of the heroes, readers are relieved. Though weapons capable of such destruction exist, there apparently are guidelines even beyond man's genius for machine guns—evil undoes itself, an idea that Tolkien would certainly have approved. King has managed to remind readers of their own Hollywood heroes, shown how Mafia thugs will never measure up to those standards, and introduces a new kind of heroism to the fight—that of Eddie and Roland taking on these men with their superior firepower, even though they are outnumbered and forced to fight naked. These are the new American heroes, King suggests. The junkie and the cowboy, who do not even need clothing, certainly have no need of Hollywood's Amazing Rambo Machine. They are a throwback to those hazy days in the American psyche of western men with single bullets who faced down evildoers in dusty streets. King has created a new type of hero here, but he has done so by drawing on the American consciousness of its own popular culture. This is not the first time King will subtly shift something recognizably American into something quintessentially America.

When Eddie crosses over into Roland's world, he allows readers to see Mid-World through American eyes. The things that Eddie longs for—fried chicken being second only to his fix of heroin—are recognizable things to Americans. Since he has been sucked out of his natural environment and thrown into a strange and dangerous place, Eddie keeps readers afloat with his constant chatting, his running commentary, and his unmistakable accent that puts readers back on solid ground. Take a New Yorker out of the city and all he does is talk about how much better things were back home—that's an attitude that most Americans can understand. Eddie's perspective also lets readers see things using modern terminology. He describes the doorway view into 1960s Macy's as a movie scene filmed

Five : The Dark Tower *Connections*

with the smooth steady camera shots familiar to modern moviegoers. Taking a strange concept like seeing through another person's eyes in a doorway and comparing it to a movie allows readers to actually picture what Eddie sees on the beach. King has made the unfamiliar quite familiar and yet new all over again. His perspective allows readers to seamlessly follow the gunslinger across worlds, bringing a little bit of America with him.

Lady of Shadows

Odetta Holmes/Detta Walker introduces a new level to the story, not because of her duality, though that is a study in itself, but because she reminds readers of a time in American history that many are eager to forget. As a black woman living through the Civil Rights Movement, Odetta gives modern readers a chance to reconnect to some of this country's troubled past. Sure, American readers know about the movement. They have probably heard of Jim Crow laws and protests. They may even recall Dr. Martin Luther King's speech about his dream, and they probably appreciate getting the day off of work or school to celebrate the man's birthday. Still, much of King's readership will only have a vague notion of what these things mean, much like Eddie can only put Odetta's experience into the echoed words of a Bob Dylan song. King manages to bring more than a new character to his story in the Lady of Shadows—he resurrects a very believable spirit of the struggle for equality. When Odetta remembers her time in Oxford Town, when she describes the angry men who held her for three days, the details of her experience bring the entire Civil Rights Movement crashing into the present.

Readers have probably seen movies about the time, and certainly they have heard the speeches or reports of the things that went on; but King brings the gritty reality of the past into the present with images of Odetta's fouled panties, her recollection of the men banging against the jail bars, and her knowledge that there is a huge difference between talking about a revolution in a cozy living room and actually being imprisoned for one's beliefs by vicious men. King is able to bring an increasingly distant past to life for American readers through his use of language and his descriptions of the prison where Odetta is held for so long. The men who abuse her never really break the law of the time. Modern readers expecting horrific accounts of abuse, rape, and torture are nearly relieved to see that

Odetta escapes with nothing more than a soiled pair of panties. And yet, on reflection, that slowly becomes even worse. Odetta has not been beaten physically, but she has been emotionally bruised, spiritually ruined, and morally wronged. To treat her as an animal in a cage is to demean her very humanity, and then to have the readers almost feel relieved that she was not treated worse forces Americans to consider their own perceptions. Is it really better to be treated as subhuman? True, Odetta does escape with her life—something that many in her situation did not manage to do. But the readers' reaction to her survival, and their perception of her treatment, gives life in the '60s an immediacy that American readers may never have experienced in their school history classes.

The Boy

King often brings the underbelly of American society to light in his novels, and his introduction of Jake Chambers is no exception. At first impression, Jake has a good life. His parents are wealthy. He attends a prestigious private school. He has been given opportunities in life that will lead him down the path of success—or at least success as many Americans perceive it. That is, Jake will continue to have the best education, he will grow to be a strong and smart businessman, and he will make a lot of money to support his own family in the manner that he himself was raised. On the surface, this seems like a wonderful life, even the American Dream.

Unfortunately, readers soon come to understand, Jake's life is not wonderful. His parents are virtual strangers to him. Now this is not to say that some children feel distant from their parents—that seems a universality of teenage existence, after all—but Jake's situation is not hormonal. Jake's parents are strangers because he rarely sees them. His father works all the time. His mother is always involved in some social event or another, "comforting" some sick friend, or simply ignoring her baby boy. The only person with whom Jake has any real interaction is the housekeeper, a woman who isn't even his nanny and is paid only to keep the apartment clean. Yet this is the person to whom Jake shows his good grades on papers; and, being a good employee and a generally nice person, Mrs. Greta Shaw takes on this role with the same attitude with which she approaches the dishes and the vacuuming. When Jake has a meltdown at school and flees

Five : The Dark Tower *Connections*

during his final, it is Mrs. Shaw who tries briefly to comfort him when he gets home and has to face his angry parents. Still, their relationship isn't close enough for any real emotion, so Jake watches her leave, feeling even more empty than before. Jake is not alone in this situation or in this feeling. Many American children find themselves in this predicament. In a society which values financial gain more than familial success (a lot of the time), Jake is only one of many children who find themselves under insane amounts of pressure from family to succeed in school and yet rarely connect emotionally to the same family members who expect so much of them. As long as Jake performs well and doesn't cause problems, his parents can safely ignore him. They have done their job, as they see it — the kid is in a good school. It is up to him to do the rest, and unless they need to step in, there is no pressing need to get any more involved with Jake's life. So when Jake starts to lose his mind due to the split in his memory (he did or did not get killed by a car), he is alone to face the consequences. In fact, one of Jake's biggest fears is that eventually he will go crazy enough for other people to tell. He doesn't seem to fear insanity; for Jake, having his father talk about how the kid lost his mind is infinitely worse. For a child completely disconnected from his parents, Jake still wants his father's approval. Unfortunately, Elmer Chambers is not the kind of man to approve of a child who walks out during exams. Jake's predicament echoes a very recognizable American attitude that readers will understand.

The description of Jake's ultra-successful father is another layer that readers will recognize. Elmer Chambers is a high-powered executive. He speaks of his son using the language of corporate America, and Jake often feels himself to be nothing more than another commodity on his father's list of material possessions. Jake isn't even "Jake" to his father; when Elmer thinks of his offspring, it is always in terms of "the kid." Not that readers expect such a man to have a loving nickname for his only boy, but they at least hope for Elmer to think of Jake as a person. Any attempts to see compassion in this man are a waste of time, readers realize after a moment. Whether he is too busy plotting his next bold business endeavor or too high on the cocaine he uses to keep him going, Elmer Chambers is a shadow to his son and to readers. Sadly, he is the epitome of American success. His family lives in a fancy apartment. His child attends a prestigious school. He is a respected and feared man in his professional life. Yet his son barely knows him. Jakes does know about the gun his father keeps in his office, the gun he has never fired. Perhaps cocaine fueled-paranoia prompted the purchase of the weapon, but Jake's only real connection to his father boils down to this gun. For the rest of his life, Jake Chambers does use his father's gun, a perversion of the idea so idolized in American consciousness. Instead of earning those guns in some test of manhood, as Roland did, Jake simply takes the gun when he leaves home, and not because he wants something of his father's to bring with him. Jake simply thinks the gun might be good for protection. Family bonds have broken down in this relationship. And even more ironically, Jake finds a real father figure in Roland, the man who sacrificed him with hardly a thought on the first encounter. King suggests that the territory of fathers and sons is convoluted and complex, and the echo of a father in America can only be replaced by another shadow of fatherhood. For King, the ideal is clearly nonexistent, and the fact that Roland is the closest Jake can get to a father figure is a depressing observation of the American condition.

The introduction of Jake Chambers will also remind readers of another cultural institution that is distinctly American — that of the ultra private, ultra refined, ultra selective Piper School. As a student of this esteemed educational facility, Jake is expected to thrive, to succeed academically and socially so that he may impress his classmates (who will all later become colleagues in the professional world he is certain to dominate) and satisfy his parents. The Piper School is everything Americans expect from such a private institute; students are expected to adhere to very strict rules of behavior and decorum. Everything from the proper way to excuse oneself to use the restroom to the way one wears the starched uniform is laid out in painstaking detail for students to follow. Deviation from the norm is not acceptable, and in Jake's situation, allowing others to see that he is slowly losing his mind is completely unacceptable — to those at the school and to his parents, but also to Jake himself. As much as he privately rebels against the strict code of conduct at Piper, Jake doesn't want to disappoint anyone. He doesn't want them to see what he perceives as weakness — his mental turmoil — and when he realizes that he is about to be exposed by his final essay, he flees the school, unable to face the reactions of people who realize that he has finally lost it. Jake's plight is a reflection of the enormous amounts of pressure some parents and schools place on students to succeed in America today. Even though Jake has a bona fide problem, he can't discuss it with anyone without fear of being judged too harshly, and rather than try to seek help from his elders, as the society seems to suggest he can, Jake knows that even to mention

Five : The Dark Tower *Connections*

what is happening to him will only lead to further degradation and condemnation. Students at the Piper School may be encouraged to seek help on the surface, but underneath that offer Jake senses something sinister, a somewhat malicious intention that will only use any confessions of weakness against him — a system that will exploit his fears and display his shortcomings for all to see.

In light of this kind of environment, it is terribly ironic to see Jake's teacher's reaction to the dreaded final essay. Though the words are ghostly echoes of the madness taking over Jake's mind, the teacher chooses to see his essay as a profound work of genius, a work far beyond his age group and grade level. By turning the thing that Jake was certain would reveal his encroaching insanity into an object that earns him the respect and admiration of the Piper School, King makes an ironic commentary on the nature of education. Jake actually is losing his mind, and the essay is a reflection of that downward spiral, a random and babbling series of ideas that do not make sense beyond the context of the Dark Tower and the quest to save it. Instead of seeing this madness for what it is, though, the teacher reads beyond the lines, seeing a depth that was not intended nor, one could argue, is even present in the text. This is a tendency of some intellectuals — to read into things perhaps more than should be or, honestly, can be done. Rather than see the nothing that is before her, Jake's teacher finds ideas buried in the text — or, more likely, buried in her own mind and loosely suggested by the text. King seems to be mocking higher education here and certainly the notion of the intellectual, a theme repeated endlessly in *The Stand*. Whenever there are people with a lot of book smarts, King seems to suggest, readers will find some kind of hypocrisy, self-delusion, or, in some cases, even blatant fictionalizing — a need to find more in some things than there is, to read into situations more than is intended. And even after this deep excavation of partial meaning has been pulled from the original, King suggests, some intellectuals will insist that those who cannot see the "deeper meaning" are missing something obvious — an attitude echoed by Jake's teacher's comment about how he must have fled school because he worried that such advanced use of symbolism would not be understood by his teacher. She reassures him that she can see his brilliance and hints that anyone who cannot is lacking in some way; the terrible irony here is that there is nothing to see, and her reassurance that she can see what he *really* meant is disturbing on another level altogether. Either intellectuals are so skilled at injecting meaning into meaninglessness, or Jake's madness really is genius in a way even he can't comprehend. Neither option is very reassuring—not for Jake, not for the American educational system, and certainly not for King's readers.

Not in Kansas Anymore

When the ka tet emerges from the wreckage of Blaine's Barony Coach, readers are shocked to find them standing on a platform in Topeka, Kansas. Echoes of *The Wizard of Oz* aside for the moment, King has brought this intrepid group out of a world that resonates with American imagery straight into America. The only question left is which America they have stumbled into. Is this the America of Eddie's 1980s? Is this the future of Jake's 1970s or Susannah's 1960s? Is it yet another dimension of the country, one more in an infinite multiverse of Topekas in a million possible Kansases?

The heroes are surprised and saddened to see that this Topeka is one that has been ravaged by a great plague. This is the world of *The Stand*, a familiar place indeed, and as the group passes by family clusters of corpses huddled together as they attempted to flee the inevitable, the enormity of the devastation is visited anew by readers familiar with this story. The newspaper headline places the timeline somewhere after the end of the summer during which Mother Abagail and the Dark Man have their confrontation, but echoes of that struggle are everywhere. From the spraypainted warning to "watch out for the walkin' dude" on a sign to the piles of decaying bodies, Roland's companions wonder which one of their worlds has met this fate, and even the possibility that it was one of theirs unnerves them. Even though they have bid farewell to their world, to their original place in the universe, it still bothers them to consider that that place, however willingly abandoned for Roland's world and his quest for the Tower, may have met such a fate.

They are relieved to discover that this ravaged world is not the one they came from. Small details make the distinction: Jake spots a bumper sticker for the Kansas City Monarchs instead of the Royals; Eddie notices a Takuro Spirit, a car company, make, and model that no one recognizes; a machine sells Nozz a La instead of Coke or Pepsi. These little things assure the travelers that this is not the world they came from, but Roland easily undermines their relief when he observes that this plague could be in the future of any of their worlds, and Jake is dismayed to think of his parents dying in such a way. The boy hasn't really thought of them in a very long

Five : The Dark Tower *Connections*

time, and they are already dead to him for all intents and purposes, yet the possibility that they may really die of a plague like this one is nearly unbearable. He clings to the idea of the differences, hoping against hope that this Topeka is not his Topeka, that these people are true strangers. Even with that belief, Jake, the boy who has seen much and survived even more, is deeply disturbed by the death he sees at the train station. Susannah is even more affected by the losses, and she fixates on the pages of obituaries in the newspaper, marveling at how hard these doomed people tried to honor their dead, even at the end. A woman who has been hardened by trials that would have destroyed many, Susannah is considerably tougher than the average person, and yet she too is overwhelmed by the loss before her.

All of the travelers are affected by the world of *The Stand*. King suggests that such loss of life is horrific, and though readers know that — of course they know that — he reminds them in a surprising way. It is one thing to know intellectually that there has been a great loss of life and to watch a story of death and destruction play out. It is another thing entirely to watch the effects of that loss on someone else, to see how they react to the situation. Readers may mourn the loss of America in *The Stand*, but they realize anew just how awful such a thing could be when they see Jake, Susannah, and Eddie try to rationalize how it couldn't be "their" America that has been lost. Witnessing loss through an alternate perspective brings it even more into focus for readers.

The connections to the world of *The Stand* do not end with the platform in Topeka. Even earlier in the Dark Tower series, King has hinted that these worlds will soon collide. At the end of *The Wastelands*, the Ageless Stranger, who calls himself Richard Fannin, comes to collect the Tick Tock Man as his servant. He asks him to say, "My life for you"— Trashcan Man's mantra. Apparently in King's worlds villainy and servitude cross all boundaries, and evil always survives to start again. When the ka-tet meet the man in black again in *Wizards and Glass*, this time in the glass palace from *The Wizard of Oz*, Roland's arch-nemesis calls himself Randall Flagg, and the man who seduced Gabrielle Deschain claims responsibility for the plague that has ravaged this "world next door" to the world of Eddie, Susannah, and Jake — a world that could be the America that readers currently live in. Stephen King manages to bring this world into sharp focus, raising essential questions about life and death, reminding readers of American history and culture, and asking them to consider what it really means to stand.

SIX

All God's Chillun' Should Stand

There has been much speculation about King's obsession with heroic children in his works. Does King use children simply because they are innocent? Do they inherently possess some power of goodness, while the sad and deluded adults in the world have forgotten what power they once had? King certainly enjoys having children stand against overwhelming evil. The notion of the Stand — that is, the ultimate confrontation with Evil — is not something that began in the novel of the same name. King has been toying with the idea since his earliest work. Even by the time he was twelve and discovered his dad's stash of fantasy horror novels, including Lovecraft, he was already writing tales about heroic kids.[1]

In one of his earliest stories, "Jhonathan and the Witchs," King's child hero manages to kills three witches by outsmarting them and earns himself a nice prize in the process. Though clearly derivative of Grimm and following the standard fantasy mode (hero is given seemingly impossible quest by king, and hero succeeds in quest using magical/supernatural means and earns the reward), this story shows that King's love for young heroes started when he himself was a young man. As he says in *Danse Macabre*, "Kids have the ability to think around corners," and that quality allows them to face evil in a different way than their adult counterparts, sometimes more successfully because they are still young, still in that process of becoming, still able to see outside the box of maturity and into the impossible possibilities.[2] King explains that both *IT* and "The Body" share the same thematic elements that he recalls from his own childhood: "love and terror and finding a hand to hold when things get hard and living in the world hurts."[3] King's characters often consider the demarcation between childhood and adulthood, concluding that there is something inherently magical about being a kid, something pure that transcends simple innocence to become a powerful weapon against evil. The trouble is trying to regain this sense of intuition as an adult, and a lot of King's famous stands involve children successfully facing evil and then suffering the consequences of that stand long into a haunted adulthood. For King, adults have lost that sense of knowing what to do, and while they stumble about trying to find their way, evil grows stronger. Unless the adults can recapture their childhood selves, often overcoming childhoods filled with violence and dysfunction, King suggests there is no hope of victory. A suicidal stand by adults against an indestructible evil is a familiar scene in a King novel.

In fact, King seems to delight in making his characters face impossible odds and indescribable evils. This in itself is nothing new to the horror genre, certainly. For the most part, characters must face an adversary in some fashion or there isn't much of a story. Yet, King takes this standard event and turns it into something more in his work. His characters do not merely fight the bad guys in some massive showdown; they face down evil with courage and honor, often knowing that to do so means certain death. Sometimes King's heroes will be rescued by some divine hand, but a lot of the time King is glad to sacrifice his heroes for the good fight. For someone who rivals the BBC in his willingness to kill off main characters, King's reception by his readers is curious. In a world where audiences do not generally enjoy watching the bad guy win (unless the bad guy is really cool and the good guys are stuffy parodies of Justice), King's readers accept that his heroes die in their battles with aplomb. There is no outcry to rescue Gardener as he lies in a puddle of his own blood in the launching spaceship at the end of *The Tommyknockers*. There is no movement to spare Eddie when he faces the spider-like embodiment of IT. Readers of King accept that his heroes will fall, and sometimes not even fall well (remember Eddie's fate in *The Dark Tower?*), but this is not the issue that King concerns himself with. It does not matter if the character lives or dies for King; instead, it matters how he conducts himself during that final encounter. King's characters stand, at their own peril, and sometimes the fight goes their way, and sometimes it does not. Either way, evil is defeated for the moment, so it seems worthwhile...almost. Some readers may ask themselves why such sacrifice is necessary if the hero falls and evil returns anyway. This is the brilliance of King's Stand. The important thing isn't that people die, for people die every single day and sometimes while not even doing something worthwhile; the important thing is that for one brief moment the people stand up for Right and Good and what Roland of Gilead would call the White.

Because the same scenario presents over and over again in King's work, some critics may be tempted to see King as repetitive and unoriginal in his storytelling. This would be an unfair characterization, however. One might just as easily denounce William Faulkner as being repetitive because he uses the same time and place and (ultimately) family in his work, or call Ernest Hemingway unoriginal because his heroes are always stoic military men. Each time an author uses the same idea in a different work, he is usually approaching the concept from another angle, examining the ideas from another perspective, or adding another level of depth to the theme. This is what King has done with his idea of the Stand. Though it is clearly spelled out in the book that bears the title, this idea of good facing against evil is certainly not new in any work — not in Western literature at any rate. King's approach to this inevitable showdown is different from that of his predecessors and followers, and he raises important questions as a result of this archetypal event.

What is worth standing up for? Who is worthy enough to stand? How will the effects of the stand ripple across the characters' lives in the future? Can evil ever truly be defeated? These are all points that the stand raises, ideas central to King's work from his earliest childhood stories to his recent bestsellers. Specifically, though, King seems to enjoy having a non-traditional hero stand at the crucial moment. He likes the idea of children standing up against evil. The quartet in "The Body" face off against dangerous hoodlums to protect their find — and, moreso, to defend that find's right to decency. The children in *IT* stand against an unspeakable evil. The boys in *Dreamcatcher* hold their ground against bullies for the sake of a retarded boy that they don't even know. Though the concept of standing is not so specifically developed as it is in the novel that bears the name, King certainly enjoys the idea of innocence against evil, often allowing the innocent to be permanently altered by the stand.

Sometimes these changes are beneficial, but more often than not, King's heroes are somehow ruined for the world as a result. Though King doesn't really expand on the events after the end of "The Body," readers do find out what happens to the boys — and here is one occasion where at least some of them are improved by their actions (that is, after they receive their due punishment for their stand). All of the boys are severely beaten, but the end result is somewhat reassuring. Gordy is a successful writer, Chris is a lawyer, albeit a dead one by the time of the story's telling, and at least Vern and Teddy didn't meet a messy end right away. The children in *IT* grow up to be dysfunctional adults unable to truly live their lives, blessed with financial and social success but always haunted by the memory of what they can't recall—and they don't even know that they've forgotten. Still, they made a promise, an oath to stand again if the time came, and that binding tie is what brings them all back to Derry for one final faceoff, for one more chance to really stand and be true. The boys from *Dreamcatcher* are haunted by the "one good thing" they did in their lives, and everything after that moment seems silly in comparison. It is a hard thing to reach the pinnacle of one's life in junior high school, when every moment afterwards is a look back to that finest hour, a yearning to be so brave and strong and true again, and to have it Matter the way it did that day.

In these stories King suggests that though the stand is a noble thing, it sometimes has long-term consequences for those involved, and not all of those effects are positive. In fact, standing against evil during one's childhood in a Stephen King tale often leads to lifelong dysfunction and discontent, a sense that once there was a chance to do something Great, and everything since then is just a pale shadow, an imitation of living that cannot ever be more than a mere echo of that one shining moment of Glory. Yet, for King, the stand is still worthwhile. Even though characters are forever scarred, even though evil continues to exist, even though the stand is more a gesture than anything that has a big effect on the world, it is still vitally important. If people can still choose to stand against those odds, knowing the costs, or at least accepting them afterwards as they truly come to understanding, then perhaps, King suggests, there is hope for humanity after all. This is one of the key elements of *The Stand* and an idea that reverberates across King's multiverse, appearing in novels and stories throughout his career.

"The Body": Ray Brower Meets a Train

"The Body" is one of King's more well-known short stories, probably because the movie *Stand by Me* was fairly successful. As for inspiration for the story, King's mother suggests that, as a 4-year-old, "King may have seen a playmate killed by a train."[4] This might be the image behind the death of Ray Brower, but ultimately it isn't important. The how and why of Ray Brower's death is insignificant; what matters is that the boys go on a journey to see a dead body—that is, to confront Death while in the midst of Life. The boys don't acknowledge this consciously, however; to them the trip is just for kicks, four boys off to see a body the same way boys might poke a dead animal or watch a spider scuttle across a clubhouse floor. For readers, this "innocence" on the part of the quartet allows them a choice: They can read the story as a story, or they can read into the story to see what it means underneath. King never demands that his readers invest more time and effort than they wish. If they want to read about a trip into the woods, some juvenile hijinks, a little bit of boyhood trauma, and a good showdown, they can, and a thoroughly enjoyable read it will be. However, if they want, readers can choose to think about the events as they unfold. Readers can consider this trip to see Ray Brower as a way to confront mortality, a chance for the boys to mature into young men. Of course, not all of the boys will grow up, but there is the potential for growth, as there always is in life, and if Vern and Teddy do not grow up to be the same kind of men that Chris and Gordy do, well, they had a chance to stand once. The fact that they ran away is telling but ultimately believable. Not everyone can stand against evil. Sometimes the universe asks too much and people fail (Consider Stan Uris in *IT*). King seems to suggest that the very act of standing does make good, heroic children into good-hearted, heroic adults. Not every child will be able to withstand the pressures of the confrontation, but children are always given some kind of choice — even if that choice is hard to see, with Fate shoving them forward.

The stand in "The Body" begins in much the same way that many King stories do — by an accident of fate or chance. The boys do not set out to do something important. They are not seeking anything noble. In fact, they embark on their journey into the woods for a rather macabre reason — they want to see the body of Ray Brower. The trip is not intentionally made for any high moral purpose. They do not set out to do a good thing. In fact, it is debatable as to whether they actually did a "good" thing in the end, but the essence of the stand is the same. Four young boys stand their ground against overwhelming odds, defending what is theirs against those who would take it from them. Granted, they are defending their right to finding the body, their right to become heroes in the eyes of the townspeople, but ultimately the showdown between Gordon LaChance and Ace Merrill has very little to do with Ray Brower. Gordon and Chris decide that they must defend their find, that the body is theirs, and therefore it is their responsibility to decide what to do about it. They do not stand up against the older boys because they actually want the noto-

Six : All God's Chillun' Should Stand

riety of finding the missing boy or even because they decide it is the "right" thing to do. Instead, Gordon is overwhelmed with the need to defend his find, to not allow someone to take what he feels is his by right.

Similar to many children scarred by their childhood, Gordon and his friends suffer long-lasting effects from their stand. Some occur almost immediately, as each boy suffers retribution from the older boys as soon as he gets home. Gordon is savagely beaten by Ace Merrill. Chris ends up in the emergency room after his own brother tosses him down the stairs. Teddy and Vern, even though they ran from the stand, are also caught and physically punished for being present in the woods. This violence is an important element of King's Stand. Even though the boys know that there will be consequences, even though they know without a doubt that the older boys will find them and punish them, they still stand, damning the consequences. Like Larry and Ralph facing their doom on a stage in Las Vegas, these boys accept that such a beating is a natural consequence of their actions, and they gladly acquiesce to that price. Granted, they are not asked for their lives, as Larry and Ralph are, but they do stand at the expense of their friendship.

Unlike the characters in *IT* and *Dreamcatcher*, however, who find that standing up against evil is the thing that keeps them together, the connective thread that binds them after all the years, Gordon and his mates do not stay close friends, or even friends at all. Teddy and Vern vanish into the ranks of classmates, becoming just another face in the halls, someone they once took a trip into the woods with; and King suggests that the journey to find the body, and the ripple effects of that grisly discovery, does not affect these two much. Teddy stays the same crazy kid, following the path that everyone had predicted. Vern falls into alcoholism and teenage stupidity. Both boys end up dying without having been changed by that moment in the woods. Gordon and Chris, on the other hand, both change profoundly. For Gordon, that stand in the woods marked the moment his innocence vanished. The Gordon who returns home is an older one, a young man who finally understands his parents' grief, who can come to terms with the tragedies in his life. For Chris, this stand is the beginning of his transition from general screw-up to law school graduate. It's as if once they stand up against the bullies, the older boys in the town, these two can stand against anything.

"The Body" is certainly a classic Bildungsroman, a coming-of-age tale recognizable to most readers, whether they know the literary term or not. Often the process of becoming an adult in traditional literature involves some kind of confrontation with grown-up situations. Young men in fantasies slay mythical creatures. Young women in romances meet dashing men and get married. In every story of a young person, something happens that transforms that child into an adult. In this respect, King's stand is nothing new. However, just because something has been done in literature, and done so often that a confrontation of sorts is a stage of Joseph Campbell's classic hero myth description, does not mean that it cannot have new meaning. Readers of King's stories can relate to the idea of young men growing up by confronting death. For a country whose young men for several generations "grew up" during a World War or similar conflict, the notion that boys become men when they face their own mortality is a given cultural expectation. Even the more recent idea that boys become men through confrontation — typically school yard confrontation — is something American readers will expect and accept in a story. King has twisted this expectation a little bit though. Instead of facing detention for standing against Ace and his gang, Gordy and Chris face death, or at least certain bodily harm. The older boys are certainly capable of killing these four young men in the woods. No one would know. Gordy and Chris are quite alone. The fact of the gun saves them from immediate peril, but they still have to survive the beatings. Some American readers, though, would nod in approval at this, recalling their own school days of bullying and standing. Granted, most readers' confrontations will not be over a dead boy or anything so dramatic, but the idea of facing the big bad boy on campus certainly resounds in American consciousness. In this way King has taken a normal coming-of-age story, blended it with American cultural growing pains, and made something new with the addition of a corpse — tradition meets cultural memory meets horror.

IT: *Clowns, Sewers, and Spiders*

Whenever Americans are asked about a Stephen King horror novel, they inevitably respond with *IT*. A novel that exploits fears, from clowns and mummies to werewolves and blood (not to mention any number of other noted fears in the American population), *IT* tells the story of a small group of children who face an ancient evil twice — once during a hot summer in their youth and again as adults who know they must finish the task. The novel is told through a series of overlapping flashbacks—switching from present to past and back again so that the build-up to the first confrontation mirrors the later one and gives readers a double climax at the end of the story.

IT resounds with Faulknerian overtones. Tony Magistrale notes the connections between the set-up of *The Sound and the Fury* and *IT*: "King employs a similar interrupted narrative style throughout *IT*, as the history of the Losers' Club and the monster that is the town of Derry is slowly and thoroughly made clear for the reader in a series of dramatic childhood flashbacks and recapitulations."[5] King also subtly adds overt Faulkner references in the names of those lost at the Black Spot fire. Mike's father tells him of the boys of E Company—Alan Snopes, Everett McCaslin, Horton Sartoris—men who meet their end in a fire set by angry racists in an eerie echo of Faulkner's often twisted South. Not to say that referencing Faulkner in itself makes King's work literary, but for those readers who know, this allusion is a gentle nod to the literary establishment. In addition, King's organizational structure in *IT*, the jump of time from present to past, is another familiar feature to readers of Southern American literature. However, the use of flashbacks to tell a story is not unique to Faulkner, and King is not the first writer to use this method of narration in a story, so the style is not overtly derivative. Instead, the use of a traditional literary narrative style adds another level of sophistication to King's work. For those readers who wish to recall the denizens of Yoknawpatawpha County as they read, this is a pleasant nudge, a knowing smile; but for those who do not know their Faulkner, King does not demand a knowledge of those tales. He acknowledges the tradition before him, but he does not refer to it in a way that requires readers to understand stream of consciousness and untangle multiple threads of narrative—standard reading procedures in any of Faulkner's novels. Again, King has used a literary technique, yet his readers can choose to pursue that depth of meaning or not. The story is told either way, and whether readers chuckle a little at the mention of someone named Sartoris and a fire in a barn-like building ceases to matter.

The Losers' Club

Bill Denbrough echoes King himself in that he is a writer of horror novels, but there is more to this character than a mere shadow. The hero of *IT* and the driving force behind the Losers' Club decision to stand and fight is largely due to Bill's personal charisma, but it is also a result of that Other that works through all of the children. The notion of some force to counterbalance IT is a common thought in King's multiverse. For all evil there is some good; for all that is Darkness there is the White. That force remains largely anonymous in this tale, but it is definitely present, and whether it is some kind of predetermined fate or destiny or something consciously pushing events into motion ceases to matter.

There is always the specter of the Turtle, in this and in other King novels, but that creature only seems to tell the characters what they already know, secrets they understand but are afraid to consider until the moment demands they must. When Bill is being dragged into the Deadlights, the Turtle offers him advice, but it is platitudes, information that Bill already knows by virtue of being a decent human being: He can do this; they all need to stick together; Stand and be True, etc. Even in *The Dark Tower* series, the Turtle is more a symbol than a vibrant, active force in the universe. It may nudge, it may suggest, and it may remind characters of things they may want to ignore, but ultimately the power of the Turtle is extremely limited to moral support and symbolic power. Heroes in King's novels must find the strength to stand within themselves. The universe may nod and wink at them, but there are rarely magic wands of power or secret incantations to save the day. The children must stand as they are, plain and simple, before evil, bolstered only by innocence and courage and the need to do the right thing.

What the Club is mostly aware of, though, is that they are all being pushed into the stand, prodded along a specific path towards their final confrontation. King suggests that this Other force is not necessarily a good force, as it certainly doesn't save any lives or offer any definite aid. It simply makes sure that they are in the right place at the right time, using Bill and his tragically dead brother as steam for the machine. Bill is even aware that he is being used, wondering that just as IT has latched onto Henry, a boy who has been victimized by forces his entire life, the Other is using him, using his anger over George's death as ammunition to fuel the need for a stand.

Each member of the Club has a special power: Bill has his deadly charisma, the ability to make his friends willing to die for him. The gunslinger suffers from the same double-edged blessing — he easily attracts followers, but he has to watch as they willingly lay down their lives in the

Six : All God's Chillun' Should Stand

name of his cause. Beverly is a good shot, and it is she who wounds IT in the werewolf guise, nearly destroying the creature for good and inspiring the fear that causes IT to flee for the first time in its existence. Ben can build things. His engineering skills forge everything from the underground "treehouse" to the silver bullets. Eddie can find the way to things—a precursor to Pete's ability to see the Line in *Dreamcatcher*. Stan has the ability to keep them grounded, with his birds and his belief in the ordinary world. Richie can always make them laugh—a crucial skill when standing against an ancient evil. King seems to suggest that the most powerful weapon against some kinds of evil is to laugh at it, to make jokes, and that is the heart of the ritual of Chud. Even Mike has the special role of record keeper. He stays behind, forgoing the success and fortune that would have waited for him beyond Derry, and chooses to man the post, to watch and make sure that IT does not return; and when IT does, it is Mike who calls the troops back into battle.

Each member of the Losers' Club has an ability that makes up for a deficiency in another member. This interconnected web of strengths and weaknesses makes them even stronger as a unified force. Though Bill is terribly afraid of getting lost, he knows that he need never fear when he is with Eddie—he observes at one point that Eddie seems to have an internal compass in his head that always points in the right direction. Is it the Turtle who benignly directs this Line? King never explains, but as each child realizes his or her special ability, he or she also realizes that for whatever is lacking in themselves, there is another to fill that role. This cements their relationship, their need for one another, and makes them a serious force to be reckoned with when they stand against IT.

When Eddie stands against his mother in the hospital, he realizes that he is not entirely alone in his confrontation. He feels like "there had been something working in him, working through him."[6] Eddie does not think this force is evil in itself, but it is powerful and frightening, intimidating enough to cow his mother into submission; and just like Bill before him, Eddie realizes that this newfound ability is an extension of the stand that lays before him. It is almost as if the universe itself realizes that the Loser's Club must stand together as a group and conspires to give them the power to try. If only Eddie could tap into that power after the first confrontation with IT, perhaps his life would have been happier. Though he is financially successful, readers get the sense that much of Eddie's life since he left Derry has been filled with fear, and even the security of a profitable limousine company and a somewhat loving wife is not enough to make him truly happy. In fact, Eddie isn't happy until he is reunited with the friends he had forgotten, a joy that is perverted by the fear of what comes next. Then again, Eddie Stands in the end, sacrificing himself for his friends, and he is glad to die in Beverly's arms, comforted by the thought that this time they truly have destroyed the evil in Derry.

IT's Minions

Many of the characters in *IT* are not entirely under their own control. The adults are subject to a bone-deep need to obey the town itself, victims to the evil in a subconscious way, and able to commit horrific deeds without much in the way of consequences. The people of Derry have been engaging in wanton bloodshed for centuries, often standing by as violence happens, but occasionally joining in that action, and always without any long-term consequences. Sure, the residents of Derry "Stand" against the Bradley Gang, ruthless bank robbers, but the premeditated and almost jovial manner in which they cut down the men and women that afternoon is wrong on a fundamental level, so wrong that when the few people who will admit that it even happened discuss it, they all claim to have been out of town that week. IT allows the townspeople to indulge in some kind of primordial need to kill or to stand by and allow the deaths of others.

IT does not always subtly encourage people to do IT's bidding. Sometimes it is very specific in its orders. Take Henry Bowers, for instance. The son of an insane veteran, and subject to his father's whims and violent temper, Henry does not stand much chance of being a normal person. To make matters worse, Henry becomes the pawn of IT, hearing IT's orders in his mind as he hunts down the Losers' Club. Because IT has only the power of suggestion beyond the realm of the sewers (though IT can definitely roam a little when it faces children), IT needs someone on the outside to help defeat the heroes. As a child, Henry hears the voice from drainpipes, a voice that suggests and then demands that he perform for IT. When he is older, Henry lives in fear of that voice, of the clown's face, and when he escapes to kill the adult Losers, he does so as much out of fear of IT as to do IT's bidding. By the end, Henry is a pathetic creature, one almost worthy of sympathy...until readers recall how Henry broke

Eddie's arm — twice — and was not afraid to brandish his knife at the only nice old woman in Derry. Granted, the would-be Samaritan quickly flees the scene when Henry rushes at her, but at least there was a moment when readers could feel that not every single adult in Derry is doomed. There are some good people left in the world.

Unfortunately for the Losers, they have a tendency to surround themselves with unsavory people instead of the few who are willing to lend a helping hand. An excellent example of this self-destructive behavior is Beverly's husband, Tom Rogan. A man who regularly beats Beverly for trivial offenses, Tom is easily taken in by IT's whispering, and he is ruthlessly sacrificed as a pawn. In fact, his only use to IT is to bring Audra to the sewers. After that task is done, Tom dies of a heart attack, a result of the shock of seeing IT in the flesh, or at least the only flesh IT can really have in this plane of existence.

"You Can't Be Careful on a Skateboard"

King definitely understands the nature of childhood, and that knowledge is reflected in his characters. When Bill tells a young boy to "be careful"—that classic parental line of warning—he is quickly admonished with a wisdom that is lost in adulthood. Life itself is dangerous, and sometimes it is not possible to be careful. Perhaps the very joy of living life is in taking that chance, knowing that everything may go horribly wrong and doing it anyway. Riding a skateboard is a classic childhood activity, but King has turned this innocent pastime into something more, a symbol for a more pragmatic outlook on life, an understanding that there is no safety net. The rider can and probably will fall, time and again, but the important thing is to get up, dust oneself off, and get back on. If a person spends too much time being careful, he runs the risk of becoming Eddie Kasprak, a man with a brave core who has been warped by an overbearing mother into an apparent weakling who cannot withstand the traumas of childhood. Yet even Eddie manages to stand when it matters, first against the leper, then against Henry Bowers, and eventually against the spider-like form of IT itself. In the end, Eddie rides the skateboard, sacrificing himself to save his friends, facing his fears and dying a hero's death beneath the city.

When Bill contemplates this choice to get back on the proverbial skateboard, he hesitates. The adult in him imagines the worst — he will fall, he will be humiliated, he will be hurt — but Bill is enough of a realist to recognize that those feelings do not mean defeat for the grown-up Losers' Club. Men approaching forty should not be hopping on skateboards without first considering the consequences and, more importantly, first considering the reason to get on the thing in the first place. In today's world of countless Youtube videos of people hurting themselves doing stupid things, it is easy to forget that most important question: Why get on the skateboard in the first place? Bill has no one to impress, no trick to perform. He is not Tony Hawk; skateboarding is not his life. It is a relic of his childhood, and even when he was younger, Bill was not into skateboards. He risked his young neck riding Silver, a bike that would humble most full-grown adults. Bill is not seriously tempted to recapture his youth by getting on a skateboard, an act that would be overtly symbolic and probably end badly. Bill does not need that kind of courage to face IT; instead, he needs to use the wisdom he has gained in his life to decide which battles are worth fighting. IT must be destroyed, there is no question, and that risk must be taken, but foolish risks without obvious benefit are not worth it. Now, Bill does decide later on to take a risk, but this time it is for something worthwhile: He must rescue Audra from the Deadlights. He has to regain his childhood and ride Silver, but this time he takes the risk knowing the consequences, knowing that his efforts may be in vain, knowing that despite everything he knows, he has to try, and the trying is what matters. You can't be careful on a skateboard, but you can certainly decide it's worthwhile to take a risk. In King's work, a person never knows if he will survive the stand, but he always has a choice. Heroes decide to stand, but they don't have to; they can choose to run and hide like everyone else. The decision to stand and deal with the aftermath is what makes them heroes.

Grown-Ups Are the Real Monsters

King emphasizes that children are special because of their ability to accept the world around them. Everything is new to a child, so a little bit of the supernatural does not upset any worldview — kids don't have a worldview to upset quite yet. Ben muses on this as he stands outside the Derry Public Library as an adult:

Six : All God's Chillun' Should Stand

Kids were also better at incorporating the inexplicable into their lives. They believed implicitly in the invisible world. Miracles both bright and dark were to be taken into consideration, oh yes, most certainly, but they by no means stopped the world. A sudden upheaval of beauty or terror at ten did not preclude an extra cheesedog or two for lunch at noon.[7]

This sense of wonder and acceptance is what allows kids to face evil and survive, King suggests. The entire world is a mystery, filled with unknowns, and so children can accept anything without too much turmoil. They may know that something is not right, as the Losers Club recognizes the alien nature of IT, but they are not paralyzed by disbelief as many adults would be. The classic terror of the horror genre, the inability to believe that evil can and does exist in the real world, does not affect children. They know something lives under their bed, and they see the eyes watching them from the closet at night. A world filled with fantastical places that they have never visited must also be filled with amazing creatures they have never seen. That does not imply that they cannot believe in their existence. As people age, however, that openness to the oddness of the world fades.

As adults, something from the realm of horror is enough to derail sanity. Grown-ups assume they have the world figured out, so when they see something beyond their expectations, as King puts it, the wires overload and "your mind kept coming back to it, pawing it lightly like a kitten with a ball of string...until eventually, of course, you either went crazy or got to a place where it was impossible for you to function."[8] The adults who see IT either die from the shock or completely ignore what they are seeing. Then again, the residents of Derry often ignore unpleasant things; whether because they live so deep inside the field of IT's influence or because the town itself is corrupt at the heart, the children of Derry have learned not to rely on the adults to help them. It does not seem to matter if the threat is a crazed parent, wayward boys, or a deranged clown — the kids in this town must stand on their own.

When Eddie Kasprak has a private meeting with the pharmacist Mr. Keene, he learns one of his childhood's greatest truths: Adults are the monsters. Readers may be conflicted at this point. On the one side, it is wrong for Eddie to continue to be deceived about the nature of his sickness. He has a right to know that he isn't "really" sick, despite his mother's insistence that he is a delicate boy. Then again, who is Mr. Keene to disrupt Eddie's delicate worldview? Is it acceptable for a stranger to interfere in a person's private business? Is it Mr. Keene's place to reveal the twisted nature of Eddie's relationship with his mother? King raises serious questions with this episode.

Readers may applaud the pharmacist for taking the initiative, for giving Eddie a choice in his treatment. At least Eddie is told the truth about his medicine, and what he does with that knowledge is up to him. Mr. Keene's conscience can rest easy — he is no longer actively participating in the deception of a child. He is circumspect in the delivery of this information. He does not embarrass Eddie in public, he does not reveal the secret in front of anyone, and he gives Eddie the somewhat adult treatment of a serious talk over drinks. Of course, the drinks are milkshakes and Mr. Keene is not an equal with Eddie, but as far as giving the boy an honest appraisal, the pharmacist does his best to give Eddie the illusion of adulthood. King hints at something more sinister below the surface of this meeting, however. By the end of the discussion, Eddie is certain that part of Mr. Keene is thoroughly enjoying himself as he rips gaping holes in the boy's self-image. The pharmacist essentially tells Eddie that the boy has a mental problem, that his asthma is all in his head, and that everything Eddie thinks is true about himself and his position in the world is not true. Part of Eddie has suspected this, for he is not struck dumb into disbelief by this admission. The rational part of his mind quickly accepts what Mr. Keene tells him, not because he trusts the man but because the medicine says it should be taken as needed. Eddie knows that any real medicine would have limits, or the user would overdose. He accepts that the reason there are no limits on his prescription is because a person cannot overdose on water vapor, and that means that the pharmacist is telling the truth — and somehow delighting in the fact of his role in the revelation. Mr. Keene may not intend to be mean-spirited, but to Eddie there is something evil in Mr. Keene's behavior, something twisted and monstrous that enjoys destroying Eddie's self-confidence, that is thrilled to tell Eddie that his illness is contrived and that his mother is irrational.

Readers may be confused by this episode, as well as somewhat unnerved to find that Mr. Keene is not the only adult to secretly enjoy delivering bad news. It is easy to justify the telling — the child has a right to know, he is old enough to make his own decisions, the deception has gone on long enough, etc. — but there is something creepy about Mr. Keene's insistence on the truth, even when it is obvious that Eddie does not want to know. Eddie doesn't want to notice, but he realizes that his

Six : All God's Chillun' Should Stand

"asthma attack had tasted better to him [Mr. Keene] than his half-finished coffee soda."[9] If he is truly acting in Eddie's self interest, he should see that the boy is upset and leave it alone, wait a little while for him to grow up some more and perhaps grow more amenable to harsh realities. But Mr. Keene does not pause. He does not even seem to entertain second thoughts about informing Eddie. Instead, he hammers home the point that Eddie's medicine is a placebo, a grand invention for senior citizens but a gross injustice against a boy Eddie's age. He then uses this meeting as a platform to espouse his personal theories about money-grubbing physicians and overbearing mothers, topics which really have no place in Eddie Kasprak's situation. As Eddie notes, "Grownups could be so hateful in their power sometimes."[10] Readers may begin to wonder about Mr. Keene at this point, but then again, perhaps readers should doubt a man who participated in the slaughter of the Bradley Gang in his youth. Mr. Keene is an old-time resident of Derry, and if IT has infiltrated the town as completely as the Loser's Club thinks, then he is an extension of that evil, if only in an ordinary way. Mr. Keene honestly believes he is doing the right thing, but he felt the same way when he and a number of other Derry residents calmly and coldly premeditated the assassination of a small group of men and women one summer day. Adults in a King novel can never truly be trusted by the child heroes, even when it appears that they are trying to help. Adult help often becomes more trouble than it is worth.

American Horrors

It is easy to see why so many King readers think of *IT* as his ultimate horror novel. The story is filled with stereotypical horror elements—clowns, spiders, sewers, werewolves, lepers, mummies, even big prehistoric birds; each of these is guaranteed to elicit a shiver just by virtue of what it is. And that is before King begins to work with them. Clowns are an easy target; we even have a word for the fear of clowns—coulrophobia—and it is fairly common in American society. This does seem a bizarre thing to be afraid of; after all, clowns are meant to entertain children, evoking memories of childhoods spent marveling when the circus was in town. Clowns are supposed to make kids laugh, to bring them joy through their silly antics and painted faces. Is Stephen King to blame for this new image of twisted clowns, of lips, painted red with blood, hiding razor-sharp teeth? A look at the American history of clowns shows that clown phobia entered mainstream society around the time of three major events. The first was the degeneration of Weary Willie, the clown alter-ego of three generations of Emmett Kellys—the last of whom ended his career with a homicide—aided, so he claimed, in part by Willie. Second, John Wayne Gacy certainly did not help the American consciousness regarding clowns and their homicidal behavior, though he was never officially a clown beyond volunteer events. Finally, Stephen King published *IT*, the quintessential killer clown novel. The decades that followed have been filled with evil clowns, so much so that in a study of 250 children done by the University of Sheffeld in 2008, many subjects found a clown motif "frightening and unknowable."[11]

This fear could be traced back to the idea of masks, of a face hidden beneath a face that doesn't change, and that is exactly the horror of *IT*. Pennywise is just a mask, one of many, but one specifically designed to lure in unsuspecting children. Of course, *IT* takes place in the late '50s, when pop culture's perception of clowns included Bozo and encouraged warm memories of popcorn at the circus. The children who live in Derry during this cycle of IT's killing spree are not armed with the fear that modern readers have. They have not seen a movie about a killer clown offering balloons to innocent kids, nor have they heard the stories of real-life clowns running amok.

The Losers' Club know enough of IT to fear Pennywise, but this is only because they sense the unnaturalness of the evil. Other children get a hint that something is slightly wrong, but they are overwhelmed by their positive memories of the circus and the certainty that nothing in the world will really hurt them. The Losers' Club is different. Each of them knows that the world can and will hurt them. Bill has lost a beloved brother. Ben has been teased and tormented for his weight, Eddie for his weakness, and Richie for his mouth. Mike and Stan have been the victims of racial and ethnic hatred. Even Beverly has been victimized by her overprotective and abusive father. They know enough of the realities of the world to obey that sixth sense of warning, and that allows them to survive this trick.

The idea of the mask endures throughout the novel, though, as readers discover that Pennywise is only one identity of a dozen designed to frighten children. When the heroes finally confront IT in the flesh in this world, they face a huge spider—another popular American phobia, though this one much older than Stephen King can take credit for. Then again, Bill realizes that even the spider isn't IT's true form, but the closest it can manage, or perhaps the best his brain can conceive without losing his sanity. Even revealed in its lair, IT is still hidden beneath yet another mask.

The novel is filled with horrific imagery and haunting Evil, but as far as American pop culture is concerned, facing down the monster in a climactic stand is the only way for Good to triumph. Perhaps readers can hold King partially accountable for this recent phenomenon of fearing clowns, but it is only one cause of many for those sleepless nights that readers can lay at King's door.

Dreamcatcher: *Aliens, Old Friends, and Hunting Cabins*

In *Dreamcatcher*, King describes how a quartet of young boys stand for a brief moment, and how that action affects the rest of their lives. For Jonesy, Henry, Beaver, and Pete, that one moment when they did a good thing has long-lasting ripples, endowing each of them with a special ability of sorts and cementing their relationship so that they are still as close as ever nearly three decades later. In a world where high school friends fade into memory, these boys maintain a connection they forged in junior high, and it is the one moment of "doing the right thing" that allows them to stay so close.

When the boys stumble upon the bullies tormenting Douglas Cavell, they have no real reason to get involved. By doing so, they are risking life and limb. In the testosterone-fueled hallways of junior high and high school, for younger boys to face off against older boys often ends badly for those who have not yet sprouted into puberty. When Jonesy, Henry, Beaver, and Pete turn the corner around Tracker Brothers in their quest for a glimpse of Tina Jean Schlossinger's pink parts, they do not expect to find a chance to take a stand against evil. They are engaged in an everyday action of teenage lust, hunting for forbidden photos of naked women, and not at all concerned with standing up for the ideals of Good and Right. Yet, King has them switch immediately from this somewhat devious intention to a noble quartet willing to sacrifice bodily health and junior high reputation to rescue a boy they don't even know — and a retarded boy at that.

True, there is something compelling about Douglas Cavell, something that almost forces the boys to act in his defense, but there is more to this stand than simple coercion. When they see Richie Grenadeau trying to make Dudditz eat a piece of dog excrement, their sense of moral outrage is instantaneous and visceral. It doesn't matter that the victim is a boy from the Retard Academy, a stranger whose Scooby Doo lunchbox they came across. It doesn't matter that the boys tormenting Dudditz are older and stronger. What matters is that stronger people are abusing a half-naked terrified boy who cannot defend himself, and the sheer indecency of the act is what prompts them to intervene. They cannot simply walk away, like the people of Derry have been doing for centuries when it comes to evil in their town. Faced with human evil, the boys are compelled by their sense of decency and Right to stop it.

It is true that Jonesy, Henry, Pete, and the Beav have less to fear from Richie Grenadeau and his pals than Gordy and his gang when facing Ace Merrill. Unlike the boys in "The Body," these Derry-ites are not very far from civilization. Pete can run to get an adult's help for his friends, and as they point out, to Richie's dismay, Pete is a very fast runner. Adults and aid are within reach, but an even more powerful deterrent to the older boys is that the would-be heroes know their names. Realizing that they may get beat up for their trouble, the boys settle on one thing that Richie cannot combat—the ability to tell on them. The threat that others will know that they have been torturing a defenseless boy is enough to encourage the cretins to abandon their game and their prey. There are promises of retaliation, of course, but in this story that payment never comes. Unlike Gordy and his friends, who suffer broken bones and hospital visits, this foursome is never confronted by Richie and his pals again. For a crew to stand and not face immediate consequences may seem like a good thing, but this is a Stephen King novel, and just because the payment has not been demanded yet, that does not mean it will not be harsh.

For a little while, though, it seems that the boys have been blessed by their interference. Each boy inherits some kind of psychic ability—Pete can see the "line," the others can read minds—and the bond between them is solidified. The boys are even allowed to become town heroes when they use their collective "gifts" to find a missing girl. That seems to be the highlight of their lives, though. After saving Dudditz and finding Josie, the quartet slides into an ever-downward spiral of depression. By the time readers meet them in adulthood, Pete is an alcoholic; Beaver is lonely and dysfunctional; the smartest member, Henry, is suicidal; and Jonesy is recovering from a catastrophic accident that has left him handicapped in more ways than a limp. Despite these tragedies, the boys still get together every year. The things they learned on the day they saved Dudditz still bind them together. The catchphrase "No bounce, no play" is from the wall behind Tracker Brothers, a saying they first encountered on the day they met Dudditz. The echoes of this one good deed reverberate through every encounter they've had since then.

Horror Lives Everywhere Every Day

Dreamcatcher contains other elements familiar to King's readers—horror, certainly, and death and mayhem, of course, but also an uncompromising military, this time under the leadership of Kurtz (a character oddly reminiscent of the tortured military man in Conrad's *Heart of Darkness*). There are aliens as well, this time the embodiment of evil in the form of Mr. Gray and his plot to infect everyone through the water supply, but there are also quintessential American elements that readers will recognize. The quartet spends time every year at a hunting cabin deep in the woods. Hunting cabins and manly getaways are familiar fare to readers from New England. Hole in the Wall has been in Beaver's family for generations, a place for his father to come with his friends, and for Beaver to bring his friends when he grows older. Oddly reminiscent of Faulkner's concept of hunting (especially Ike McCaslin in "The Bear"), readers will identify with the idea of getting away to nature, kicking back in the woods with a hunting rifle and a beer, enjoying card games and shooting the breeze with old friends as the fireplace rustles and the cold November wind blows outside. King interrupts this idyllic retreat with an alien invasion, of course, subtly reminding readers of all the everyday dangers that lie beneath the simple trip into the woods. Hunters get lost in the woods for days, eating whatever they can find. Hunters mistake other hunters for deer and accidentally shoot one another as the snow and cold confuse the mind while they wait in tree stands. Anyone wounded while at a remote hunting cabin is on his own, hoping that he can get help before it's too late. Snow-filled mountain roads prove dangerous even for off-road vehicles as they return from town to the distant getaway. And all of these dangers preclude the presence of aliens in the forest. These are ordinary terrors that Americans face every time they pack their hunting equipment.

King takes readers down another fearful path in *Dreamcatcher*—one slightly different than the typical alien invasion — in the manner of Mr. Gray's plot. The aliens here do not intend to dissect the humans or use them in experiments, or anything that readers normally expect from this genre. Instead, Mr. Gray's goal is annihilation, a common enough goal, ultimately, but he intends to use the humans as incubators for his own dying race. Even this plot device is not so original — aliens in fiction always have some kind of ultimate endgame. What makes Mr. Gray unique in this genre, and for American readers, is that he does not remain a bigheaded gray alien. His physical form dies, and his essence invades Jonesy, taking him over like a Bodysnatcher. This is another kind of horror for readers. Instead of fearing the alien, the Gray Boy, the obviously identifiable threat, they must instead fear Jonesy, a character they like and respect. King forces his readers to fear not the big bad monster outside but the sinister presence within. It is one thing to destroy foreigners, external creatures; it is another thing entirely to cheer for the destruction of Jonesy, a man who has already suffered a great deal in his life. True horror is fear of the self, after all. In watching Jonesy struggle to preserve his consciousness, readers must acknowledge the Mr. Gray in all of them, the alien evil that seeks to pervert the cause of Good and Right. The Puritans would probably call this force the Devil, and no doubt there would be some whipping involved, but the notion of an evil infiltrating the mind of an otherwise good man is an old idea in American consciousness, but one no less fearful for its age and familiarity.

Of course, the story all comes down to that stand Jonesy made in his youth and the abilities that Dudditz (or at least helping Dudditz) bestowed upon him. His psychic abilities allow him to remain himself, locked inside a small room in his head, and the connection with his friends allows them to overcome Mr. Gray. Even in this, though, there is sacrifice, as Beaver and Pete lose their lives facing this threat.

Last Stand

Standing in a Stephen King novel is fraught with peril, but children who stand are particularly blessed and cursed. These precocious kids are always rewarded in some way, but they also pay steep costs for their bravery. Gordon and Chris, the Losers' Club, and the gang at Hole in the Wall are not the only children King has facing overwhelming odds, but any

Six : All God's Chillun' Should Stand

time there is a group of children there is a certain kind of power as well, and sometimes it can be used to defeat the darkness for a little bit longer. Then again, this is Stephen King, and so that same group of children can twist their power for evil ends (*Children of the Corn* anyone?). Either way, children in a King novel are a force to be reckoned with, especially when they stand.

Final Thoughts

The Stand is essentially a novel about change and how people react to transitions. Some can adapt to a new way of living, and some can only struggle to make the new world mirror the old. Despite the way the world may change, though, King suggests that humanity will remain the same creature. Some people will fight for good, others will stand by and allow evil to thrive, but there will always be enough on both sides for a decent battle to occur. This is an outlook that both damns and saves humanity, but perhaps it is the only view that a modern American audience can truly believe, and this philosophy is what has made *The Stand* a fan favorite among King's readers. Perhaps fans appreciate *The Stand* so much because there is enough in it for everyone to get into. For readers into science fiction, there is the idea of a government-created super flu that wipes out most of the human race. For those who enjoy epic fantasy, there is a battle between good and evil fought by a few chosen heroes. For readers interested in social commentary, there is a great deal of talk about human nature and society in general. For those who are fascinated by politics, there is a chance to view government in the making from the ground up. For those who just want a good story filled with good characters, there is a huge cast constantly trundling across the pages, each fascinating in turn, and they all do their part to move the story along.

The Stand is not the next Great American Novel by any means. It is flawed. For instance, it is quite long, which is not a criticism in itself, but there are times when the action drags and readers begin to wonder if the story will ever get going again. This slow pacing is most clear when King blows up most of the Free Zone Committee with a bomb — he said that he didn't know where to go with the story, and that it had somehow turned into a record of rebuilding society (an interesting point, but not one he

Final Thoughts

wanted to focus the rest of the novel on), so the only thing to do was blow up a few characters and jumpstart the action again.

Still, my intention was to find out if *The Stand* had the depth expected of a serious literary work — themes, imagery, symbols, a certain "arresting strangeness" and resonation with readers — that is, the things that a literary critic looks for when considering a text. In short, the answer is a solid yes. From considerations of politics and government to the nature of the soul and spirituality, King's novel covers a great deal of thematic material. His writing is filled with imagery that further expands his points, whether he is calling on readers' knowledge of Tolkien with his "red Eye" descriptions or the casual way he mentions a dead cat and a rat in order to suggest a litany of subtext. As for symbols, *The Stand* resounds with them; from corn to cars and dead electrical sockets to the full moon, each concept reminds readers of something else that further enhances their understanding of the story.

Not only does King raise essential questions with this novel, he also creates a world believable enough to echo in his other novels. The world of *The Dark Tower* is a rich tapestry of King's multiverse, but it is the world of *The Stand* that readers recall as the band of heroes stands outside a train station in Topeka, Kansas, and hopes, prays even, that this desolate lost world is not the one they abandoned. Even though each of Roland's ka-tet has willingly left his world behind and accepted Mid-World as a new home, the idea that their past has led to such a future is appalling, and all of them are glad to find clues that this ravaged world is not the one they knew and loved. It is the world next door, perhaps, but not the exact one, and there is comfort in that. For a group of travelers who face the ultimate quest — to save all universes — to be so disturbed by King's plague-riddled world speaks volumes about the impact of this novel on American readers. Even the heroes are bothered by the concept.

As far as concepts are concerned, King has taken the idea of the stand against evil and refined it in the many novels that comprise his work. He does this particularly well when dealing with children, and especially clearly in "The Body," *IT*, and *Dreamcatcher*. Each of these novels resounds with American sensibilities as it explores the subtleties of standing in one's childhood, the echoes of youth resounding across the entire lifetime, sometimes a mark of honor and pride, and sometimes a badge of shame and despair. However the children fare in their stand, though, King connects with his adult readers on a fundamental level as he makes childhood fears real once again.

Final Thoughts

I began with questions about why King is not taken very seriously by the academic establishment, and I have come to the conclusion that his writing style and his popularity have joined together in setting him firmly away from other literary greats. Still, King is very much a man of the times, and he is not the only writer to not be taken seriously in his day. There is the possibility that in a few decades academics will turn to his work with the same passion and hindsight that they turned to Herman Melville or John Steinbeck. Certainly, if and when that attention does shift to Stephen King and his phenomenon, critics will not be disappointed. In fact, they may find standing up with the King to be a rather rewarding experience.

Chapter Notes

Introduction

1. Gary Hoppenstand and Ray B. Browne, eds., *The Gothic World of Stephen King* (Bowling Green, OH: Bowling Green State University Popular Press, 1987), p. 2.
2. Ibid.
3. Kassia Kroszer, "Reading Books: 3 Out of 4 Americans Do It," Booksquare, Aug. 23, 2007, accessed 4 Oct. 2007, http://www.booksquare.com/reading-books-3-out-of-4-americans-do-it/.
4. "Literary Reading in Dramatic Decline," National Endowment for the Arts News Room, July 8, 2004, accessed 4 Oct. 2007, http://www.nea.gov/news/news04/ReadingAtRisk.html.
5. Harold Bloom, ed., *Stephen King: Modern Critical Views* (Philadelphia: Chelsea House, 1998), p. 3.
6. Steven Spignesi, *The Essential Stephen King* (Franklin Lakes, NJ: New Page Books, 2001), p. 10.
7. Stephen King, *The Stand. Complete and Uncut Edition* (New York: Doubleday, 1990), p. viii.
8. Hugh C. Holman and William Harmon, *A Handbook to Literature*, 6th ed. (New York: Macmillan, 1992), p. 298.
9. Harold Bloom, *The Western Canon* (New York: Riverhead Books, 1994), p. 3.
10. Ibid.
11. King, *The Stand*, p. ix.
12. Suzanne Ellery Greene, "Best Sellers," in *Handbook of American Popular Culture*, vol. 2, ed. M. Thomas Inge (Westport, CT: Greenwood Press, 1980), p. 31.
13. Werner Jaeger, *Paideia: The Ideals of Greek Culture*, vol. 1, trans. Gilbert Highet (New York: Oxford University Press, 1945), p. i.
14. Ibid., p. xxiii.
15. Ibid., p. xxvii.
16. H. I. Marrou, *A History of Education in Antiquity*, trans. George Lamb (New York: Sheed and Ward, 1956), p. 9.
17. Ibid., p. 12.
18. Andreas Huyssen, *After the Great Divide: Modernism, Mass Culture, Postmodernism* (Bloomington: Indiana University Press, 1986), p. vi.
19. Greene, p. 37.
20. T. S. Eliot, "Tradition and the Individual Talent" (1920), *Quotidiana*, ed. Patrick Madden, accessed 17 Oct 2011, http://essays.quotidiana.org/eliot/tradition_and_the_individual/.

21. Jonathan Culler, *Literary Theory: A Very Short Introduction* (New York: Oxford University Press, 1997), p. 27.
22. Ibid., p. 31.
23. Ibid., p. 35–36.
24. Qtd. in Culler, p.36.
25. Culler, p. 37.
26. Paul Johnson, *Intellectuals* (New York: Harper and Row, 1988), p. 309.
27. Ibid., p. 342.
28. Hoppenstand and Browne, p. 5.
29. Edwin F. Casebeer, "The Art of Balance: Stephen King's Canon," in *Stephen King*, ed. Harold Bloom (Philadelphia: Chelsea House, 1998), pp. 207–208.
30. Mark Edmundson, "Narcissus Regards a Book," *The Chronicle Review*, Jan. 30, 2011, pp. B10-B11.
31. Ibid., p. B11.
32. Casebeer, p. 209.
33. Michael R. Collings, *The Many Facets of Stephen King* (Mercer Island, WA: Starmont House, 1985), p. 13–14.
34. Douglas E. Winter, *Stephen King: The Art of Darkness* (New York: New American Library, 1984), p. 3.
35. Tim Underwood and Chuck Miller, eds., *Stephen King Goes to Hollywood* (New York: New American Library, 1987), p. 9.
36. Qtd. in Greg Smith, "The Literary Equivalent of a Big Mac and Fries? Academics, Moralists, and the Stephen King Phenomenon," *The Midwest Quarterly* 43.4 (Summer 2002): p. 330.
37. Ibid.
38. Qtd. in Collings, *The Many Facets of Stephen King*, p. 335.
39. David Punter, *The Literature of Terror: A History of Gothic Fictions from 1765 to the Present Day* (New York: Longman, 1980), p. 4.
40. Winter, p. 4.
41. Ibid., pp. 3–4.
42. Ibid., p. 8.
43. Ibid., p. 5.
44. Stephen King, *Danse Macabre* (New York: Berkeley, 1981), p.14.
45. Punter, p. 3.
46. Qtd. in Brenda Miller Power, "An Ethnography of an Event," in *Reading Stephen King*, eds. Brenda Miller Power, Jeffrey D. Wilhelm, and Kelly Chandler (Urbana, IL: National Council of Teachers of English, 1997), p. 7.
47. "Books: King of Horror," *Time Magazine*, Oct. 6, 1986, accessed 23 Aug. 2011, http://www.time.com/time/magazine/article/0,9171,962461,00.html.
48. Ruth Franklin, "Stephen King and I," *The New Republic*, Nov. 5, 2000, p.50.
49. Ibid.
50. Francine Fialkoff, "King Holds Court at the NBAs," *Library Journal*, Dec. 1, 2003, p. 92.
51. Frank McConnell, "Just Doing It: Stephen King's Craft," *Commonweal* 118.57 (Jan. 25, 1991): p. 57.
52. Ibid.
53. Bloom, *Stephen King*, p. 3.
54. Ibid., p. 2.
55. Ibid.
56. Ibid.
57. The tendency to examine King's work according to publication does not allow

critics to truly see King's creative process. Many of his works were written and published in chaotic order, and so lumping together novels published in the same few years rarely reflects the actual order in which King formulated and wrote them. This need for a chronological overview tries to categorize King into stages of writing that do not correspond to the actual stages he experienced.

58. Darrell Schweitzer, ed., *Discovering Modern Horror Fiction II* (Mercer Island, WA: Starmont Publishers, 1988), p. 1.
59. Michael R. Collings, *The Stephen King Phenomenon* (Mercer Island, WA: Starmont House, 1987), p. 61.
60. Stephen King, "I Want to Be Typhoid Stevie," in *Reading Stephen King*, eds. Brenda Miller Power, Jeffrey D. Wilhelm, and Kelly Chandler (Urbana, IL: National Council of Teachers of English, 1997), p. 14.
61. Ibid., p. 15.
62. Ibid.
63. King, *The Stand*, p. ix.
64. Ibid., p. xii.
65. Collings, *The Many Facets of Stephen King*, pp. 109–110.
66. King, *The Stand*, p. 458.
67. Grant qtd. in Collings, *The Many Facets of Stephen King*, p. 110.

Chapter One

1. King, *The Stand*, p. 23.
2. Ibid., p. 25.
3. Ibid., p. 31.
4. Ibid., p. 130.
5. Ibid., p. 67.
6. Linda J. Holland-Toll, *As American as Mom, Baseball, and Apple Pie: Constructing Community in Contemporary American Horror Fiction* (Bowling Green, OH: Bowling Green State University Popular Press, 2001), p. 178.
7. King, *The Stand*, p. 71.
8. Ibid., p. 668.
9. Ibid., p. 353.
10. Ibid., p. 207.
11. Ibid., p. 223.

Chapter Two

1. King, *The Stand*, p. 4.
2. Ibid., p. 57.
3. Ibid., p. 58.
4. Ibid., p. 59.
5. Ibid., p. 43.
6. Ibid., p. 93.
7. Ibid., p. 87.
8. Ibid., p. 154.
9. Ibid., p. 449.
10. Ibid., p. 516.

11. Ibid., p. 514.
12. Ibid., p. 201.
13. Ibid., p. 371.
14. Ibid., p. 518.
15. Ibid., p. 342.
16. Ibid., p. 347.
17. Ibid., p. 387.
18. Ibid., p. 471.
19. Ibid., p. 836.
20. Ibid., p. 117.
21. Ibid., p. 365.
22. Ibid., p. 521.
23. Ibid., p. 181.

Chapter Three

1. Winter, p. 4.
2. King, *The Stand*, p. 1067.
3. Ibid., p. 1067.
4. Ibid., p. 202.
5. Winter, p. 2.
6. King, *The Stand*, p. 622–623.
7. Collings, *The Many Facets of Stephen King*, p. 67.
8. King, *The Stand*, p. 209.
9. Ibid., p. 1045.
10. Ibid., p. 1047.
11. Ibid., p. 1053.
12. Ibid., p. 1081.
13. Holland-Toll, p. 199.
14. Ibid., 215.
15. King, *The Stand*, p. 459.

Chapter Four

1. Bloom, *Stephen King*, p. 2.

Chapter Five

1. Stephen King, *The Drawing of the Three* (New York: Signet Books, 1987), p. 37.
2. King, *The Drawing of the Three*, p. 60.

Chapter Six

1. Paul Mandelbaum, ed., *First Words: Earliest Writing from Favorite Contemporary Authors* (Chapel Hill, NC: Algonquin Books, 1993), p. 286.
2. Qtd. in Mandelbaum, p. 285.

3. King, "I want," p. 17.
4. Mandelbaum, p. 285.
5. Tony Magistrale, *Landscape of Fear: Stephen King's American Gothic* (Bowling Green, OH: Bowling Green State University Popular Press, 1988), p. 114.
6. Stephen King, *IT* (New York: Signet Books, 1986), p. 766.
7. Ibid., p. 510.
8. Ibid.
9. Ibid., p. 738.
10. Ibid., p. 740.
11. Finlo Rohrer, "Why Are Clowns Scary?" *BBC Magazine*, Jan. 16, 2008, accessed 21 Aug. 2011, http://news.bbc.co.uk/2/hi/7191721.stm.

Bibliography

Bloom, Harold. *The Western Canon.* New York: Riverhead Books, 1994.
Bloom, Harold (ed.). *Stephen King: Modern Critical Views.* Philadelphia: Chelsea House, 1998.
Blue, Tyson. *The Unseen King.* Mercer Island, WA: Starmont House, 1989.
"Books: King of Horror." *Time Magazine,* 6 October 1986. Web. 23 August 2011.
Casebeer, Edwin F. "The Art of Balance: Stephen King's Canon." In *Stephen King,* edited by Harold Bloom, 207–217. Philadelphia: Chelsea House, 1998.
Collings, Michael R. *The Many Facets of Stephen King.* Mercer Island, WA: Starmont House, 1985.
_____. *Stephen King as Richard Bachman.* Mercer Island, WA: Starmont House, 1985.
_____. *The Stephen King Phenomenon.* Mercer Island, WA: Starmont House, 1987.
Collings, Michael R., and David Engebretson. *The Shorter Works of Stephen King.* Mercer Island, WA: Starmont House, 1985.
Crawford, Gary William. "Stephen King's American Gothic." In *Discovering Stephen King,* edited by Darrell Schweitzer, 41–45. Mercer Island, WA: Starmont House, 1985.
Culler, Jonathan. *Literary Theory: A Very Short Introduction.* New York: Oxford University Press, 1997.
Davis, Jonathan P. *Stephen King's America.* Bowling Green, OH: Bowling Green State University Popular Press, 1994.
Edmundson, Mark. "Narcissus Regards a Book." *Chronicle of Higher Education* 57, no. 22: B10–B11.
Eliot, T. S. "Tradition and the Individual Talent." 1920. *Quotidiana.* Ed. Patrick Madden. Accessed 17 Oct. 2011, http://essays.quotidiana.org/eliot/tradition_and_the_individual/.
Fialkoff, Francine. "King Holds Court at the NBAs." *Library Journal* 128, no. 20: 92.
Franklin, Ruth. "Stephen King and I." *The New Republic* 223, no. 19: 50.
Greene, Suzanne Ellery. "Best Sellers." In *Handbook of American Popular Culture,* vol. 2, edited by M. Thomas Inge, 31–50. Westport, CT: Greenwood Press, 1980.
Holland-Toll, Linda J. *As American as Mom, Baseball, and Apple Pie: Constructing Community in Contemporary American Horror Fiction.* Bowling Green, OH: Bowling Green State University Press, 2001.
Holman, C. Hugh, and William Harmon. *A Handbook to Literature,* 6th ed. New York: Macmillan, 1992.
Hoppenstand, Gary, and Ray B. Browne (eds.). *The Gothic World of Stephen King.* Bowling Green, OH: Bowling Green State University Popular Press, 1987.
Huyssen, Andreas. *After the Great Divide: Modernism, Mass Culture, Postmodernism.* Bloomington: Indiana University Press, 1986.

Bibliography

Indick, Ben P. "Stephen King as Epic Writer." In *Discovering Modern Horror Fiction I*, edited by Darrell Schweitzer. 56–67. Mercer Island, WA: Starmont Publishers, 1985.
Ingebretsen, Edward J. *Maps of Heaven, Maps of Hell: Religious Terror as Memory from the Puritans to Stephen King*. Armonk, NY: M.E. Sharpe, 1996.
Jaeger, Werner. *Paideia: The Ideals of Greek Culture, Vol. I* (translated by Gilbert Highet). New York: Oxford University Press, 1945.
Johnson, Paul. *Intellectuals*. New York: Harper and Row, 1988.
King, Stephen. *Danse Macabre*. New York: Berkley Books, 1981.
_____. *Different Seasons*. New York: Signet Books, 1983.
_____. *The Drawing of the Three*. New York: Signet Books, 1987.
_____. *Dreamcatcher*. New York: Scribner Books, 2001.
_____. "I Want to Be Typhoid Stevie." In *Reading Stephen King*, edited by Brenda Miller Power, Jeffrey D. Wilhelm, and Kelly Chandler, 13–22. Urbana, IL: National Council of Teachers of English, 1997.
_____. *IT*. New York: Signet Books, 1986.
_____. *The Stand. Complete and Uncut Edition*. New York: Doubleday, 1990.
Kroszer, Kassia. "Reading Books: 3 Out of 4 Americans Do It." *Booksquare* 23 (August 2007). Web. 4 October 2007, http://www.booksquare.com/reading-books-3-out-of-4-americans-do-it/>.
Lant, Kathleen Margaret, and Theresa Thompson. *Imagining the Worst: Stephen King and the Representation of Women*. Westport, CT: Greenwood Press, 1998.
"Literary Reading in Dramatic Decline, According to National Endowment for the Arts Survey." *National Endowment for the Arts News Room*, 8 July 2004. Web. 4 October 2007, http://www.nea.gov/news/news04/ReadingAtRisk.html>.
Magistrale, Tony. *Landscape of Fear: Stephen King's American Gothic*. Bowling Green, OH: Bowling Green State University Press, 1988.
Mandelbaum, Paul (ed.). *First Words: Earliest Writing from Favorite Contemporary Authors*. Chapel Hill: Algonquin Books of Chapel Hill, 1993.
Marrou, H. I. *A History of Education in Antiquity* (Translated by George Lamb). New York: Sheed and Ward, 1956.
McConnell, Frank. "Just Doing It: Stephen King's Craft." *Commonweal* 25 (January 1991): 57–59.
Power, Brenda Miller. "An Ethnography of an Event." In *Reading Stephen King*, edited by Brenda Miller Power, Jeffrey D. Wilhelm, and Kelly Chandler, 3–12. Urbana, IL: National Council of Teachers of English, 1997.
Punter, David. *The Literature of Terror: A History of Gothic Fictions from 1765 to the Present Day*. New York: Longman, 1980.
Rohrer, Finlo. "Why Are Clowns Scary?" *BBC Magazine*, 16 January 2008. Web. 21 August 2011.
Schweitzer, Darrell (ed.). *Discovering Modern Horror Fiction I*. Mercer Island, WA: Starmont Publishers, 1985.
_____. *Discovering Modern Horror Fiction II*. Mercer Island, WA: Starmont Publishers, 1988.
_____. *Discovering Stephen King*. Mercer Island, WA: Starmont House, 1985.
Smith, Greg. "The Literary Equivalent of a Big Mac and Fries? Academics, Moralists, and the Stephen King Phenomenon." *The Midwest Quarterly* 43, no. 4: 329–45.
Spignesi, Stephen J. *The Essential Stephen King*. Franklin Lakes, NJ: New Page Books, 2001.
Underwood, Tim, and Chuck Miller (eds.). *Bare Bones: Conversations on Terror with Stephen King*. New York: McGraw Hill, 1988.
_____. *Stephen King Goes to Hollywood*. New York: New American Library, 1987.
Winter, Douglas E. *Stephen King: The Art of Darkness*. New York: New American Library, 1984.

Index

academia 8, 37, 128–129, 131, 142–144
allegory 44–45
Americans 6, 39, 42–43, 44, 46, 47, 54–59, 63, 69, 70, 72–73, 74, 80, 85, 89, 92, 107, 108–109, 113, 120, 122, 130, 131, 135, 136, 137, 138, 139–140, 141, 152, 166
Andolini, Jack 137
Andros, Nick 67, 68, 86–90, 92, 95–96, 115, 117, 118, 121–122, 124
anti-intellectualism 17–18, 63–64, 143
apocalyptic novel 129–130
Aristotle 132
atheism *see* skepticism

Bag of Bones 31, 128
Baker, Jane 118
Balazar, Enrico 137
Bateman, Glen 90–95, 105, 113, 116, 119, 123, 125
Bildungsroman 151–152
Blakemoor, Rita 85, 96
Bloom, Harold 5, 7, 9, 13, 33, 36, 55, 59, 127, 128–129, 130
"The Body" 146, 148, 149–152
Bowers, Henry *see* IT
Brentner, Ralph 113, 119, 120
Brentwood, Joe Bob 57–58, 66
Brower, Ray *see* "The Body"
Bruett, Lila 55–56, 61, 74
Bruett, Norm 55

Campion, Thomas 40, 55
Captain Trips *see* super flu
catharsis *see* Aristotle
Chambers, Elmer 141–142
Chambers, Jake 140–144, 145
change 85, 108, 119, 168
children 78, 146–167; *see also* innocence
choice *see* free will
Christianity 42, 44–45, 51, 86–90, 103, 107–108, 114, 120
classics 6, 127, 128

Collings, Michael 23, 30, 34, 43, 118
communicability 65–68
Crimson King 111
Cross, Nadine 51, 85, 97, 99–100, 100–102, 109, 111, 116
Cullen, Tom 86, 89, 95–98, 119
cultural studies 2, 5, 8

Danse Macabre 29, 146
Dark Man *see* Flagg, Randall
The Dark Tower 28, 110–111, 133–145
Dean, Eddie 135–137, 138
Dean, Susannah *see* Holmes, Odetta
Denbrough, Bill *see* IT
Denniger, Dr. Herbert 74
Deschain, Roland 134–136
Dorgan, Detective Second 113
doublethink 92
Dreamcatcher 148, 149, 163–166
dreams 112–116

Eagleton, Terry 14
economy 93
Edmundson, Mark 19–21
Elbert, Donald Merwin *see* Trashcan Man
Eliot, T.S. 12–13, 71
entitlement, sense of 57–58
Ervin, Andrew 7
escapism 3, 24, 27, 37–40
eucatastrophe 49, 106, 119, 120
Everyman 71, 72
evil 50, 89, 94, 99, 100, 102, 104, 106, 109–110, 114–115, 118, 125, 138, 146–147, 154, 160
The Eyes of the Dragon 110

faith *see* Christianity; spirituality
family 77–78, 84, 142
fantasy 146
fate 116–117, 150
Faulkner, William 153
feminism 79

Index

Flagg, Randall 41, 45, 47, 50, 86, 87, 88, 89, 92, 93, 94–95, 97, 100, 103–104, 105, 108–111, 114, 117, 120, 122, 125, 145
Flowers, Ray 70
formalism 2
free will 51, 90, 98, 100, 103, 106, 116–117, 149, 154, 158
Freemantle, Abagail 41, 47, 86, 87, 89, 92, 101, 107–108, 113, 120

God 90, 97, 106, 107–108, 114, 117, 119, 120
Goldsmith, Carla 77
Goldsmith, Frannie 72, 75–79, 123, 125
Goldsmith, Peter 76–78, 121
good 89, 99, 111
good vs. evil 47, 86, 87, 88, 96, 97, 113, 148, 154
Gorgeous George 102
gothic 29–30
government 58, 67, 68, 69, 70, 121–124, 130
graduate school 2
The Great Divide 7, 9–10, 130; *see also* high art/low art
Greer, Patty 66–67

Henreid, Lloyd 94–95, 102–105
heroism 70
high art/low art 21
Hirschfield, Angie 113
Hogan, Whitney 120, 122
Holman and Harmon 25
Holmes, Odetta 139–140, 145
home 83–84, 134
Homer 12
hope 125–126
Hoppenstand and Browne 5–6, 18
Horace 36, 130
horror 23–29, 48–49, 55, 65, 87, 94, 147, 159, 165
human nature 81, 90, 91, 92–93, 95, 110, 122, 124, 126

innocence 95, 96, 97, 125, 148; *see also* children
intellectual 74, 92, 98–99, 101, 102, 109, 143
IT 31, 146, 148–149, 152–163

"Jhonathan and the Witchs" 146
Joe 85, 86, 97–98, 101
journey 119, 124, 149–150

Kant 13, 59
Kasprak, Eddie 159–161; *see also* IT
Keene, Mr. 159–161

LaChance, Gordon *see* "The Body"
Lauder, Harold 98–100, 121, 123

Lawry, Julie 96–97, 124
literature 129; definition of 12–17, 130
Lord of the Rings 31, 34 46–52; *see also* Tolkien, J.R.R.
love 118

Matheson, Richard 26
media 68–70
Merrill, Ace *see* "The Body"
military 59–65, 70, 73, 130
Miller, Chuck 34
Modernism 7–8, 12–13, 76
Mordred 111
Mort, Jack 136
Mother Abagail *see* Freemantle, Abagail

Needful Things 30
Norris, Edward M. 66

Oates, Joyce Carol 127

page-turners 6, 15, 20, 23, 131
Palmer, Bob 69
Plato 12
popular culture 8, 16, 127, 130–132, 138
prizes (for literature) 7, 32

realism 39–40
Redman, Stuart 45, 54, 65–66, 68, 72–75, 86, 89, 90, 92, 116, 119, 120, 125
Rider, Jess 76, 82
Rockway, Leo *see* Joe
Rogan, Tom *see* IT
romanticism 76

Schweitzer, Darrell 34
science 91
Secondary Reality 10, 26, 43, 53, 58, 59
Shakespeare, William 7, 10, 21
Shaw, Greta 140–141
skepticism 86, 88, 89, 90
society 39, 78, 79, 91, 93
sociology *see* Bateman, Glen
spirituality 90, 136; *see also* Christianity, skepticism
The Stand (miniseries) 74
The Stand (novel) 40–46, 63, 112, 145
standing 43, 60–61, 70, 75, 82, 96, 110, 117–121, 125, 126, 146–151, 154, 158, 164, 166–167
Starkey, Bill 59–60, 65
stereotypes 71, 75, 86, 137
stoicism 73, 92
Stukey, Wayne 80, 81
success 80–81, 140, 141
super flu 39, 55, 59, 63–64, 66, 68, 69, 73, 78, 116

Index

Swann, Lucy 86, 97
Swine Flu 64

technology 67, 79, 93–94, 130, 135, 138–139
Tolkien, J.R.R. 24, 25, 37, 43, 90, 102, 138; see also Lord of the Rings
The Tommyknockers 147
tradition 127, 153
Trashcan Man 105–107, 117, 145

Underwood, Alice 80, 82, 83
Underwood, Larry 44, 79–86, 92, 96, 99, 101, 104, 113, 117, 118, 119–120, 124, 136
Underwood, Tim 34

Walker, Detta *see* Holmes, Odetta
Walkin' Dude *see* Flagg, Randall
weapons 92, 94, 125; *see also* technology
west 115
Westerns 72, 73, 115, 135, 138
Winter, Douglas 24, 27–28, 34, 115
women 78–79

PS3561.I483 S73 2012